CONTENTS

Helion & Company Limited
Unit 8 Amherst Business Centre
Budbrooke Road
Warwick
CV34 5WE
England
Tel. 01926 499 619
Email: info@helion.co.uk
Website: www.helion.co.uk
Twitter: @helionbooks
https://helionbooks.wordpress.com/

Colour Profiles: Andrey Yurgenson

Designed and typeset by Mach 3 Solutions (www.mach3solutions.co.uk)
Cover design Paul Hewitt, Battlefield Design (www.battlefield-design.co.uk)

ISBN: 978-1-804517-71-0

British Library Cataloguing-in-Publication Data
A catalogue record for this book is available from the British Library

We always welcome receiving book proposals from prospective authors.

Note: In order to simplify the use of this book, all names, locations and geographic designations are as provided in *The Times World Atlas*, or other traditionally accepted major sources of reference, as of the time of described events.

ABBREVIATIONS AND ACRONYMS

GIAP – Guards Fighter Aviation Regiment (*Gvardeiskiy Istrebitelniy Aviatsionniy Polk*)
GKAP – Guards Red-Banner Aviation Regiment (*Gvardeiskiy Krasnoznamenniy Aviatsionniy Polk*)
GMTAP – Guards Mine-Torpedo Aviation Regiment (*Gvardeiskiy Minno-Torpedniy Aviatsionniy Polk*)
HQ – Headquarters
IAD – Fighter Aviation Division (*Istrebitelnaya Aviatsionnaya Diviziya*)
IAE – Fighter Aviation Squadron (*Istrebitelnaya Aviatsionnaya Eskadriliya*)
IAP – Fighter Aviation Regiment (*Istrebitelniy Aviatsionniy Polk*)
KFK – multi-purpose boat (*Kriegsfischkutter*)
MFP – naval ferry barge (*Marinefährprahm*)
MTAD – Mine-Torpedo Aviation Division (*Minno-Torpednaya Aviatsionnaya Diviziya*)
MTAP – Mine-Torpedo Aviation Regiment (*Minno-Torpedniy Aviatsionniy Polk*)
RAP – Reconnaissance Aviation Regiment (*Razvedyvatelniy Aviatsionniy Polk*)
SAD – Composite Aviation Division (*Smeshannaya Aviatsionnaya Diviziya*)
SAP – Composite Aviation Regiment (*Smeshanniy Aviatsionniy Polk*)
ShAP – Ground-attack Aviation Regiment (*Shturmovoy Aviatsionniy Polk*)

INTRODUCTION

Why this book was written? Well, the author simply got tired of reading the same stories over and over again – the stories put together by other authors about the combat use of Kittyhawk aircraft by the Northern Fleet Air Force. It seems that different authors have a lot to tell about the design of these aircraft, their deliveries under Lend-Lease agreement, but when it comes to combat use of the Kittyhawks, all authors write the same stories. So, the author, with the support of his friends, went to a branch office of the Central Archive of the Ministry of Defence of the Russian Federation (Archive of the Navy branch) in the town of Gatchina and found documents related to the combat use of this aircraft type in the Northern Fleet Air Force.

In the battles of 1942–1943 the Kittyhawks operated as fighters. That is why the author quoted the documents and combat flight logs of the pilots of the 2nd Guards Red-Banner Fighter Aviation Regiment named after B.F. Safonov with some additions taken from the documents of the Northern Fleet Air Force Headquarters. Anyway, who would better know all the difficulties of fighting enemy aircraft than the pilots themselves and their superiors? The author managed to find most of the confirmed air victories of the Kittyhawk pilots and the names of the pilots who won them. However, since wars always bring losses, the Kittyhawks missing in 1942–1944 are also included into this book.

From the end of 1943 the Kittyhawk aircraft, while keeping its fighter role, became more frequently used as a reconnaissance aircraft and a fighter-bomber. The latter was the most interesting topic to research, and the author was able to find a large number of pilots' reports, combat flight logs and gun camera photos of strikes which gave an idea of how the pilots and their commanders saw the course and outcome of a particular battle. Documents from the American NARA archives helped to show how the enemy saw the Kittyhawks attacking their ships and vessels, and also gave the results of these strikes. On the other hand, sometimes due to the lack of German documents, not all the ground target strikes are described, as in a number of cases the documents available to the author cannot give an answer about the effectiveness of those strikes.

The author would like to thank Igor Borisenko, Josef Falk, Hans-Ulrich Henschel, Andrey Kopytkov, Aleksander Mardanov, Vyacheslav Mosunov, Vladimir Nayavt, Gennady Sloutskiy, Yuriy Rybin, Pavel Vein and all the staff at the Central Archive of the Ministry of Defence of the Russian Federation (Archive of the Navy branch) for their considerable support in the creation of this book.

HISTORICAL NOTE: THE 2ND GUARDS RED-BANNER FIGHTER AVIATION REGIMENT NAMED AFTER B.F. SAFONOV

The regiment was formed in December 1939 as the 72nd Composite Aviation Regiment of the Northern Fleet Air Force. The regiment included both fighters and bombers, and later (in 1942) even torpedo bombers. In fact, this regiment became the progenitor of all the air forces of the Northern Fleet, being later transformed into two fighter and one mine-torpedo regiments.

On 22 June 1941 the regiment was commanded by Colonel G.P. Gubanov.

On 16 September 1941 the regiment was awarded the Order of the Red Banner.

On 18 January 1942 for success in battles with the enemy the regiment received the rank of Guards and was renamed into the 2nd Guards Red-Banner Composite Aviation Regiment.

On 15 June 1942 the regiment was named after B.F. Safonov, the regiment commander, who died in an air battle on 30 May 1942.

On 14 October 1942, after the withdrawal of bomber and mine-torpedo squadrons from the regiment (they were included into the 24th Mine-Torpedo Aviation Regiment, the future 9th Guards Mine-Torpedo Aviation Regiment), the regiment was renamed into the 2nd Guards Red-Banner Fighter Aviation Regiment named after B.F. Safonov.

The regiment took an active part in the battles of 1944, for which on 31 October 1944 it was awarded the honorary name 'Pechengskiy'.

1
THE KITTYHAWK FIGHTER-BOMBER

The history of the Kittyhawk fighter-bomber began in 1936, when the Curtiss Aeroplane Company of America, part of the Curtiss-Wright Corporation, developed the Curtiss Hawk Model 75 fighter. The aircraft was fast, manoeuvrable, and easy to handle. It was accepted into service by the United States, and France soon placed an order for its armed forces. Following this, the fighter was purchased by Norway, China, Thailand, and several other nations. The aircraft's engine, armament, and equipment were adapted to suit the needs of each air force. In total, 1,300 Hawk-75 aircraft were produced. In the French Air Force, the Hawk-75 fought with some success against the Luftwaffe during the 1940 campaign. After France surrendered, Germany sold some of the captured P-36s to Finland, where they were used by the Finnish Air Force in combat against Soviet aviation from 1941 to 1944.

The commercial success of the Hawk-75, along with positive feedback from various air forces, encouraged Curtiss to develop a new fighter based on its design. A new 1,040hp Allison V-1710-33 engine was installed, resulting in the XP-40, which first flew in October 1938. Subsequent testing revealed the need for design improvements. The aircraft was then entered into a competition to supply a new fighter for the U.S. Army Air Corps. Curtiss won the contract and was awarded an order for 524 P-40 fighters. In April 1940, the P-40 entered service with the U.S. Army Air Force. It could reach a top speed of 575 km/h, climb to 4,500 metres in 5.3 minutes, and had a range of 1,529 kilometres. The original armament consisted of two 12.7mm and two 7.62mm machine guns.

In addition to the United States, the P-40 was adopted by the British and French air forces. The version supplied to these nations was modified according to their requirements. After France's capitulation, aircraft originally intended for its air force were delivered to the Royal Air Force (RAF), where they were designated Tomahawk I. Based on wartime experience, the British requested several changes, such as armoured windscreens and seatbacks. This version became known as the Tomahawk II in RAF service. These enhancements significantly improved combat survivability and were adopted by the U.S. for mass production. The resulting version was designated the P-40B by the U.S. Army Air Force.

The P-40C introduced further modifications, including two additional 7.62mm machine guns in the wings and the option to carry an external fuel tank beneath the fuselage.

However, these upgrades came at a cost to performance. The top speed of the P-40C dropped to 555 km/h. To address this, designers installed a more powerful 1,150hp Allison V-1710-39 engine, which could produce up to 1,470hp for short durations. This version was designated the P-40D in the United States and became known as the Kittyhawk in RAF service. Nevertheless, it was not widely adopted due to ongoing demands for better armament. The armament was subsequently upgraded to six 12.7mm machine guns, and the aircraft was equipped to carry a 500-lb bomb under the fuselage, with wing-mounted bomb racks added later. With its new engine, the P-40E (Kittyhawk IA in RAF terminology) reached a maximum speed of 590 km/h.

Curtiss continued to pursue improvements. One approach involved installing the 1,300hp Packard Merlin V-1650-1 engine, resulting in the P-40F. Although flight tests showed performance was nearly identical to the P-40E, it was still mass-produced.

Another development, the P-40L, was a lighter version of the P-40F. To reduce weight, two machine guns were removed, armour was reduced, and fuel capacity was cut. However, speed increased only marginally to 595 km/h, and other performance parametres remained unchanged. Around the same time, the Packard Merlin V-1650-3 engine became the powerplant of the superior P-51 Mustang, which was urgently needed by the Air Force. As a result, all subsequent P-40 variants reverted to using Allison engines, with continuous improvements to the V-1710 series. Even before the P-40L was produced, Curtiss had developed the P-40K by installing the 1,325hp V-1710-73 engine. However, its performance remained similar to the P-40E. The next major variant, the P-40M, used a 1,200hp V-1710-81 engine, which improved climb rates at medium altitudes.

The final mass-produced version was the P-40N. By 1943, the aircraft was considered obsolete as a front-line fighter. Nevertheless, the designers applied the lessons learned from the P-40L to create a lighter version with improved performance. The top speed increased to 608 km/h, and both vertical and horizontal manoeuvrability were enhanced. Initially armed with four 12.7mm machine guns, later variants carried six. While early P-40Ns were powered by the V-1710-81 engine, later versions used the V-1710-99 (P-40N-20) and V-1710-115 (P-40N-40), with output remaining at 1,200hp.

Th e P-40N was the most numerous variant, with over 5,000 produced out of a total of around 14,000. It became the principal aircraft of the Soviet Northern Fleet Air Force, where Soviet pilots achieved their greatest successes with the type.

P-40s saw action across all major theatres of the Second World War—engaging enemy aircraft in Europe, Africa, and the Pacific. While considered an average performer, the P-40 proved robust, reliable, and capable of taking on most adversaries. It was equally effective in ground attack roles: setting Rommel's supply trucks ablaze in North Africa, attacking Japanese cargo vessels in Asia, and strafing transport junks in China. Surviving P-40s frequently appear in war films, often portraying themselves.

The first P-40s arrived in the Soviet Union in September 1941, transferred by the RAF. As the British designated the aircraft "Tomahawk," Soviet documents often referred to the type as *Tomahouk*, *Tomagauk*, or *Kittyhauk*, regardless of the variant. The name *Kittyhauk* became standard in Northern Fleet Air Force records only from late 1942, likely after it was clarified that the Fleet had received P-40Es, whereas army units had earlier variants. Between 1942 and 1944, the USSR received approximately 2,700 P-40s (some sources list 2,069), of which 291 were assigned to the Navy Air Force.

The 2nd Guards Red-Banner Aviation Regiment (2nd GKAP, *Gvardeiskiy Krasnoznamenniy Aviatsionniy Polk*) was the first Northern Fleet unit to receive Kittyhawks, in April 1942. The regiment's first victory came on 17 May 1942, when Guards Lieutenant Colonel B.F. Safonov shot down a Luftwaffe Ju 88. The 2nd GKAP operated Kittyhawks until May 1943. While the aircraft was judged superior to the Hurricane, it was considered inferior to the Airacobra, and the regiment later transitioned entirely to the latter. The 255th Fighter Aviation Regiment (255th IAP, *Istrebitelniy Aviatsionniy Polk*) also operated Kittyhawks. Despite flying combat missions, the unit failed to record any aerial victories and was re-equipped with Airacobras in 1943.

The Kittyhawk fared better in reconnaissance roles. The 118th Reconnaissance Aviation Regiment (118th RAP, *Razvedyvatelniy Aviatsionniy Polk*) used modified Kittyhawks with aerial cameras from 1943.

In October 1943, the 78th IAP received three Kittyhawks from the 255th IAP, but as it was undergoing reformation, the aircraft—alongside several Hurricanes—were transferred to the 27th IAP. After reorganisation, the 78th IAP returned to combat in 1944, now fully equipped with Kittyhawks.

The 27th IAP also began operating Kittyhawks in October 1943. Initial results were poor: four aircraft were lost to enemy action and one to technical failure in November alone, with four pilots killed and no enemy aircraft shot down. The regiment's first aerial victory came only on 3 March 1944, when Senior Lieutenant M.I. Boychenko downed a Bf 109 over an Allied convoy.

The 78th IAP scored its first kills with Kittyhawks on 23 April 1944, when Captain M.N. Veryovkin and Junior Lieutenant Komashko each shot down a Bf 109 while escorting a convoy. Despite meeting 1944 fighter standards, the Kittyhawk was still considered inferior to the Airacobra and Yak-7B by Northern Fleet HQ. However, the Kittyhawk proved highly effective as a fighter-bomber. Its long range and six heavy machine guns made it ideal for 'free hunting' missions against enemy shipping and coastal targets. Kittyhawk operations concentrated on the Varanger Fjord and the north-east coast of Norway, reaching as far as Gamvik. Strikes were conducted on both large convoys and small vessels. A typical 'free hunter' group comprised four to six aircraft—one or two with cameras—and the rest armed with FAB-100 bombs. Targets were identified independently and attacked using skip or dive bombing tactics.

Larger strikes (10–12 aircraft) were mounted against known targets, with two aircraft monitoring the results. These carried either two FAB-100 bombs or one FAB-250; however, the latter reduced range due to the absence of an external fuel tank.

Skip bombing involved a 1,000–1,500m approach, diving at 45–50 degrees, then levelling off at 600m to drop bombs from 15–25m at 150–200m range. Dive bombing began at 2,000–2,500m with a 70–75 degree dive, releasing FAB-100s from 800–1,500m and exiting at 600–1,200m. Large strike groups (up to 30 aircraft) attacked land targets such as those in Kirkenes, with a mixed load of FAB-250 and FAB-100 bombs. These formations were typically escorted by Kittyhawks of the 27th or 78th IAP, or Airacobras from the 2nd GKAP.

A special note must be made regarding the 12.7mm Browning machine guns, which fired 750 rounds per minute and launched 42–49g bullets. Nicknamed "circular saws" in American propaganda, these weapons inflicted severe damage on enemy vessels, disabling crews and equipment and even causing critical damage to steam systems on larger ships.

In summary, the Kittyhawks of the Northern Fleet performed admirably in the strike role. However, their limitations as fighters by 1944 standards led to their replacement in that role, with their success as fighter-bombers owing much to the dedicated training and tactics developed by the 78th and 27th IAPs.

Kittyhawks prepared for transfer under the Lend-Lease Act.

Top: Kittyhawk of the Northern Fleet Air Force takes off.

Centre: Wing-mounted machine guns of the Kittyhawk.

Bottom: Kittyhawk fitted with additional fuel tank.

2
GERMAN SHIPS AND AIRCRAFT

The primary adversaries of the Northern Fleet Air Force were German naval vessels and Luftwaffe aircraft.

The largest Kriegsmarine vessels involved in combat operations against the Northern Fleet were typically patrol and anti-submarine ships converted from requisitioned fishing trawlers. These vessels belonged to the 59th, 61st, 63rd, and 65th Patrol Boat (*Vorpostenboote*) Flotillas (each operating between seven and eleven vessels at different times), and the 12th Submarine Hunter (*U-Jagd-Boote*) Flotilla (with eight to nine vessels in service across various periods). These converted trawlers had displacements of up to 1,500 tonnes and could reach speeds of 12–15 knots. They were usually armed with a single 75mm or 88mm cannon and several automatic anti-aircraft guns, including quad-mounted variants, with the total number of anti-aircraft weapons sometimes reaching 20. Though originally trawlers and thus possessing good seaworthiness, German reports highlighted their poor manoeuvrability. The ships carried a large stock of depth charges for anti-submarine warfare, and some were equipped with sonar. One such vessel, submarine hunter UJ-1210, was sunk by Kittyhawk fighter-bombers on 16 May 1944. Due to their size and resemblance to merchant ships, these trawlers were often mistaken by Soviet pilots for cargo vessels, sometimes estimated at displacements of up to 8,000 tonnes. However, the reverse also occurred: patrol ships were occasionally misidentified as small patrol motorboats, even when no such boats were present in the convoy.

Another class of vessel frequently encountered by the Northern Fleet Air Force was the purpose-built minesweeper (*Minensuchboot*), constructed in various series for the Kriegsmarine between 1933 and 1945. These minesweepers had displacements of up to 1,000 tonnes and speeds ranging from 16 to 18 knots, depending on the series. They typically carried two 105mm guns (except for the M40 series, which could carry only one) along with several anti-aircraft guns, including quad-mounted units. Equipped with both contact and non-contact minesweeping gear (magnetic and acoustic), many were also fitted with sonar and depth charges. During the period in question, the 5th, 9th, and 22nd Minesweeper Flotillas (*Minensuchflottille*)—each with up to 20 ships—were engaged in combat operations against the Northern Fleet. Due to their silhouette, these ships were often mistaken for destroyers by Soviet pilots. Unlike their Baltic Fleet counterparts, however, Northern Fleet aircraft did not succeed in sinking any of these minesweepers, though many were damaged to varying degrees.

The picture of German naval forces would be incomplete without mention of smaller warships that also engaged in combat with Northern Fleet aircraft. One notable class was the motor minesweeper (*Räumboot*). Built in multiple series, these vessels had displacements of 120–250 tonnes. Originally intended as minesweepers, their robust seaworthiness and versatility led to their extensive use as convoy escorts and in engagements against Soviet aircraft and torpedo boats. Thanks to their powerful engines, *Räumboote* could achieve speeds of up to 20 knots. They were typically armed with one 37mm and several 20mm anti-aircraft guns. When performing minesweeping duties, they were also fitted with appropriate gear and depth charges. These vessels were often misidentified by inexperienced pilots as generic 'patrol boats'. The 5th, 7th, and 21st Motor Minesweeper Flotillas (*R-Bootsflottillen*) participated in operations against the Northern Fleet, with around 15–20 boats typically involved. Many suffered damage, and two—R-90 and R-151—were destroyed by bombs dropped by Kittyhawks of the 78th Fighter Aviation Regiment (IAP).

In addition to the motor minesweepers, the Kriegsmarine operated a large number of *Kriegsfischkutter* (KFK) multi-purpose boats. Designed for potential post-war conversion into fishing vessels, three wartime variants were in use: patrol, anti-submarine, and minesweeping configurations. KFKs had displacements of 100–150 tonnes and cruising speeds of around 9 knots. Armament generally included one 37mm or 40mm cannon and several 20mm anti-aircraft guns. Depending on the variant, they were fitted with heavier armament (patrol boats), minesweeping equipment, or sonar and depth charges. KFKs served in the Kirkenes Harbour Protection Flotilla (*Hafenschutz-Flottille Kirkenes*), which in mid-1944 was reorganised as the 67th Patrol Boat Flotilla (*Vorpostenflottille*), operating up to 20 vessels. One of these, V-6706, was sunk by Kittyhawks of the 78th IAP on 16 October 1944.

Alongside purpose-built craft, the Germans also commandeered a number of small Norwegian ships for use as patrol vessels and minesweepers.

Because of the complete absence of a railway network and the limited development of paved roads in northern Norway, the German command relied heavily on coastal transport between garrisons using small ships, high-speed landing barges, and motorboats.

The high-speed landing barges (*Marinefährprahm* or MFP—naval ferry barges) warrant particular attention. Approximately 50 were operational in the Northern Fleet's area of operations. In early 1944, the 22nd and 23rd Landing Ship Flotillas (*Landungsflottille*) operated in the region; by summer, they had been reorganised into the 5th and 6th Flotillas. MFPs displaced between 220 and 400 tonnes and had cruising speeds of around 10 knots. Lightly armoured around the engine room and superstructure, MFPs came in two main types: artillery and transport. Artillery variants were equipped with two 88mm guns and two quad-mounted 20mm anti-aircraft guns. Only five such craft were present in the two flotillas operating in the north. These ships had proven effective in repelling Soviet air attacks in both the Baltic and Black Seas. Transport versions carried one 75mm or 88mm gun and several 20mm anti-aircraft guns. Their structural resilience made them highly survivable—hits from one or even two FAB-100 bombs often failed to cause significant damage, and the vessels were usually able to reach repair facilities under their own power.

Both the MFPs and Norwegian motorboats were responsible for transporting supplies to German garrisons along the occupied Norwegian coast, making them prime targets for Kittyhawk fighter-bombers. However, this presented a moral and operational dilemma: Norwegian motorboats also carried civilian goods, and it was often impossible to distinguish whether a given vessel was transporting military or civilian cargo. The total number of Norwegian motorboats used for supply purposes during the war remains unclear, as does the number sunk.

A note must be made regarding the interpretation of German documentation. Statements such as "the aircraft crews observed fire, but German sources did not confirm it" should be approached with caution. Although a large number of documents detail German naval operations, the author did not have access to the logbooks of all individual ships involved. Most available records came from flotilla-level reports, which often omitted detailed accounts of damage sustained in combat.

Crew losses must also be considered. Minesweepers and submarine hunters typically had crews of 60–70 men, while motor minesweepers and landing barges were crewed by around 25. Thus, the death or injury of even a small number of sailors could significantly reduce a vessel's combat effectiveness.

As for aerial combat, the main opponent of Soviet fighters was *Jagdgeschwader* 5 (JG 5), the 5th Luftwaffe Fighter Wing, which operated Messerschmitt and Focke-Wulf aircraft. Formed in 1942, JG 5 was primarily tasked with countering Soviet air activity in the northern theatre. The unit included many experienced pilots and posed a serious threat to the Northern Fleet Air Force.

However, it must be noted that by 1944, the Luftwaffe was significantly weaker than it had been in 1941–42. This is evident from the phenomenon of "overclaiming"—the tendency for pilots to report more kills than were actually achieved. In the earlier years of the war, Luftwaffe claims exceeded Soviet losses by a factor of two or three, or sometimes corresponded closely to real figures. By 1944, claims exceeded actual Soviet losses by almost tenfold. Despite legendary accounts of Luftwaffe aces, many of their victories occurred under conditions of numerical superiority, and even then, there were often large discrepancies between claims and confirmed Soviet losses. When Soviet pilots held the numerical advantage, outcomes could be equally disastrous for the Germans. Furthermore, anti-aircraft fire from German ships and coastal batteries also contributed to Soviet aircraft losses and should be considered when evaluating Luftwaffe claims. In the author's opinion, records of German aircraft losses in 1944 are often unreliable, making it difficult to draw definitive conclusions regarding aircraft shot down or damaged. Nonetheless, in recent years, access to documents from the U.S. National Archives and Records Administration has shed new light on German losses. In addition to Luftwaffe archives, materials from the German Army and Navy have also become available, offering valuable insights into individual air battles. Credit is due to Western historians working in this field, particularly the research of Eric Mombeek. As more records are uncovered, the list of verified Soviet aerial victories is likely to grow.

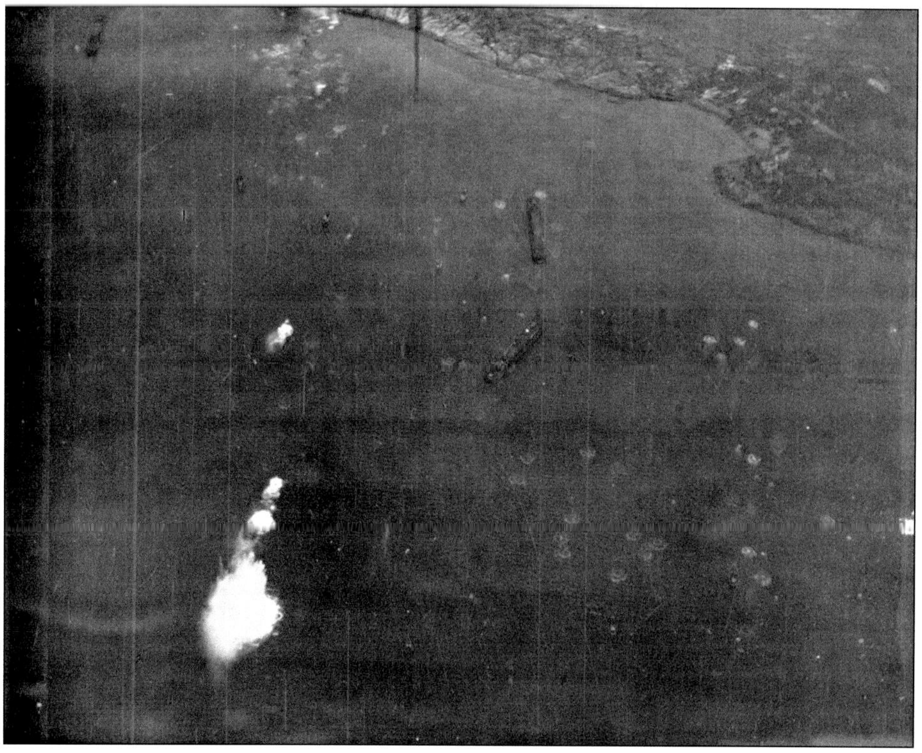

Top: A high-speed artillery landing barge under attack by aircraft of the Northern Fleet Air Force.

Bottom: Aircraft of the Northern Fleet Air Force attacking German high-speed landing barges.

3
KITTYHAWKS IN 1942

The pilots of the Northern Fleet Air Force were in high spirits at the beginning of 1942. Victories of the Soviet Army all along the front line and successes in the battles against Luftwaffe in the North gave hope for a successful continuation of the fighting. However, early in the spring of 1942, Soviet pilots began to encounter Messerschmitt Bf 109 fighters, which were clearly superior to their predecessors in the flight characteristics. Very soon it became clear that the Germans had begun to convert their units in the North to a new version of this fighter – Bf 109F. There was nothing particularly new about this aircraft. It had been in use in the central sections of the front since 22 June 1941, but it was new to the northern battle area. It soon became clear that, as a Soviet report stated, "This aircraft type [Bf 109F] is superior to its predecessor [Bf 109E] in horizontal and vertical speed. In comparison with our Hurricane aircraft, the Bf 109 is superior in horizontal and vertical speed; however, it is inferior in firepower and horizontal manoeuvrability".

By then the main fighter aircraft in the Northern Fleet was the British Hawker Hurricane, and it was obvious that it had to be replaced. The Allies supplied P-40 fighters under the Lend-Lease Agreement, which was referred to as the *Tomahouk* or *Tomagauk* in Soviet documents. However, the first P-40 fighters to enter service with the Northern Fleet Air Force were the P-40E-1 aircraft, which were referred to as Kittyhawks in the Royal Air Force. This name soon entered the lexicon of the Northern Fleet pilots.

The oldest regiment in the Northern Fleet Air Force – the 2nd Guards Re Banner Aviation Regiment – was the first to receive Kittyhawks. The regiment was formed in December 1939, originally as the 72nd Composite Aviation Regiment. It included both fighters and bombers, and later (in 1942) even torpedo bombers. In essence, this regiment became the ancestor of the Northern Fleet Air Force. The 24th Mine-Torpedo Aviation Regiment (*Minno-Torpedniy Aviatsionniy Polk,* MTAP) – the future 9th Guards Mine-Torpedo Aviation Regiment (*Gvardeiskiy Minno-Torpedniy Aviatsionniy Polk,* GMTAP), 78th IAP, 27th IAP and a number of other units were formed on its basis.

On 22 June 1941 the regiment was commanded by Colonel G.P. Gubanov. The regiment took part in hostilities, engaging in air combats with Luftwaffe aircraft and carrying out bombing and assault strikes on German troops and ships.

On 24 June 1941 Senior Lieutenant B. Safonov, piloting a I-16 fighter, shot down a Ju 88 aircraft (W.Nr. 8173) of the 6. *Staffel, II. Gruppe, Kampfgeschwader* 30 (6./KG 30 – this designation system will be used for Luftwaffe units further in the text – *Translator's note*). This was the first victory of the Northern Fleet fighter aviation in the war that had just started.

On 21 July 1941, six SBs of the 72nd Composite Aviation Regiment (*Smeshanniy Aviatsionniy Polk,* SAP) led by Captain K.D. Pogodin attacked German ships in the port of Kirkenes and sank the German transport *Wandsbeck* (2,183grt). Although the transport was later refloated and repaired by the Germans, it can be considered the first ship sunk by the Northern Fleet Air Force.

On 18 January 1942, for successes in fighting the enemy, the regiment was reorganized into the 2nd Guards Combined Red-Banner Aviation Regiment of the Northern Fleet Air Force. The following is a quote from the war diary of the 72nd SAP:

> April–May 1942: A new Kittyhawk fighter has been received from the United States, studied and mastered by the personnel (12 flight crews) of the 2nd Fighter Aviation Squadron (*Istrebitelnaya Aviatsionnaya Eskadriliya,* IAE). The commander of the 2nd GKAP Guards Lieutenant Colonel Safonov was the first who studied and flew the Kittyhawk aircraft; he later personally trained the rest of the flight crews of the 2nd IAE. Assembly and studying of the aircraft were performed in conditions of systematic attacks by the enemy and intense combat work; no outside technical assistance was provided.

Credit must be given to Guards Lieutenant Colonel B.F. Safonov. He was charged with the difficult task of converting his regiment with the new type and decided to personally test the new aircraft to determine its strong and weak points. In May 1942, the first P-40 s/n 775 arrived at the regiment's location. The first Kittyhawk was assembled by 11 May 1942, and B.F. Safonov made several flights on it.

From the combat flight log of the 2nd GKAP:

> 11 May 1942.
> 21:04. Take-off of one Tomahawk, flight around the airfield. The pilot: Commander of 2nd GKAP Lieutenant Colonel Safonov.
> 21:23. Landing of one Tomahawk.

Four days later, B.F. Safonov flew this aircraft into battle…

Since the Central Archives of the Navy in Gatchina hold a large number of original documents, it would be logical to use them to describe the further air battles.

From combat report No.128 of the Headquarters (HQ) of the 1st IAE of the 2nd GKAP:

> 15.05.1942, 23:00, Vaenga airfield. 19:00–19:42. Take-off of three Hurricanes and one Tomahawk aircraft piloted by Safonov. Pilots Polyakov, Kuzichkin, Grigoriev. The combat task: to repulse enemy aircraft heading towards the Murmansk area. Over Mishukovo pilot Polyakov attacked a Ju 88 aircraft at an altitude of 3,000m using RS-82 rocket projectiles from a distance of 700–800m, launched one rocket projectile, observed explosions below, then the enemy aircraft went into a dive and came out of it. Polyakov followed it, began to catch up, fired one burst of machine-gun fire from a distance of 200–150m, accelerated and got closer to a distance of 50–70m, fired again, then the gunner stopped returning fire. After several bursts the port engine stopped and was emitting black smoke, the starboard engine was also damaged and left behind a trail of black smoke, then the pursuit stopped due to depleted ammunition. The pilot believes the aircraft was shot down. Pilot Kuzichkin attacked a Ju 88 when entering a dive, fired four RS-82 rocket projectiles on approach from a distance of 850m, the rockets exploded at the same altitude with undershoot of 50–70m, the Ju 88 went into a dive, Kuzichkin fired two bursts from machine guns directly at the

tail from a distance of 200–250m. The aircraft dropped bombs and began to exit the dive, it was attacked from above from a distance of 200m, two bursts were fired. Pilot Grigoriev attacked a Ju 88 using RS-82 and released four rocket projectiles from 600–700m on approach to the target. The explosions overshot at the same altitude. When the enemy aircraft was exiting the dive, it was attacked from above using machine-gun fire, directly at the tail at 30 degrees angle from 500–600m, the Ju 88 manoeuvred at low altitude and escaped. During a rough landing (aircraft tactical number 20), pilot Grigoriev broke the side strut stop of the left landing gear leg. Mission accomplished.

21:05–22:00. Take-off of three Hurricane and one Tomahawk aircraft. Regiment Commander Safonov, pilots Polyakov, Kuzichkin, Grigoriev. Loitering over the airfield. Mission accomplished.

Left: Twice Hero of the Soviet Union, Commander of the 2nd GKAP, Guards Colonel Boris Safonov in the cockpit of a Kittyhawk. Safonov was posted missing in action on 30 May 1942.

Right: Guards Senior Sergeant P.D. Klimov, Hero of the Soviet Union. The photo was taken later, when he had already been promoted to the rank of Guards Lieutenant.

From combat report No.140 of the 2nd IAE HQ, 23:00, 15 May 1942, Vaenga airfield:

Four Hurricanes, one MiG-3 (take off 19:00, landing 19:42). Senior Lieutenant Pokrovskiy, Captain Orlov, Sergeants Yaroslavtsev, Klimov repulsed the enemy air raid near Murmansk at an altitude of 3,000m. Senior Lieutenant Pokrovskiy attacked a Ju 88 with machine-gun fire from a distance 300–200m at an altitude of 3,000m down to 200m. The Ju 88 dived into the water in the area of the ships' anchorage in the port of Murmansk. Lieutenant Kuzichkin observed the crash.

Left: Guards Captain P.I. Orlov, Hero of the Soviet Union. He was killed in action on 15 March 1943.

Right: Guards Senior Lieutenant V.P. Pokrovskiy, Hero of the Soviet Union.

From the combat report of the 3rd IAE, 24:00, 15 May 1942, Vaenga-1 airfield:

19:00–19:40, four Hurricanes, pilots Panov, Pronchenko, Gredyushko, Anikin were loitering above the airfield at an altitude of 4,000m. A signal was received in the air: "Enemy aircraft are approaching Murmansk". When approaching Murmansk at an altitude of 3,500m pilots Panov and Gredyushko saw two Ju 88 aircraft. Pilot Panov attacked the leader from the front at 3/4 target aspect ratio. He fired one burst of machine-gun fire. Two bursts were fired from behind at target aspect ratio from 3/4 to 1/4 at a distance of 250–100m. The Ju 88 aircraft went into a steep dive emitting smoke. During the dive, pilot Gredyushko was attacking the enemy down to an altitude of 150m and fired four bursts of machine-gun fire. The Ju 88 crashed on the western shore of Kola Bay opposite Murmansk. Panov fired 1,380 rounds of ammunition, Gredyushko 3,000 rounds. Pilots Anikin and Pronchenko did not attack.

Based on the results of air battles of 15 May 1942, the Northern Fleet Air Force Headquarters credited one shot down and three damaged Ju 88 bombers, as well as one damaged Bf 109 credited to the pilots of the 2nd GKAP and 78th IAP. The pilots of the 2nd GKAP added the following to their personal scores: Guards Lieutenant K.T. Panov – one shot down Ju 88, Guards Senior Lieutenant V.P. Pokrovskiy and a pair of Guards Lieutenant Kuzichkin and Guards Junior Lieutenant S.T. Polyakov – one damaged Ju 88 each. In addition to the fighters of the Northern Fleet Air Force, 11 Hurricanes of the 767th, 768th, and 769th IAPs of the 122nd Fighter Aviation Division (*Istrebitelnaya Aviatsionnaya Diviziya*, IAD) of Air Defence Forces intercepted the Luftwaffe aircraft heading to bomb Murmansk. The air defence pilots shot down two Ju 88s, one Ju 87, one Bf 109, and one Bf 110 each, but lost two Hurricanes (pilots bailed out with parachutes). Army pilots also took part in repelling the attack – four Airacobras of the 19th Guards Fighter Aviation Regiment (*Gvardeiskiy Istrebitelniy Aviatsionniy Polk*, GIAP) and seven Hurricanes of the 197th IAP participated in the air battle against the Luftwaffe. Their pilots shot down two Bf 109 aircraft and damaged one Bf 109 at the cost of one Hurricane crashing during a forced landing.

The available German documents confirm the loss of one Ju 88 bomber near Murmansk. The bomber was from 4./KG 30, W.Nr. 142038, aircraft code '4D+HM', and it was shot down on its return flight, after it dropped bombs on Murmansk. The crew of *Unteroffizier* Jäger died with the exception of the navigator; he managed to reach German positions and reported that his aircraft had been shot down by enemy fighters. According to historian Alexander Mardanov, Ju 88 of the 5./KG 30, W.Nr. 142055, aircraft code '4D+LN', which had been considered lost on that day, was actually shot down on 18 May 1942.

The first Luftwaffe aircraft to be shot down by a Kittyhawk of the Northern Fleet Air Force occurred two days later, on 17 May 1942. The pilot of the fighter was Guards Lieutenant Colonel B.F. Safonov. From combat report No.129a of the 1st IAE HQ of the 2nd GKAP, 17 May 1942, 23:00, Vaenga airfield:

> 9:46–10:20. Take-off of one Tomahawk and nine Hurricane aircraft. Regiment Commander Safonov, Squadron Commander Alagurov, Wing Commander Sinev, pilots Kuzichkin, Polyakov, Krivoruchko and pilots of 2nd IAE Orlov, Bokiy, Pokrovskiy. The task: to repulse enemy aircraft near Murmansk–Mishukovo. Engaged the enemy in the air. Regiment Commander Safonov attacked a Bf 109 from a distance 200–300m from behind at 1/4–2/4 target aspect ratio and fired two to three bursts. He attacked the Ju 88 strictly from behind, opened fire from 300m and closed to 20m, the gunner did not fire, both engines emitted clouds of black smoke. The crash was not observed. Some debris flew off the bomber, all ammunition was used, altitude 3,500m. Squadron Commander Alagurov fired at a Bf 109 in a head-on attack from a distance of 200–100m using both cannon and machine guns and shot down the Bf 109, which crashed around seven to eight kilometres westward of Murmansk. Due to low engine power, he was forced to land at the home airfield at 9:58. Wing Commander Sinev attacked three Bf 109s from 80–100m distance at 3/4 frontal target aspect ratio and in head-on attack. Pilot Polyakov fired two rocket projectiles at two Bf 109s, the explosions were below the enemy aircraft. He attacked a Ju 88 by launching two RS-82 rocket projectiles from below at 1/4 target aspect ratio, the first burst was 30m to the left, the second projectile hit precisely between the wing and the cockpit, 5–10m above the target, then the Ju 88 began to lag behind, pursuit was impossible as the fighter was alone. Pilot Kuzichkin attacked a Ju 88 with rocket projectiles, released three projectiles, with 50–60m undershoot. Pilot Orlov, 2nd IAE, attacked a Ju 88 at 1/4 target aspect ratio from the tail from a distance of 200–20m, having used up all ammunition. The Ju 88 started to lag behind, but escaped into the clouds with his port engine smoking heavily. The crash was not observed. Pilot Pokrovskiy attacked a Ju 88 and a Bf 109 from behind at 200m distance. The Bf 109 was at 2/4 target aspect ratio from 200m distance. Pilot Bokiy attacked a Bf 109 from 200–250m from below. The firing was accurate. The pilot made a turn and joined his group. Then he attacked a Ju 88 at a distance of 100–150m and kept shooting until he used up all ammunition: one burst at the gunner, then at the engine of the Ju 88; the bomber disappeared in the clouds. Aircraft (tactical number 05) flown by pilot Krivoruchko did not return from the mission, the cause is under investigation.

Later it was established that Guards Junior Lieutenant Ivan Krivoruchko was killed in the air battle on that day. Basing on the results of the air combat of 17 May 1942, the Northern Fleet Air Force Headquarters credited Lieutenant Colonel B.F. Safonov with shooting down a Ju 88 and Captain V.N. Alagurov with a Bf 109. Captain P.I. Orlov and Lieutenant S.T. Polyakov scored one damaged Ju 88 each. It should be noted that the 2nd GKAP was not alone in the air engagement. In addition to the fighters of the 2nd GKAP, three Hurricanes of the 769th IAP of Air Defence Forces, two Kittyhawks of the 20th GIAP and three Hurricanes of the 197th IAP of the 14th Army Air Force participated in repelling the raid. Several fighters of the 2nd GKAP and 78th IAP took off for the battle, but could not take part in it. The Soviet fighters (including 2nd GKAP) were credited with four shot down Ju 88s, the German fighters managed to shoot down two Hurricanes – one of each of the 2nd GKAP and 769th IAP, both pilots were killed.

The Germans suffered casualties too. Pilots of seven Ju 88 bombers of the KG 30 reported that Soviet fighters had attacked them at an altitude of 5,000m. The fighter attacks forced the Germans to get rid of their bomb loads and withdraw to their airfield. But one Ju 88 did not manage to escape. This unfortunate bomber was a Ju 88, W.Nr. 142062, aircraft code '4D+LH', of the I./KG 30. According to documents, it is listed as missing over Murmansk together with the crew of *Unteroffizier* Wilhelm Teichmann. The Luftwaffe fighters also suffered losses. According to the book by Eric Mombeek, the Bf 109s of the 5., 6., and 8. *Staffeln* of *Jagdgeschwader 5* (JG 5) together with their Bf 110s escorted the Ju 88s on the bombing raid to Murmansk. A total of 22 Bf 109s took part in the mission. According to the report of the Luftwaffe pilots, between 09:50 and 10:25 they fought with 25–30 Hurricanes at altitudes of 2,000–4,000m. The German fighters scored eight shot down Soviet aircraft against the loss of one Bf 109. It was the Bf 109F-4, W.Nr. 10177, of the 6./JG 5. The pilot, *Oberfähnrich* Willi Pfranger, was taken prisoner. Guards Captain V.N. Alagurov of the 2nd GKAP was the Soviet pilot who added a victory over the Bf 109 to his combat record that day.

On 20 May 1942, the regiment received 12 brand-new Kittyhawks (s/ns 956, 958, 984, 990, 1000, 1001, 1002, 1003, 1004, 1005, 1006, 1007), so the active work was started on converting pilots to the new type. Meanwhile, the 2nd GKAP was summing up the combat results from 24 April to 23 May 1942. During this time, the Kittyhawks conducted two air battles and shot down one Luftwaffe aircraft. In the meantime, the statistics for the Hurricanes were not very encouraging – they conducted 37 air battles, shot down 17 enemy aircraft and damaged 16, while suffering 16 lost and 18 damaged aircraft. The pilots of the regiment clearly needed a new fighter aircraft.

In course of the conversion training the regiment lost its first Kittyhawk – on 29 May 1942, Guards Lieutenant D.F. Maksimov, flying Kittyhawk s/n 1002, failed to maintain direction during take-off and crashed into a DB-3f of the 36th Aviation Division of the Long-Range Aviation. The aircraft caught fire and burnt, the pilot, Guards Lieutenant Dmitri Maksimov, was killed. The next day, 30 May 1942, Lieutenant Colonel B.F. Safonov did not return from a combat mission.

From a description of air combats maintained by the 2nd GKAP:

Guards Captain V.N. Alagurov of the 2nd GKAP awaiting combat sortie.

Hurricane of the Northern Fleet Air Force.

Mission planning: The mission was planned under the direction of Regiment Commander Lieutenant Colonel Safonov. Initially it was planned that covering of the transport ships will be carried out in pairs – Lieutenant Colonel Safonov with Major Kukharenko, and Captain Orlov with Senior Lieutenant Pokrovskiy. About 30 minutes before the flight the order came 'to go on mission in a group of four'.

Approaching the target: After take-off (9:20), the aircraft set a course for Kildin Island, after reaching Kildin Island they turned 280 degrees towards the approaching aircraft. In the Set-Navolok area, after determining the aircraft type (two MBR-2s), the aircraft laid in a course for the transport ships. Major Kukharenko returned from the last stage of the mission. When approaching the convoy, it was noticed that four to six Ju 88s were diving one at a time towards the ships. There were no hits on the transport ships.

Air combat: The attacks were made while the Ju 88s were coming out of a dive. Lieutenant Colonel Safonov missed the first Ju 88 and began to attack the second bomber. The third Ju 88 approached the Kittyhawk of Safonov from the tail, and was attacked from behind by Senior Lieutenant Pokrovskiy. The fourth Ju 88 approached the Kittyhawk of Pokrovskiy from the tail, and was attacked from behind by Captain Orlov. After the first attacks, the Ju 88s attacked by Pokrovskiy and Orlov, turned left at 30 degrees from the direction of the first aircraft. Thus, Pokrovskiy and Orlov flew away from Lieutenant Colonel Safonov during the attack, and after the battle none of them saw the commander again. They could not connect him via the radio as they were working on a different wave frequency, and it was impossible to determine where he had gone. After the battle, Captain Orlov and Senior Lieutenant Pokrovskiy agreed on the radio to rendezvous over the transport ship, which they did. From there, they flew to the airfield, as the fuel reserve was running out and the ammunition was all used up. The Ju 88 dived from an altitude of 2,000m, leaving the dive at an altitude of 300–400m. The battle was fought at altitudes of 200 to 10 metres.

Air combats of individual pilots: Lieutenant Colonel Safonov radioed that he 'had screwed two', a few seconds later that he was 'beating the third' and a few seconds later again radioed 'engine damaged, going to forced ditching'.

Senior Lieutenant Pokrovskiy kept firing at a Ju 88 from behind from a distance of 200m until all of his ammunition was used up; the Ju 88 fell into the water burning.

Captain Orlov was firing machine guns at a Ju 88 from behind from a distance of 200–300m at an altitude of 30m; as a result, the port engine caught fire, the Ju 88 slowed down, Orlov passed it and when he turned around the Ju 88 was no longer in sight. The bomber presumably crashed into the water.

Note: According to the report of the Destroyer Division Commander – more than 10 enemy aircraft bombed the transport ship. One Kittyhawk crashed into the water at an angle.

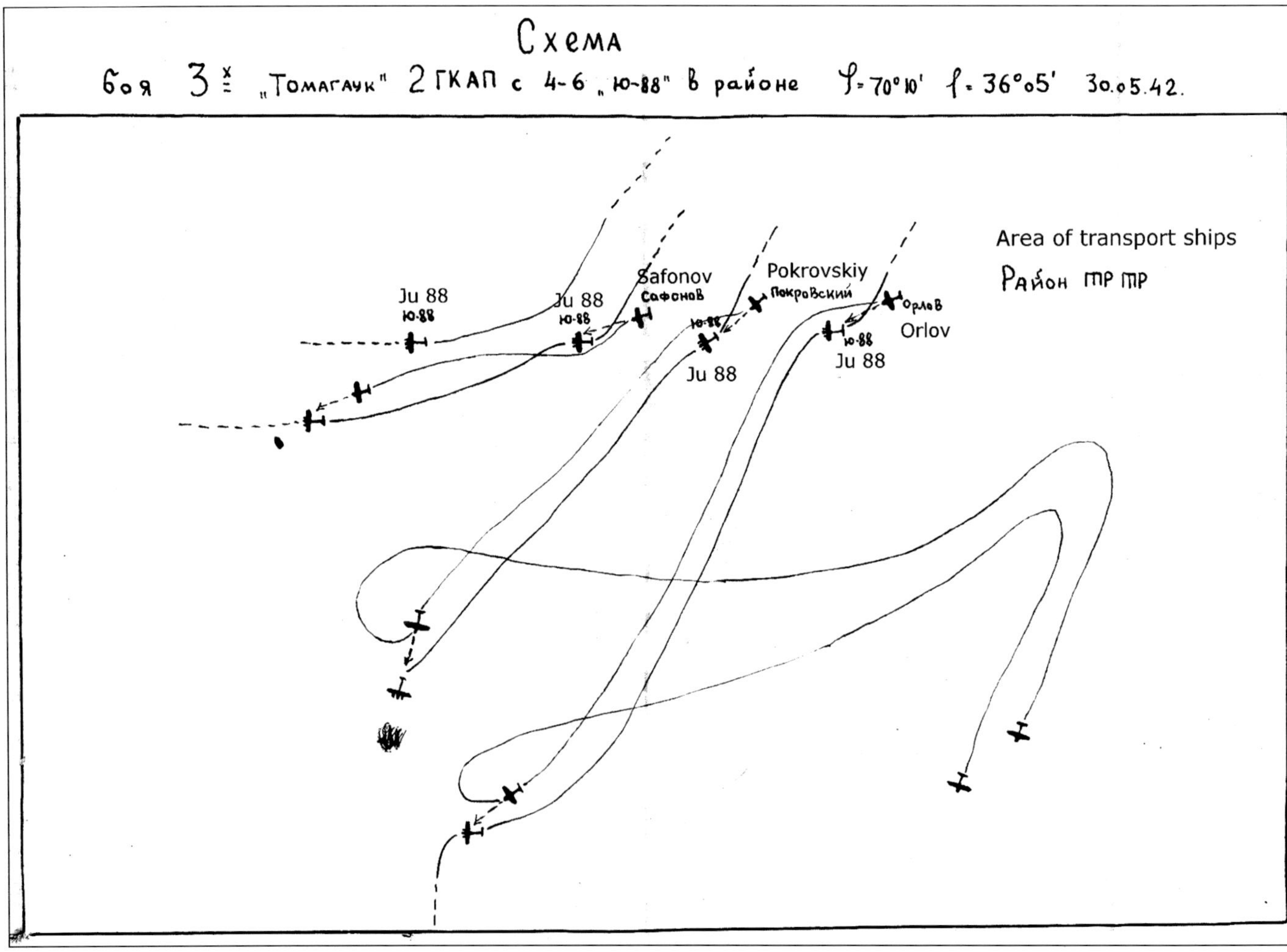

Plan of the air combat between three Kittyhawks of the 2nd GKAP and four to six German Ju 88 bombers (latitude 70°10'N, longitude 36°05'E) on 30 May 1942.

Kittyhawk on the approach to landing.

From combat report No.134 of the 1st and 2nd IAE HQ of the 2nd GKAP, 30 May 1942, 19:00, Vaenga airfield:

> 9:20–10:45. Departure of four Kittyhawk aircraft, Regiment Commander Safonov, pilots Orlov, Pokrovskiy, Kukharenko to meet the shipping convoy. Senior Lieutenant Pokrovskiy attacked a Ju 88 from behind at low-level flight from a distance of 300–200m, the aircraft caught fire and went down burning in the sea to the north-east of the Rybachiy Peninsula. In addition, two more aircraft fell burning in the same area, all ammunition was used. Captain Orlov attacked a Ju 88 from behind from a distance of 300–200m, the starboard engine caught fire, the crash was not observed. The aircraft supposedly crashed north of the Rybachiy Peninsula, in addition two more burning aircraft were observed, all ammunition was expended.

It should be noted that a pair of Pe-3 aircraft of the 95th IAP fought side by side with the pilots of the 2nd GKAP. Lieutenant V.S. Streltsov, the Pe-3 pilot, shot down a Ju 88 over the Barents Sea near convoy PQ-16. It is often claimed that the Pe-3 pilot attacked a single reconnaissance aircraft, but the operational report of the Northern Fleet Air Force states that the Pe-3 attacked four Ju 88s and shot down one of them. The report of the victory achieved by the pilot of heavy fighter was confirmed by the pilots of the 2nd GKAP. The air engagement ended with three shot down Ju 88 allocated to the group of Guards Lieutenant Colonel Safonov: Guards Lieutenant Colonel V.P. Pokrovskiy of the 2nd GKAP and Lieutenant V.S. Streltsov of the 95th IAP scored one kill each; another damaged Ju 88 was assigned to Guards Captain P.I. Orlov of the 2nd GKAP.

According to Eric Mombeek, the Luftwaffe lost two Ju 88s near the convoy. The first was a Ju 88A-4 bomber, W.Nr. 1760, aircraft code '4D+CM', of the 4./KG 30. According to German sources,

Guards Major A.N. Kukharenko. He was awarded the British Distinguished Flying Cross medal.

the aircraft was lost in the vicinity of convoy PQ-16. The crew of *Oberleutnant* Siegfried Scharff perished with the aircraft. The second was reconnaissance Ju 88D-5, W.Nr. 430244, of the 1. *Staffel (F)* of the *Aufklärungsgruppe* 124 (1.(F)/Aufkl.Gr. 124). The aircraft was severely damaged in the convoy area and crashed during landing in Kirkenes. Its crew, led by *Unteroffizier* Ludolf Schmitz, was lucky: no one was injured. It is sometimes stated that a third Ju 88 was lost in the convoy attack, but the KG 30 documents indicate that this aircraft crashed during take-off.

For a long time, it was impossible to establish the details of death of Lieutenant Colonel B.F. Safonov. However, documents from the Northern Fleet destroyer division give the following picture of the pilot's last moments. From the report of the destroyer *Grozny*:

> 09:58. Twelve Ju 88 aircraft entered a dive from an altitude of 5,000–6,000m towards the transport ships, with the sun behind them. The ships opened fire. Up to 40 bombs were dropped. The ships have no visible damage. The flag was lowered on the American transport ship. After eight minutes the firing stopped, the enemy aircraft headed westward.
>
> 10:32. A Tomahawk-type fighter attacked a Ju 88, the bomber caught fire and fell into the water.
>
> 10:35. The main command post received a report from the port anti-aircraft gun station that a Tomahawk-type fighter had fallen into the water.

Apparently, after repulsing the attack of the Luftwaffe bombers, B.F. Safonov returned to cover the convoy and attacked the German reconnaissance aircraft that had been following the convoy. From the report of the Luftwaffe reconnaissance Ju 88:

> At 10:30–10:37 I was attacked by one Pe-3 and one Hurricane aircraft. The latter approached at 100m and turned away after the machine-gun fire was opened from the reconnaissance aircraft. Smoke was pouring from the Hurricane.

The distinguished Soviet ace managed to cause fatal damage to the Luftwaffe Ju 88D-5, W.Nr. 430244, which crashed during landing; but the return fire of the gunners was fatal. The death of Guards Lieutenant Colonel B.F. Safonov, Commander of the 2nd GKAP, was a terrible tragedy to the pilots of the regiment.

The journal of the 72nd SAP of the Northern Fleet Air Force recorded: "Safonov's death caused some confusion in the ranks of our regiment. Some pilots (Captains Reutov, Alagurov) were discouraged. They lost faith in their own forces and started overestimating the enemy. Pilot Reutov said: 'If even Safonov was killed, we have no chance at all.'" But the war continued, and Kittyhawks again flew cover for convoy PQ-16.

From combat report No. 134 of the 1st and 2nd IAE HQ, 30 May 1942, 19:00, Vaenga airfield:

> 13:06–14:30. Four Kittyhawk aircraft took off: pilots Pokrovskiy, Yushinov, Ogorodov, Bychkov. The mission: to cover the convoy at sea. When approaching the ships, two Ju 88 bombers and several fighters were observed, chased but lost sight of due to the long distance.
>
> 16:55–18:27. Four Kittyhawk aircraft – pilots Pokrovskiy, Yushinov, Ogorodov, Bychkov took off to cover the ships at the entrance to Kola Bay.

The pilots who covered convoy PQ-16 were awarded a commendation by the First Lord of the British Admiralty for successfully covering the Allied transport convoy from 25 to 30 May 1942.

After the death of B.F. Safonov, the regiment continued its conversion to Kittyhawks. The regimental technicians, using a lock to suspend an additional fuel tank, created a simple attachment system to carry a FAB-100 bomb. Thus, the first step towards turning the Kittyhawks into fighter-bombers was taken. On 18 June 1942, 10 Kittyhawks (s/ns 1093, 1098, 1102, 1110, 1111, 1112, 1113, 1114, 1115, 1116) arrived at the 2nd GKAP. A little later in the same month, one more with the serial number 751 arrived.

Guards Captain V.S. Adonkin of the 2nd GKAP after a combat mission.

Between 23 May and 22 June 1942 Hurricanes of the 2nd GKAP shot down nine and damaged four enemy aircraft having lost six aircraft shot down and eight damaged. During the same period, the regiment Kittyhawks shot down four and damaged one enemy aircraft having lost only one own aircraft. The outcome was clear.

As of 22 June 1942, the 2nd GKAP had the following aircraft on its strength:

- 37 Hurricanes, of which 15 were serviceable;
- four MiG-3s, of which one was serviceable;
- 12 Tomahawks, of which 10 were serviceable;
- seven SBs, of which six were serviceable;
- nine DB-3fs, of which eight were serviceable;
- one TB-3, out-of-service;
- two U-2s, both also out-of-service.

On 23 June 1942, another Kittyhawk was lost in a crash. At 23:05 the aircraft piloted by Guards Senior Lieutenant V.P. Pokrovskiy took off for a reconnaissance mission over the Petsamo area. A few minutes after take-off the engine caught fire and the pilot was forced to land at the airfield with the landing gear retracted. Aircraft s/n 1002 was sent for repair but was eventually written off. The pilot was not injured.

The next day, 25 June 1942, another air combat took place. Four P-40s of the 2nd GKAP and seven Hurricanes of the 78th IAP repelled a Luftwaffe air raid. From the combat flight log of the 2nd GKAP:

> At 10:30 Major Kovalenko took off for a patrol mission over the airfield. After the signal for landing, he noticed one Bf 109 behind our aircraft in the north-eastern part of the airfield; Kovalenko turned to it and opened machine-gun fire from a distance of 200–150m, the Bf 109 turned right with smoke,

> slipping away. Our pilot spotted another Bf 109 and pursued it to Tuva-Guba. No crash was observed. Major Kovalenko landed at 11:05.

Kovalenko shot down the enemy aircraft when returning to the airfield – he attacked a Bf 109 that was approaching from the tail of a Hurricane of the 78th IAP. The Northern Fleet Air Force Headquarters scored one shot down Bf 109 to the combat account of Guards Major A.A. Kovalenko. German documents recorded that eight Bf 109s of the 6./JG 5 fought 10 Hurricanes in the Rosta area and scored four shot down Soviet aircraft; however, Soviet aircraft suffered no losses then.

At the end of the month, on 29 June 1942, the Kittyhawks scored one shot down Bf 109. Once again, the Guards Major A.A. Kovalenko achieved success. From the combat flight log of the 2nd GKAP:

> At 13:15 six Kittyhawks (leader – Major Kovalenko) took off for a patrolling mission above the airfield. In the Murmansk area they noticed bursts of anti-aircraft artillery fire. Major Kovalenko led the aircraft at the enemy, seven Ju 87 and 10 Bf 109 aircraft. The battle was fought against Bf 109s. Major Kovalenko fired four long bursts at a Bf 109 from a distance of 100–25 m; the enemy caught fire and crashed near Hill 407, 1–1.5km northward. Senior Sergeant Yaroslavtsev fired two long bursts at a Bf 109 from behind on the right at a distance of 150–170m; the enemy aircraft was already emitting smoke before the attack. The Bf 109, with a sharp descent and smoke, disappeared heading west, presumably shot down. The other pilots also attacked enemy aircraft, but did not see them fall. The engine on Kovalenko's aircraft vibrated a lot, he landed at the airfield in Chernopushki without oil. The propeller blades were bent, the lower cowling of the engine was deformed. The pilot was not injured. Junior Lieutenant Gaenko was forced to land at home airfield due to an oil spill on the RPM regulator contacts, which caused the engine to overspin.

Hero of the Soviet Union, Guards Captain A.A. Kovalenko near his aircraft. He was awarded the British Distinguished Flying Cross medal.

All but two of the Kittyhawks, which made forced landings, landed safely at 14:00. The Northern Fleet Air Force Headquarters credited one victory over the Bf 109 to Guards Major A.A. Kovalenko. As can be seen from the above document, the two Kittyhawks again had problems with engines and, unfortunately, these problems would haunt this aircraft type for a long time to come. At about the same time, four Hurricanes of the 768th IAP and a pair of Hurricanes of the 197th IAP fought against Luftwaffe aircraft. The pilots of the 768th IAP scored two shot down Ju 87s, but they suffered casualties as well. During the air engagement, Luftwaffe fighters shot down two Hurricanes (one of the 768th IAP and one of the 197th IAP), both pilots were killed. According to the available German documents, 23 Bf 109s of the II. and III. *Gruppen* of the JG 5 escorted nine Ju 87s. According to the German pilot reports, 17 Bf 109s fought against 15–20 Tomahawks, Hurricanes and I-16 aircraft somewhere between Murmansk and Murmashy at altitudes from 50 to 2,000m. The German pilots scored two shot down Hurricanes with no losses of their own.

On the last day of the month, 30 June 1942, Kittyhawk pilots scored two shot down Bf 109s. At 22:15, seven Kittyhawks of the 2nd GKAP flew to escort six Pe-2 bombers of the 28th Bomber Aviation Regiment to attack the Luostari airfield. At 22:44 six Pe-2s bombed the Luostari airfield from an altitude of 5,300m, 36 FAB-100s were dropped, the crews did not observe the result of the strike. Bomber crews noted heavy anti-aircraft fire in the target area. Attacks from German fighters and anti-aircraft fire resulted in the loss of two Pe-2s. One more aircraft was damaged by anti-aircraft artillery, crashed on landing and was taken to repair shops. One shot down Bf 109 was credited to the gunner of the bomber.

From the combat flight log of the 2nd GKAP:

> West of Titovka we engaged in air combat with four Bf 109s. Senior Sergeant Klimov – from behind at 200m distance and at 1/4-2/4 target aspect ratio – fired two bursts at one Bf 109F, which at that time was firing at a Pe-2 and set it on fire. From behind, at a distance of 100m, he fired one more long burst at a Bf 109F; it caught fire, turned over on its back and fell three to four kilometres to the west of Titovka. Senior Sergeant Yaroslavtsev opened fire from a distance of 200–250m at a Bf 109F from behind; it went into the clouds. At this time, he noticed two Bf 109F below, attacked the leader from behind at the target aspect ratio of 1/4 from a distance of 200–150m, released three bursts, Bf 109F went down, he caught up with it and at distance of 100m fired two more bursts. The Bf 109 crashed into a hillside five kilometres west of Titovka. Aircraft of Sergeant Yaroslavtsev got three bullet holes.

The Northern Fleet Air Force Headquarters scored one shot down Bf 109 each to the combat record of Sergeants P.D. Klimov and I.I. Yaroslavtsev. The German documents on this battle are not complete, but most likely the enemy of the Soviet pilots were the Bf 109s of the II./JG 5 which claimed one victory without its own losses.

The Kittyhawks conducted their first battle of the following month on 2 July 1942.

Four Kittyhawks (leader – Guards Sergeant P.D. Klimov) took off at 11:25 with the mission of patrolling over the airfield. From the combat flight log of the 2nd GKAP: "While patrolling over the airfield at an altitude of 6,000m north-east of the airfield we spotted a group of enemy aircraft of 10 Bf 110s and three Bf 109s, and engaged in air combat. All pilots attacked enemy aircraft, but no shot down enemy aircraft were observed". The Luftwaffe pilots were less shy. According to German documents, Bf 109 and Bf 110 aircraft of the JG 5 escorted Ju 88s during a raid on Murmansk. The German pilots reported two air battles in which they shot down one Kittyhawk.

Five days later, on 7 July 1942, one Kittyhawk did not return from a combat mission. At 15:20, six Kittyhawks (leader – Guards Captain P.I. Orlov) took off to patrol the airfield. From the combat flight log of the 2nd GKAP:

> In the vicinity of Murmansk we engaged in a combat with a group of enemy aircraft. Captain Orlov fired at the rear of a Bf 109 from a distance of 200m, the Bf 109 went into a dive, during which several more machine gun bursts were fired at it. The Bf 109 crashed near Päivä Javr Lake. The other pilots were attacking the enemy aircraft but did not observe any shot down aircraft. Sergeant Titov made a forced landing at Chernopushki airfield, his aircraft was hit in the combat. The aircraft destroyed; the pilot lightly wounded.

Guards Sergeant A.M. Titov. The photo was taken during his cadet years.

In addition to the Kittyhawks of the 2nd GKAP, six I-16s of the 27th IAP, four Hurricanes of the 767th IAP, nine Hurricanes of the 769th IAP, nine Hurricanes of the 78th IAP and 2nd GKAP, and several Airacobras of the 255th IAP engaged the Luftwaffe aircraft. Pilots of the 769th IAP shot down a Bf 109 and Ju 87, but lost one Hurricane, the pilot survived. The Northern Fleet Air Force Headquarters credited one shot down Bf 109 each to the combat record of Captain P.I. Orlov of the 2nd GKAP and Lieutenant I.I. Voinov of the 255th IAP. The only loss of the Northern Fleet Air Force was Kittyhawk s/n 1113 of the 2nd GKAP. According to German documents, the Bf 109s were providing air cover for a raid of two bomber groups, one of which bombed Murmansk and the other the Vaenga-1 airfield. The German fighter pilots of the 6. and 7. *Staffeln* of the JG 5 reported that they had shot down several Soviet fighters without losses of their own.

The air battles did not slow down. The next day, 8 July 1942, 18:15, 10 Kittyhawks of the 2nd GKAP (leader – Guards Sergeant Major N.A. Bokiy) took off to intercept Luftwaffe aircraft which were heading to bomb the Vaenga-1 airfield. They caught up with the German aircraft after the latter had already dropped the bombs. From the combat flight log of the 2nd GKAP:

> While catching up with bombers in the Kädel Javr area, we met a group of Bf 109s and Bf 110s, with which we engaged in an air battle. Sergeant Major Bokiy fired one long burst at a Bf 109 from a distance of 300–400m, the enemy aircraft nose-dived, and then again fired twice two machine-gun bursts each time from a distance of 300m. The Bf 109 descended and fled westward emitting black smoke, presumably shot down. Junior Lieutenant Laptev attacked one Bf 109 and opened machine-gun fire from above and behind from a distance of 400m, after which the Bf 109 went into a dive during which Laptev fired several more machine-gun bursts at it from a distance of 250–100m. The Bf 109 turned over onto its back and went into an uncontrolled fall. The pilot did not observe the crash. When the aircraft of Junior Lieutenant Laptev came out of a dive, the engine failed and the aircraft was forced to ditch. The aircraft sank 1.5–2m deep. The pilot was returned to his unit.

All aircraft, except for aircraft of A.Y. Laptev, landed at 19:35. The Northern Fleet Air Force Headquarters credited the shot down Bf 109 to the Junior Lieutenant A.Y. Laptev. The ditched Kittyhawk was lifted and sent for repair. The Kittyhawks most likely fought against the Bf 109s of the 6./JG 5. German documents that can shed light on this battle are not yet found.

The war continued, and 10 days later, on 18 July 1942, the pilots of the 2nd GKAP successfully encountered the Luftwaffe bombers. At 14:22 six Kittyhawks of the 2nd GKAP (leader – Guards Captain P.I. Orlov) took off for a patrol mission over the airfield. From the combat flight log of the 2nd GKAP:

> The Germans tried to make a bombing raid on the airfield, but our fighters repulsed them. On the Rosta traverse, with permission from the ground control, they engaged seven Ju 88s. Having made a head-on attack, the pilots then were choosing the targets on their own. Captain Orlov was approaching three Ju 88s from their tail and fired at one Ju 88 from a distance of 200–50m. He aimed at the gunner's position and at the port engine. The bomber was set on fire in the vicinity of Retinskoye Lake and crashed in the area south of Sayda Lake. Lieutenant Polyakov fired short bursts

at the starboard engine of one Ju 88 from behind at a distance of 300–20m, and set fire to the engine in the area of Vaenga. Polyakov continued to fire at the Ju 88 till its crash in the area of Retinskoye Lake. When falling, the Ju 88 exploded. Senior Sergeant Klimov fired two bursts at the cockpit of the leading aircraft from a distance of 500m and up to 50m, the Ju 88 turned over and went down. It crashed in the vicinity of Mishukov Hill. Sergeant Major Bokiy fired a short burst at the starboard side of a Ju 88 from a distance of 200m, then fired a second burst at the same place from a distance of 100–150m, after which he fired a burst at the tail of a Ju 88 from a distance of 150m. The bomber crashed 57km south-west of Bolshoye Uragubskoye Lake. Sergeant Golodnikov, covering Polyakov's aircraft, fired a long burst at the fuselage and cockpit of a Bf 109 from a distance of 200–250m, which turned left exposing its back. From the same distance, Polyakov fired a burst at the back of the Bf 109 that went to the ground smoking and rolling. Presumably, the aircraft was shot down in the vicinity of Arno Lake. Klimov's aircraft has one bullet hole in the wing. Golodnikov's aircraft sustained damage to gear and chain of the rudder trimmer." All Kittyhawks landed at 3:20pm.

A single MiG-3 was trying to help the Kittyhawks in this combat; the MiG-3 took off after them and was flown by Guards Lieutenant D.G. Sokolov. From the combat flight log of the 2nd GKAP:

> Over the airfield, I attacked a Ju 88 without success. I noticed that two Bf 109s were following a Yak-1, so I attacked the first one from 250m with no success. I myself was attacked by the second Bf 109. The fuel pipeline, horizontal and vertical stabilizers of the MiG-3 were damaged. I landed safely on the home airfield.

Guards Senior Lieutenant D.G. Sokolov. The photo was taken during his cadet years.

Together with the pilots of the 2nd GKAP, three LaGG-3s of the 255th IAP fought against the Luftwaffe fighters. The Northern Fleet Air Force Headquarters credited one Ju 88 each to Guards Captain P.I. Orlov, Guards Lieutenant S.T. Polyakov, Guards Sergeant Major N.A. Bokiy, and Senior Sergeant P.D. Klimov. Also, one Ju 88 each were credited to the pilots of the 255th IAP: Sergeant Major G.N. Chilikov and Sergeant D. Filippov. In addition, one shot down Bf 109 was credited to Guards Sergeant N.G. Golodnikov of the 2nd GKAP. According to German documents, 22 Ju 88 bombers, covered by fighters, dropped bombs on the Rosta settlement. Two Ju 88s, W.Nr. 2106 and W.Nr. 142090, of the *Erprobungsstaffel*/KG 30 were shot down in the course of this mission. Their crews died. The Luftwaffe bombers were covered by 24 Bf 109s of the II. and III. *Gruppen* of the JG 5, and the pilots of the Bf 109s claimed three Soviet fighters shot down. During this battle the Northern Fleet Air Force lost one LaGG-3 of the 255th IAP, but its pilot managed to leave the doomed fighter by parachute. Whether the German fighters sustained losses is not known.

On the next day, 19 July 1942, six Kittyhawks (leader – Guards Senior Lieutenant V.P. Pokrovskiy) took off at 13:37 to patrol over the airfield. From the combat flight log of the 2nd GKAP:

> In the area of Kädel Javr Lake at an altitude of 6,500m our pilots spotted a group of enemy aircraft, turned on them, the enemy aircraft turned to the west. On the return route, in the Mishukovo area, Sergeant [Lieutenant – *Author's note*] Polyakov attacked one Bf 109 from a distance of 300–400m from behind with no success.

All Kittyhawks landed safely at 15:20.

The Northern Fleet Air Force Headquarters did not credit any victories to the pilots of the 2nd GKAP on that day. The pilots of the 20th IAP at the same time also had air engagements with Luftwaffe fighters and bombers. The Northern Fleet Air Force Headquarters credited three Ju 88s and two Bf 109s to the pilots of the 20th IAP. According to German documents, 24 Ju 88s of the KG 30 under cover of 25 Bf 109s and several Bf 110s aircraft of the JG 5 made a strike on the Rosta settlement [a settlement in Murmansk region, now a district in the northern part of Murmansk – *Author's note*]. The Luftwaffe fighters claimed to have encountered Soviet aircraft and shot down two Soviet fighters. According to available archive documents, Luftwaffe aircraft sustained no casualties on that flight.

The Kittyhawks fought their last battle in July 1942 on 29 July. Four fighters (leader – Guards Lieutenant S.T. Polyakov) took off at 17:27 for a patrol mission. Further details are described in the combat flight log of the 2nd GKAP: "In the vicinity of Mishukovo we spotted 8–10 Bf 110s. Lieutenant Polyakov fired three to four bursts at a Bf 110 strictly into the tail from a distance of 500–400m. The Bf 110 fled westward." All Kittyhawks landed safely at 18:50.

The Kittyhawks were barely involved in this air engagement, while the rest of the Soviet aircraft were unsuccessful in that battle. In addition to the Kittyhawks of the 2nd GKAP, four Yak-1s of the 20th IAP, seven LaGG-3s of the 255th IAP, four Kittyhawks and one Airacobra of the 19th GIAP, four Hurricanes of the 767th IAP and three Hurricanes of the 769th IAP of Air Defense Forces flew to intercept the enemy forces. Soviet pilots did not claim victories over Luftwaffe aircraft, while three Hurricanes of 769th IAP of Air Defense Forces did not return from that combat. For two pilots of this regiment the battle was their last one. According to German documents, 14 Ju 88s of the KG 30, covered by 11 Bf 110s and 13 Bf 109s of the JG 5, attacked the Rosta settlement. The German fighters engaged in an air battle with Hurricanes and, according to the pilots' report, one was shot down. The German aircraft suffered no losses.

The Kittyhawks conducted their first battle in the last month of summer on 5 August 1942. A trio of fighters (leader – Guards Lieutenant P.D. Romanov) took off at 12:40 and fought a short battle against German fighters. From the combat flight log of the 2nd GKAP: "I fired one long burst at three Bf 109s from a distance of 200–300m at the target aspect ratio of 4/4, south-east of Romanov airfield. The fighters fled towards Murmansk." All Kittyhawks landed safely at 13:50. Naturally, the Northern Fleet Air Force Headquarters did not credit the victories for the 2nd GKAP. At the same time, four Hurricanes of the 78th IAP engaged in air combat against Bf 109s, and two pilots, Senior Lieutenant Kh.I. Abishev and Lieutenant P.L. Kolomiets scored one alleged victory each over the Bf 109s. However, the 78th IAP lost one Hurricane and the other was damaged. In addition to the Northern Fleet Air Force fighters, seven Hurricanes of the 767th IAP and three Kittyhawks of the 768th IAP were engaged in the combat. The pilots of the 768th IAP claimed one shot down Bf 109, but one Hurricane and one Kittyhawk did not return from the battle; their pilots bailed out with parachutes. According to German sources, 14 Ju 87s of the I. *Gruppe* of the 5th *Sturzkampfgeschwader*, under the cover of 24 Bf 109s of the JG 5, attacked Soviet batteries in the Litsa Bay. According to Luftwaffe fighter pilots' reports, they had an air engagement with Soviet fighter aircraft near Murmansk and claimed seven victories with no own losses.

Two days later, on 7 August 1942, the fighters of the 2nd GKAP engaged in combat against German 'hunters'. At 17:45 five Kittyhawks (leader – Guards Senior Lieutenant A.V. Kuzichkin) took off on patrol mission over the airfield. From the combat flight log of the 2nd GKAP:

> We engaged two Bf 109s over the airfield. Guards Lieutenant Kuzichkin attacked a wingman of the Bf 109s in a dive from a distance of 100–150m, while the Bf 109s were approaching six LaGG-3s from behind. He fired six machine-gun bursts, the engine of the Bf 109 caught fire, the enemy aircraft abruptly descended and disappeared in the clouds. Presumably, the Bf 109 was shot down. Sergeants Grigoriev and Titov fired at a Bf 109 unsuccessfully. During the battle the canopy of Titov's aircraft was torn off and he made a forced landing at the home airfield. The aircraft has one splinter hole in the starboard wing and two dents in the wing centreplane. All other Kittyhawks, except for the aircraft of Guards Sergeant A.M. Titov, landed at 18:50.

Together with the Kittyhawks, seven I-16s of the 27th IAP and eight Yak-1s of the 20th IAP fought against the Bf 109s. Basing on the results of the air combat, the Air Force Headquarters credited one presumable victory over the Bf 109s to Lieutenant A.V. Kuzichkin of the 2nd GKAP and Lieutenant V. Ageichev of the 27th IAP each. The Northern Fleet aviation lost one Yak-1 of the 20th IAP, its pilot died. According to German documents, the Ju 87 dive bombers, covered by 21 Bf 109s of the JG 5, attacked Soviet artillery batteries near Murmansk. During the air battle the Luftwaffe fighter pilots claimed four victories with no losses of their own.

Three days later a new combat occurred. On 10 August at 13:35 five Kittyhawks (leader – Guards Captain P.I. Orlov) took off to patrol the airfield and encountered enemy fighters. From the combat flight log of 2nd GKAP:

> On patrol over Polyarnoe at an altitude of 1,500m we fought against four Bf 109s, and we encountered six Bf 109s over the airfield at an altitude of 2,500. All pilots attacked enemy aircraft; no crashes were observed. At 14:02 Guards Sergeant Major Romanov made an emergency landing at the own airfield due to engine vibration. The remaining Kittyhawks landed at 15:00.

Simultaneously with the fighters of the 2nd GKAP, 10 LaGG-3s of the 255th IAP and eight Yak-1s of the 20th IAP fought against the Luftwaffe fighters. Following the results of the air combats, the Northern Fleet Air Force Headquarters credited one shot down Bf 109 to Sergeant Major S.D. Fillipov. The losses of the Northern Fleet Air Force were one damaged LaGG-3. According to German documents, six Bf 110s under cover of 20 Bf 109s bombed Varlamovo. In the target area, the Luftwaffe pilots engaged in an air combat against the Soviet fighters and claimed two victories without their own losses.

Four days later, on 14 August 1942, another air battle occurred. Five Kittyhawks (leader – Guards Major I.K. Tumanov) flew patrols over the airfield at 11:37. From the combat flight log of the 2nd GKAP:

> While on the patrol near Mishukovo we noticed eight Ju 87s, four Bf 110s and 10 Bf 109s flying at an altitude of 4,000–5,000m. Anti-aircraft artillery was firing barrage fire. Enemy aircraft saw our fighters and turned away, heading 300 degrees. Guards Major Tumanov, flying a Tomahawk aircraft, had the engine cut-off at take-off and made a forced landing

Guards Major I.K. Tumanov, Commander of the 2nd GKAP, awarded with British Distinguished Flying Cross medal. He was was killed in action on 6 December 1942.

at our own airfield. At the end of the runaway the aircraft hit the bushes, resulting in broken landing gear, tailwheel, and one aileron, and bent propeller. The aircraft is subject to medium repairs.

The other Kittyhawks landed at 12:45 with no problems.

The other participants of the events did not do any better in combat than the pilots of the 2nd GKAP. In total, nine LaGG-3s of the 255th IAP, five Yak-1s of the 20th IAP, two Airacobras and four Kittyhawks of the 19th GIAP flew to intercept German aircraft in addition to the Kittyhawks of the 2nd GKAP. The Soviet pilots claimed no victories; neither did they suffer any losses. German documents indicate that nine Ju 87s of the I. /StG 5, covered by 18 Bf 109s, attacked Soviet anti-aircraft battery positions. The pilots of the Bf 109s reported an air engagement with Soviet fighters in which they did not claim any victory but suffered no losses either. Note that the Ju 87s, according to Soviet reports, dropped bombs near the front line to no avail.

Another battle on 21 August 1942 resulted in serious losses in the 6./JG 5, and these losses to an elite unit were inflicted by the Kittyhawks pilots of the 2nd GKAP. It all started with a routine patrol over the airfield. At 16:08 four Kittyhawks (leader – Guards Captain D.A. Reutov) took off. From the combat flight log of the 2nd GKAP:

> We engaged in air combat against a group of Bf 109s over the airfield. Guards Captain Reutov approached a Bf 109 in a climb from behind (distance of 50m) and fired one burst of machine-gun fire into its back, after which the Bf 109 descended to the south emitting smoke. When exiting the engagement, while following the enemy, he fired two machine gun bursts from a distance of 200–300m, made a combat turn and headed to his group. He attacked the second Bf 109 from a distance of 100–150m, from behind and above, and released one machine-gun burst, the Bf 109 turned to the west leaving a trail of white smoke, then turned to the south with a descent. Both Bf 109s were heavily damaged or shot down. Sergeant Major Bolshakov fired two machine-gun bursts at a Bf 109 from behind and above at the target aspect ratio of 2/4 from a distance of 100–150m. At the end of the combat at 16:45 he attacked the second Bf 109 at an altitude of 300–500m from a distance of 200–300m from behind and fired seven bursts from above. The enemy aircraft was pursued until all ammunition was used. The Bf 109 fell down west of Polyarny. Sergeant Yudin attacked the enemy aircraft, but did not observe any crashes. At 16:50, Pokrovskiy made an emergency landing at home airfield due to engine cut-off. Yudin's aircraft has two cannon shot holes and up to 20 bullet holes.

All Kittyhawks, except for the aircraft of Guards Senior Lieutenant V.P. Pokrovskiy, landed safely at 17:17.

Together with the Kittyhawks of the 2nd GKAP, seven I-16s of the 27th IAP and four LaGG-3s of the 255th IAP fought against the German fighters. Following the results of the air combat, the Northern Fleet Air Force Headquarters credited one shot down Bf 109 each to Guards Captain D.A. Reutov and Sergeant Major P.V. Bolshakov, and also to the pilot of the 27th IAP Captain V.A. Ageichev. The losses of the Northern Fleet Air Force were two LaGG-3s of the 255th IAP, whose pilots survived, and two damaged I-16s of the 27th IAP which were directed for repairs. The army fighters could not reach the battle site in time, as they had no time to gain altitude due to the late warning. According to German documents, 10 Bf 110s under the cover of 14 Bf 109s of the II. and III. *Gruppen* of the JG 5 attacked Murmashy airfield. The heavy Bf 110s dropped their bombs on the airfield, missed the target by a couple of kilometres, and began to depart to the west. The remaining Bf 109s were engaged in combat against the approaching fighter aircraft of the Soviet Navy. Luftwaffe pilots claimed 14 victories over Soviet fighters, but admitted the loss of two Bf 109s. The first was a Bf 109F-4/trop, W.Nr. 10101, tactical number 'Yellow 6'. It was flown by *Oberleutnant* Hans-Diether Hartwein, Commander of the 6. *Staffel*. He managed to make an emergency landing 35km west from Murmansk in the area of Urd Lake but was missing after landing. The second lost aircraft was Bf 109F-4, W.Nr. 10161. Its pilot, *Feldwebel* Albert Brunner, piloted the damaged aircraft to Motovka, where he bailed out by parachute and managed to reach the German positions. Another Bf 109, piloted by *Feldwebel* Rudolf Müller, was damaged in the engagement but returned to the home airfield.

Guards Captain D.A. Reutov. He was killed in combat on 26 December 1942.

The air battles continued with the same intensity in September. Two of them took place on 8 September 1942. The first of them occurred around midday. Three Kittyhawks (leader – Guards Lieutenant S.T. Polyakov) took off at 12:30 to patrol over the airfield. From the combat flight log of the 2nd GKAP:

> We fought an air battle over the airfield against a group of Bf 109Fs. Lieutenant Polyakov fired three bursts at one Bf 109F from a distance of 300m, at the target aspect ratio of 3/4–4/4. I did not observe the result of the attack. Guards Sergeant Major Bokiy fired two bursts at Bf 109 from a distance of 200m strictly from behind at the moment when he was ascending, and the enemy aircraft turned to the left. During the combat, the aircraft of Sergeant Golodnikov lost a side hatch cover due

to heavy overload when entering a spin. Following the order of the wing leader, I landed at 13:02.

All other Kittyhawks, except for N.G. Golodnikov's aircraft, landed at 13:40.

A total of 44 Soviet fighters flew out to intercept the enemy: four Hurricanes and one Kittyhawk of the 122nd IAD of Air Defense Forces; four Airacobras of the 19th GIAP, four Hurricanes of the 197th IAP and six Hurricanes of the 837th IAP of the 14th Army Air Force; six Hurricanes of the 78th IAP, seven LaGG-3s of the 255th IAP, five Yak-1s of the 20th IAP, three P-40s of the 2nd GKAP and four I-15bis' of the 27th IAP of the Northern Fleet Air Force. Not all of them took part in the engagement. The Northern Fleet Air Force Headquarters credited one shot down Bf 109 to the pilot of the 255th IAP, Sergeant Major S.P. Popov. The Northern Fleet Air Force lost one LaGG-3 of the 255th IAP, whose pilot managed to bail out by parachute. In addition to the pilots of the Northern Fleet Air Force, the pilots of the 19th GIAP (who did not claim the kill) shot down a Ju 88 of the KG 30, according to available German archive documents. According to German sources, that day the Ju 88s, under cover of the Bf 109s of the II. and III. *Gruppen* of the JG 5, bombed targets near Murmansk. One Ju 88 did not return from the mission. Pilots of the Bf 109 fighters reported an air battle against Soviet fighters between Murmashy and Varlamovo. The JG 5 added 14 victories to their score without own losses.

The second battle that day was fought by the Kittyhawks in the afternoon. As in the morning, three Kittyhawks (leader – Guards Lieutenant S.T. Polyakov) took off on a patrol mission over the airfield at 15:35. From the combat flight log of the 2nd GKAP:

> We spotted a Bf 110 over the airfield at an altitude of 6,000m we which we attacked in turn. Guards Sergeant Major Bokiy from a distance of 200–400m at the target aspect ratio of 1/4 fired five bursts. Lieutenant Polyakov fired five to six short bursts from rear and below from a distance of 300–500m at the same Bf 110, which got away into the cloud heading to Ura-Guba. Above the airfield, I fired two bursts of machine-gun fire at a Bf 109 from the front and below, from a distance of 200–300m; the fighter escaped heading towards Polyarnoe. Sergeant Golodnikov was covering the aircraft of Polyakov and Bokiy, he did not fire.

This time all Kittyhawks landed safely at 16:56.

No victories were credited to the pilots of the 2nd GKAP, and things were no better for the other naval fighter pilots. A total of 13 fighters of the Northern Fleet Air Force took off: four LaGG-3s of the 255th IAP, two Yak-1s of the 20th IAP, three Kittyhawks of the 2nd GKAP and four Hurricanes of the 78th IAP. They were not successful, but suffered no losses either. The pilots of the Air Defense Forces and 14th Army were not lucky as well. Five fighters of the 122nd IAD of the Air Defense Forces (four Hurricanes and one Kittyhawk of the 767th and 768th IAPs) fought four Bf 109Fs to no avail. Meanwhile, 15 Army fighters (four Airacobras of the 19th GIAP, three Hurricanes of the 197th IAP and eight Hurricanes of the 837th IAP) engaged the Luftwaffe fighters. As a result, the pilots were credited with one shot down and two damaged Bf 109s at the cost of three Hurricanes, with two Soviet fighter pilots killed and one wounded. The German documents indicate that Bf 109s of the II. and III. *Gruppen* of the JG 5, covering Ju 88s of the KG 30 attacking targets near Murmansk, fought several air combats against Soviet fighters. The Bf 109 pilots claimed 11 victories with no losses of their own.

On the next day, 9 September 1942, the Kittyhawk pilots had to repulse an attack of German bombers on their airfield. A pair of Kittyhawks (leader – Guards Lieutenant S.T. Polyakov) took off at 11:00 and attacked Luftwaffe Ju 88 bombers. From the combat flight log of the 2nd GKAP:

> I spotted six or seven Ju 88s in the northern part of the airfield. While pursuing them in the area of Belokamenka, we engaged in combat against four Bf 109s which were coming from left and above on intersecting courses. Lieutenant Polyakov attacked one Bf 109 from a distance of 250–300m strictly from the tail, fired four or five bursts, and the enemy's aircraft descended into the clouds. The second Bf 109 was attacked head-on. The Bf 109 avoided the fight and left the combat scene to the west. Senior Sergeant Klimov attacked one Bf 109 from a distance of 200m at the target aspect ratio of 1/4 and fired two bursts from the rear and bottom. The Bf 109 went into a glide. Further pursuit was stopped as the aircraft lost speed and dropped the wing. The aircraft of Lieutenant Polyakov has one bullet hole.

Both Kittyhawks landed at their airfield at 12:00.

All in all, 18 fighters of the Northern Fleet Air Force took part in repulsing the Luftwaffe air strike at Vaenga-1 airfield: three Yak-1s of the 20th IAP and two Kittyhawks of the 2nd GKAP, five LaGG-3s of the 255th IAP, four Hurricanes of the 78th IAP and four I-16s of the 27th IAP. No victories were credited to the pilots of the Northern Fleet Air Force, but they suffered no losses either. Sixteen fighters of the 14th Army Air Force took off to help the Fleet fighters: three Airacobras and two Kittyhawks of the 19th GIAP, two Hurricanes of the 197th IAP and nine Hurricanes of the 837th IAP. The pilots of the 837th IAP claimed one victory over the Bf 109, but one of their Hurricanes was directed for major repairs after landing. The pilot was not injured. During the combat the pilot of the Airacobra of the 19th GIAP, Junior Lieutenant E.A. Krivosheev, rammed Bf 109F-4, W.Nr. 8245, of the 6./JG 5, flown by *Obergefreiter* Günther Hoffmann. As a result of the ramming both pilots were killed. According to German documents, Ju 88 aircraft of the KG 30, covered by Bf 109s of III./JG 5, bombed the Vaenga-1 airfield. The Luftwaffe bombers were successful: two Pe-3s and one DB-3f were destroyed at the base, and one DB-3f had to undergo major repairs afterwards. The Luftwaffe bombers suffered no losses. The German pilots of the Bf 109s reported shooting down 17 aircraft during an air combat against Soviet fighters, losing one of their Bf 109F-4s, W.Nr. 8245.

The Germans did not become complacent and two days later, on 11 September 1942, launched a new attack on Soviet airfields. At 15:24, four Kittyhawks (leader – Guards Major A.A. Kovalenko) flew out to intercept Luftwaffe bombers. What happened next is recorded in the combat flight log of the 2nd GKAP:

> While on patrol over Varlamovo, 11 Ju 88 were spotted. Captain Pokrovskiy fired one machine-gun burst at a Ju 88 from a distance of 400–500m. Captain Reutov fired one burst at a Ju 88 from a distance of 400–500m. While attacking they were themselves attacked from behind by Bf 109 fighters; and Major Kovalenko fired one machine-gun burst at one of them. The Bf 109s departed on a 270 degrees course. The bombers could not be intercepted after the bombing raid. At 16:00 Captain Alagurov made a forced landing at the airfield due to the engine cut-off in the air."

All of the Kittyhawks, except for V.N. Alagurov's, landed at 16:50.

However, the Kittyhawks were not the only group of Soviet fighters engaged in the combat with German aircraft at this time. The four Yak-1s of the 20th IAP fought against a pair of Bf 109s to no avail, and six LaGG-3s of the 255th IAP fought a group of Ju 88s and Bf 110s. After the air engagement, the Northern Fleet Air Force Headquarters credited one shot down Ju 88 and two Bf 110s to the pilots of the 255th IAP. Thirteen Army fighters took off to support the pilots of the Fleet: two Airacobras, two Kittyhawks of the 19th GIAP and eight Hurricanes of the 837th and 197th IAPs. The pilots of the 19th GIAP and 197th IAP fought a short battle against the Bf 109s, but were unsuccessful. Fortunately, no losses were sustained by either the Navy or Army fighters in this battle. German documents state that Bf 109 aircraft of the 6. and 8. *Staffeln* of the JG 5 escorted the Ju 88s and Bf 110s that day to attack a Soviet airfield near Murmansk. The Luftwaffe pilots claimed four victories without their own losses. However, it is not entirely clear about the loss of one Bf 110, which made an emergency landing that day. If the data corresponds to the reports of Soviet pilots, it was shot down by the pilots of the 255th IAP.

On 22 September 1942 the Kittyhawks again were engaged in combat against Luftwaffe fighters. At 12:58 two groups of Kittyhawks of four aircraft each (leader – Guards Major I.K. Tumanov and Guards Captain V.N. Alagurov) were on patrol mission near the airfield. From the combat flight log of the 2nd GKAP:

> We engaged a group of Bf 109Fs over the airfield. Klimov fired two bursts at a Bf 109F. The aircraft went westwards. Bokiy fired from a distance of 200m, at the target aspect ratio of 2/4, at two Bf 109Fs which were approaching the aircraft of the regimental commander from the tail. The aircraft turned to Mishukovo, at this time Bokiy was attacked himself, banked to the left, escaped the attack and fired one burst at a Bf 109 from a distance of 300–400m. No results of the attack were observed. Sergeant Yemelyanov' aircraft was hit in the air combat, the pilot was wounded and taken to hospital, the aircraft is sent for repairs. In the vicinity of the airfield, we engaged in air combat against a group of Bf 109Fs. Captain Alagurov fired one burst from top and behind at a Bf 109F from a distance of 250–300m. Sergeant Shvetsov fired one burst at a Bf 109s from a distance of 300m at the target aspect ratio of 3/4 and the second burst from a distance of 400–500m. No results were observed.

The Northern Fleet Air Force Headquarters did not score any victories. Simultaneously with the pilots of the 2nd GKAP, seven LaGG-3s of the 255th IAP engaged in air combat against the Bf 109 aircraft. As a result, one LaGG-3 was shot down and its pilot was killed. According to available German documents, the Bf 109 aircraft of the 7. and 8. *Staffeln* of the JG 5 were performing a 'free hunting' mission at that time. The pilots of the 8. *Staffel* reported an engagement against Kittyhawks and Hurricanes in which they shot down five Soviet fighters without any losses of their own.

Five days later, on 27 September 1942, the Luftwaffe fighters managed to inflict a serious defeat on the Northern Fleet Air Force. Unfortunately, two Kittyhawks of the 2nd GKAP were lost on that day. At 12:00, six Kittyhawks (leader – Guards Captain V.N. Alagurov) took off to intercept enemy aircraft. From the combat flight log of the 2nd GKAP:

> There was an air combat against six Bf 109Fs near the airfield. Captain Alagurov fired three bursts at a Bf 109F from a distance of 300–400m in the head-on attack. The group of Bf 109Fs headed into the sun. At an altitude of 3,500m I noticed a parachutist and two Bf 109Fs diving at him. I began to chase the last Bf 109F but they made a combat turn and left upwards. Sergeant Major Bokiy fired two bursts at two Bf 109Fs from the rear and below at the target aspect ratio of 2/4 from a distance of 300–400m; the enemy aircraft climbed away. In a group of six, I attacked a Bf 109F from a distance of 100–200m, I fired one burst at it, lost speed and went into a spin. I recovered after two spin turns and noticed two Bf 109Fs, then spotted three more Bf 109Fs above, and went to attack the latter. I attacked the rear fighter from a distance of 400–500m and was attacked by a Bf 109F myself. I avoided the attack by making a left turn, and then I saw a parachutist under attack from above by a Bf 109F, so I fired one burst at it at the target aspect ratio of 2/4 from a distance of 200m. I drove the Bf 109F away from the parachutist and escorted the latter to the ground. Sergeant Yudin was attacking the enemy aircraft that were approaching the wing leader from behind, and made several attacks from a distance of 300–400m. The Bf 109Fs escaped the attacks by climbing away. Senior Sergeant Klimov protected the tails of wing leaders until one Tomahawk joined them; then he began to choose a target. He attacked a Bf 109F, fired four bursts from a distance of 200–300m at the target aspect ratio of 1/4, from below and head-on. He made the next attack on the group of Bf 109Fs, and then he noticed that the wingman was alone, so he started to attack lonely enemy aircraft individually, knocking them out from under the tails of Yaks and LaGGs. He was flying alone until landing. Senior Sergeant Grigoriev and Sergeant Shvarev were shot down in the air battle. The aircraft were on fire, the pilots bailed out with parachutes. Grigoriev was lightly wounded, Shvarev received slight bruises. The aircraft flown by Sergeant Major Bokiy suffered damage to the spar, stabilizer, rudder, port wing, tail; the trimmer was knocked out, the skin was torn off the starboard wing and the aileron was damaged. The aircraft needs a medium repair, the pilot was unharmed."

The Kittyhawks, except for the two lost in the battle, landed at 13:30. Kittyhawks s/ns 1102 and 1110 did not return from the battle.

At the same time as the Kittyhawks of the 2nd GKAP, the pilots of the 255th IAP fought against the Luftwaffe in this air combat. The Northern Fleet Air Force Headquarters credited a victory over a Bf 109 to Lieutenant V.G. Tovstoy of the 255th IAP basing on the results of the air engagements. According to the reports from the ground observation posts, Lieutenant G.N. Chilikov of the same regiment shot down a Bf 109 by ramming it, but also lost his life. In addition to the aircraft of G.N. Chilikov, another LaGG-3 was shot down, according to the pilots' reports, by friendly anti-aircraft artillery. The pilot managed to bail out of the aircraft with parachute. The fighters of the 14th Army Air Force took off to help the Naval pilots, but were unable to catch up with the Luftwaffe aircraft. According to German documents, the Bf 109s of the 5., 6., 7. and 8. *Staffeln* of the JG 5 covered the Bf 110s and Ju 88s in a bombing raid on the Murmashy airfield. That raid caused no losses at the airfield. The Luftwaffe fighter pilots claimed eight victories with no losses of their own. However, a number of German documents mention damage to a Bf 109F-4 W.Nr.7583 of the 7./JG 5. The aircraft sustained 50% damage, but whether this occurred during take-off or landing at Luostari airfield remains unclear.

The second air combat of the Kittyhawks on that day was far less dramatic. Three aircraft (leader – Guards Sergeant P.D. Klimov) took off at 16:21 to patrol the airfield. From the combat flight log of the 2nd GKAP:

> At an altitude of 2,000m we spotted two Bf 109Fs, approached them from tail, but they zoomed away. We fired two bursts at them from behind, from a distance of 400–500m. At an altitude of 4,500m, I spotted a Bf 109F, turned to it, but the Bf 109F began to leave with a climb. We followed it to Ura-Guba at an altitude of 5,000–6,000m and continued the engagement over the airfield. At 17:29 Sergeant Titov made a forced landing at home airfield due to engine failure.

All Kittyhawks landed at 17:39.

Five aircraft of the 20th IAP fought together with the Kittyhawks in the same air combat against the Bf 109s – they lost one Yak-1, but the pilot managed to bail out with parachute. The pilots of the 2nd GKAP and 20th IAP did not claim any victories. Pilots of the 14th Army Air Force also flew to intercept Luftwaffe fighters. Five Hurricanes were flown by the 837th IAP, nine Tomahawks by the 20th GIAP, and one Airacobra by the 19th GIAP. As a result of the air combat, the pilots of the 20th GIAP scored two shot down Bf 109s, the 20th GIAP – one shot down Bf 109, and the pilots of the 837th GIAP scored one damaged Bf 109. There were some casualties, too. Two Hurricanes of the 837th IAP were shot down, one pilot was killed, the other was wounded. Two Tomahawks of the 20th IAP were shot down, with one pilot killed and the other unharmed. According to German documents, the Bf 109s of all three *Staffeln* of the III./JG 5 fought against Soviet aircraft at that time. The Germans claimed 20 victories over Soviet fighters without sustaining any losses.

Air battles in the Polar skies continued; the next one took place two days later, on 29 September 1942. At 12:45 two Kittyhawks (leader – Guards Sergeant Major P.V. Bolshakov) took off for a patrolling mission in the Murmansk area. From the reports of these missions:

> In the Rosta region I was in air engagement against a group of Bf 109s. Sergeant Titov fired two short bursts at a Bf 109 at an altitude of 6,000m, at the target aspect ratio of 2/4 from a distance of 1,500m. I did not observe the result of the attack. Sergeant Major Bolshakov fell into a spin during the approach to attack, the cockpit canopy came off.

Both Kittyhawks landed at 14:00.

Together with the Kittyhawks of the 2nd GKAP, three I-16s of the 27th IAP, four LaGG-3s of the 255th IAP, and two Yak-1s of the 20th IAP fought against the Luftwaffe aircraft. The Northern Fleet Air Force Headquarters credited one shot down Bf 109 each to Major P.A. Panin of the 255th IAP and Major N.I. Khryashkov of the 27th IAP. All the aircraft were able to return safely to their airfields. The army fighters did not take part in the battle this time. Luftwaffe bombers were attacking the Varlamovo airfield. They were covered by fighters from the 5., 6. and 8. *Staffeln* of the JG 5 that fought air battles near Varlamovo and Murmansk. The Luftwaffe pilots claimed five victories without their own losses.

Meanwhile, in October 1942 the 2nd GKAP began to receive new Airacobra fighters. Very soon it would become clear that they were superior to the Kittyhawks in both flight and performance characteristics. The regiment pilots were mastering the new fighter type at the Yagodnik airfield under the guidance of Major A.N. Kukharenko, the regimental deputy commander.

At the end of October, the Kittyhawk pilots managed to achieve another success. This happened on 30 October 1942. At 15:15 five Kittyhawks flew out on a patrol mission. They engaged Bf 109 aircraft in the Western Litsa area. As a result of the air combat, the Northern Fleet Air Force Headquarters credited Guards Sergeant Major N.A. Bokiy with one shot down Bf 109. From the report of Guards Sergeant Major N.A. Bokiy:

> I made one attack from the rear from a distance of 200–300m; the Bf 109 entered a spiral. I made one more attack on exiting from the spiral, from a distance of 250–200m. In the vicinity of Ura-Guba I came close to a distance of 200–300m and made three attacks strictly to the tail, the Bf 109 emitted black smoke, and I made another attack from a distance of 200–100m. The aircraft went down in the area of Zapadnaya Litsa.

At about the same time, three LaGG-3s of the 255th IAP engaged the Luftwaffe fighters. They were unsuccessful, but lost one aircraft and its pilot. According to available information, the aircraft from the Army and Air Defence Forces regiments were not involved in the combat. According to German documents, it can be concluded that the combat with the Soviet fighters was fought by the Bf 109s of the 6./ JG 5, which escorted the Bf 110 heavy fighters. The Luftwaffe pilots reported that they fought against the Kittyhawks and shot down four of them, with no losses of their own.

On the following day, 31 October 1942, Guards Senior Sergeant P.D. Klimov managed to achieve two victories over Luftwaffe bombers in one flight. At 12:08 four Kittyhawks took off to patrol the Murmansk area. Nearly one hour later, at 13:00 the Guards Senior Sergeant P.D. Klimov in pair with the Guards Sergeant V.L. Yudin noticed a group of three Ju 88s near Murmansk, approached them, attacked on head-on courses and shot down one Ju 88. From the pilot's report:

> I fired one long burst at a Ju 88 cockpit, flying at an altitude of 5,000m, on head-on courses. The Ju 88 was shot down and crashed near Murmansk." Then he unsuccessfully attacked the second Ju 88. Soon, after spotting the second group of up to 14 Ju 88s, P.D. Klimov approached the trailing aircraft from the rear and above. From the pilot's report: "I fired two bursts at one Ju 88 from above from a distance of 200m. The aircraft went into a left spiral, so I continued shooting at it with short bursts from a distance of 50m. The Ju 88 turned over, went into a dive and crashed near Murmansk.

Other than two Kittyhawks of the 2nd GKAP, no Soviet fighters engaged in air combat that day, so the Northern Fleet Air Force Headquarters credited two shot down Ju 88s to the combat record of Guards Senior Sergeant P.D. Klimov. According to available German documents, a group of Luftwaffe bombers of the KG 30 hit targets near Murmansk. A Ju 88A-4 bomber, W.Nr. 142128, aircraft code '4D+JR', of the III./KG 30 did not return from a combat mission. The crew of *Leutnant* Lothar Werner was missing along with the aircraft. It should be noted that the fighter pilots of the Army and Air Defence Forces regiments did not claim victory over this aircraft, as no victories were claimed by them at that time at all.

One week later, on 5 November 1942, Guards Sergeant Major N.A. Bokiy scored another presumed shot down Bf 109. At 12:30 four Kittyhawks of the 2nd GKAP flew out on a patrol mission. At about 13:00 they engaged Luftwaffe fighters, and Guards Sergeant Major N.A. Bokiy attacked a Bf 109. From the pilot's report: "I fired one long burst on head-on courses from a distance of 150–100m. I hit the enemy aircraft which was presumably shot down."

At the same time with Kittyhawks of the 2nd GKAP, four LaGG-3s and two Yak-1s of the 255th IAP engaged in air combat against the Luftwaffe aircraft. Basing on the results of the air engagement, the Northern Fleet Air Force Headquarters credited one shot down Bf 109 to the Sergeant Major A.F. Vlasov of the 255th IAP, and a presumably shot down Bf 109 to the Guards Senior Sergeant N. A. Bokiy. The losses of Northern Fleet Air Force amounted to one LaGG-3, which made a forced landing. Army fighters also took off to repel the attack. Four Airacobras and three Kittyhawks were flown by the 19th IAP, and five Hurricanes by the 197th IAP. The pilots of the 19th IAP claimed the kill of one Bf 109, while the 197th IAP shot down two Ju 87s and damaged one more dive bomber. The Army fighters suffered no losses. According to German documents, Bf 109s of the 6., 8. and 9. *Staffeln* of the JG 5 took off that day for 'free hunting' in the Murmansk area. The Luftwaffe pilots reported two air combats in which they supposedly shot down three Soviet aircraft without losses of their own.

On the next day, 6 November 1942, the commander of the 2nd GKAP, Guards Major I.K. Tumanov was killed in action. At 17:47 he took off alone to bomb the Luostari airfield. Having dropped the bomb on the target, he was on the way back. At 18:10, according to observations from the ground, his aircraft caught fire in the air and crashed near Vaenga. The committee which investigated the crash came to the conclusion that the destruction of Kittyhawk s/n 1000 and the death of its pilot, Guards Major Ivan Tumanov, were caused by the collision with the ground.

As the bad weather wasn't suitable for air combat, the Kittyhawks scored the next victory only a month later. This occurred on 6 December 1942. At 12:18 four Kittyhawks flew out on a patrol mission. In the vicinity of the airfield, Guards Sergeant Major N.A. Bokiy spotted a Bf 109 and attacked it. From the pilot's report: "I fired two bursts from below, from a distance of 300m. The second burst definitely hit the enemy aircraft. The Bf 109F was damaged." This aircraft is not mentioned in the operational report of the Northern Fleet Air Force Headquarters and appears only in the documents of the 2nd GKAP. The German documents indicate that the fighters did not engage in air combat against Soviet aircraft. It is probable that Guards Sergeant Major N.A. Bokiy attacked a Bf 109 reconnaissance aircraft, but no archive documents on operations of Luftwaffe reconnaissance units in the North have been found yet.

The next air combat took place nine days later, on 15 December 1942. Guards Senior Sergeant P.D. Klimov, who was flying alone on a bombing mission at Luostari airfield, on his return was radioed and directed to a Ju 88 aircraft and followed it to Nyal Javr Lake. In the area of Zimnyaya Motovka P.D. Klimov attacked the enemy aircraft: "I fired a long burst from a distance of 250m from below and rear, at the target aspect ratio of 1/4. The second attack was made from the right side from a distance of 100–150m, with a long burst. I observed the flames from both engines. The third attack took place at low altitude. I lost sight of the enemy aircraft near Zimnyaya Motovka, presumably the Ju 88 crashed into a hillside." Northern Fleet Air Force Headquarters credited the kill of a Ju 88 to Guards Senior Sergeant P.D. Klimov. From the records of the 2nd GKAP: "The Commander of the Northern Fleet Air Force, Major General for Aviation Kuznetsov, announced a commendation to Comrade Klimov for shooting down an enemy aircraft at night for the first time in the Northern Fleet." German documents show that a Ju 88A-4, W.Nr. 144001 of the I./KG 30 was damaged during a combat with a Soviet fighter aircraft near Murmansk. The gunner, *Unteroffizier* Xavier Meyer, was wounded.

On 17 December 1942 the Kittyhawks were close to starting a record of damaged and sunken German ships. At 13:04 two Kittyhawks (leader – Guards Captain V.N. Alagurov) took off to bomb the transports in the port of Kirkenes. In the area of Kibergnes Cape they attacked a German convoy. Here are the reports taken from Soviet and German documents. From the mission report of Guards Captain V.N. Alagurov:

> At 13:15 in the area 10–15km south-east of Kibergnes Cape we spotted a convoy: two transport ships up to 10,000 tonnes, three tankers, two patrol boats, two torpedo boats. Course 45 degrees, speed – eight knots. One unidentified aircraft

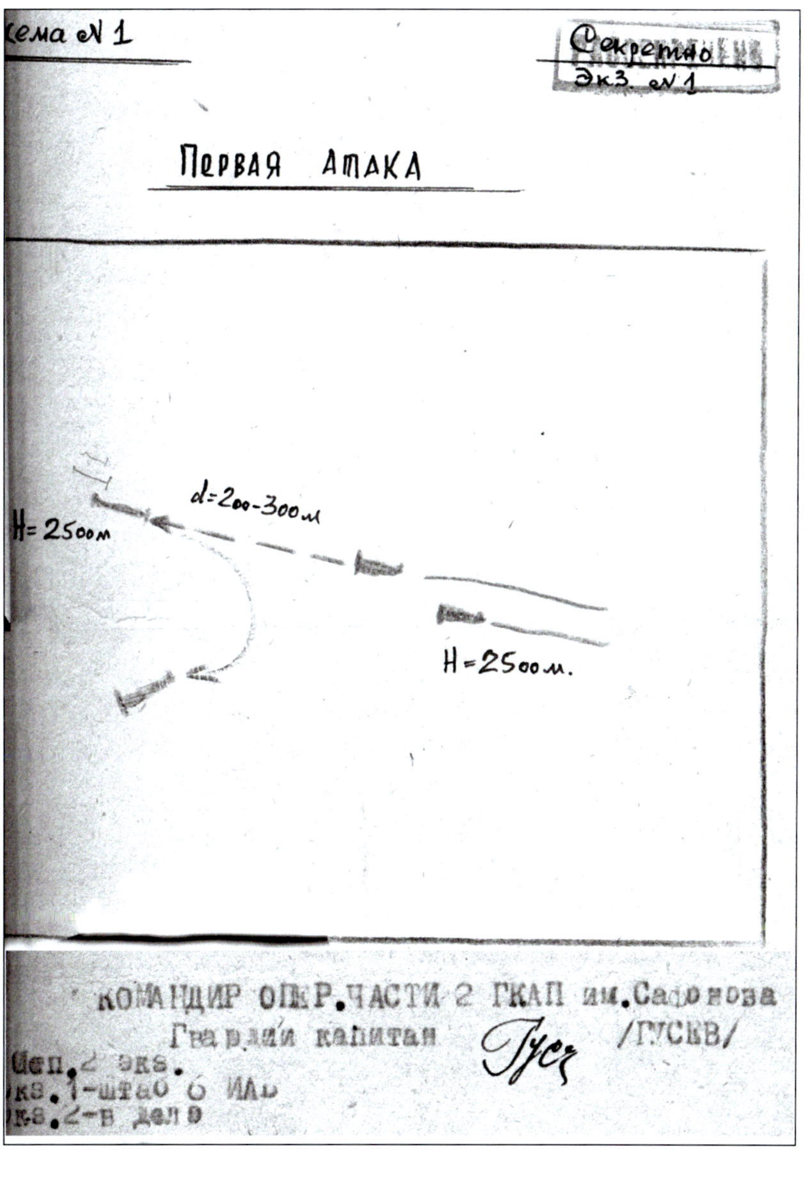

Plan of the air combat of the 2nd GKAP Kittyhawks (piloted by Guards Sergeant Major N.A. Bokiy and Guards Sergeant A.M. Titov) on 6 December 1942. The first attack.

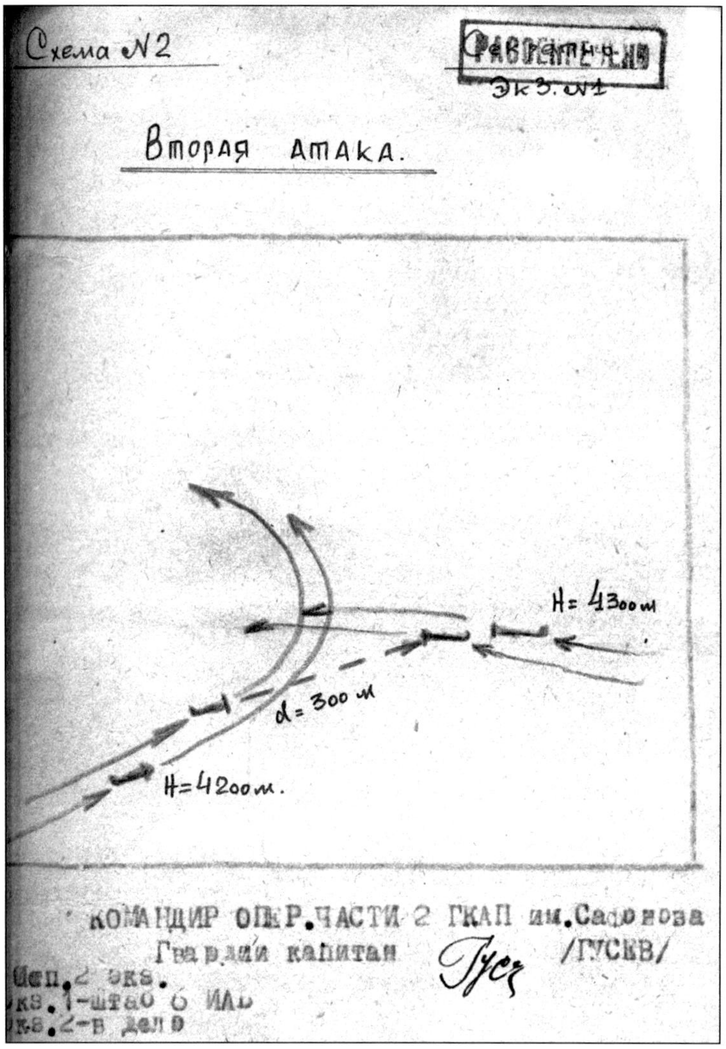

above the convoy. We attacked the convoy in pairs: from an altitude of 600m, Captain Alagurov attacked a large transport ship, while sergeant Yudin – a patrol boat. We dived 600–300m, dropped two FAB-100 bombs, on withdrawal we observed two columns of black and white smoke near the ships. We were shelled by air defence artillery, directed to the sea and headed to Vaenga airfield.

From the report of the German convoy commander:

> The convoy consisting of the transports *Rabat*, *Geste*, *Tenerife*, tanker *Mowenriff*, patrol boats V-5906, V-6109, V-6112 and motor minesweeper R-167 left Kirkenes at 7:20 and proceeded to Tromsø. At 9:40 the R-167 left the convoy, a little later the minesweeper M-301 joined the convoy at Eckerö. From 10:50 one Ju 88 provided air cover. At 11:38 there was alarm: in sector AC8483 (South-West to Kiberg) a pair of Spitfires attacked the convoy and dropped two bombs. No damage. Anti-aircraft fire was not opened as we were afraid of hitting Junkers.

Both Kittyhawks landed safely at Vaenga airfield at 14:21. This attack was unsuccessful, but it was the first one!

Left: Plan of the air combat of the 2nd GKAP Kittyhawks (piloted by Guards Sergeant Major N.A. Bokiy and Guards Sergeant A.M. Titov) on 6 December 1942. The second attack.

Below: Plan of the air combat of the Kittyhawk piloted by Guards Sergeant P.D. Klimov of the 2nd GKAP against a single Ju 88 in the area of Nyal Javr Lake – Zimnyaya Motovka (at night) on 15 December 1942.

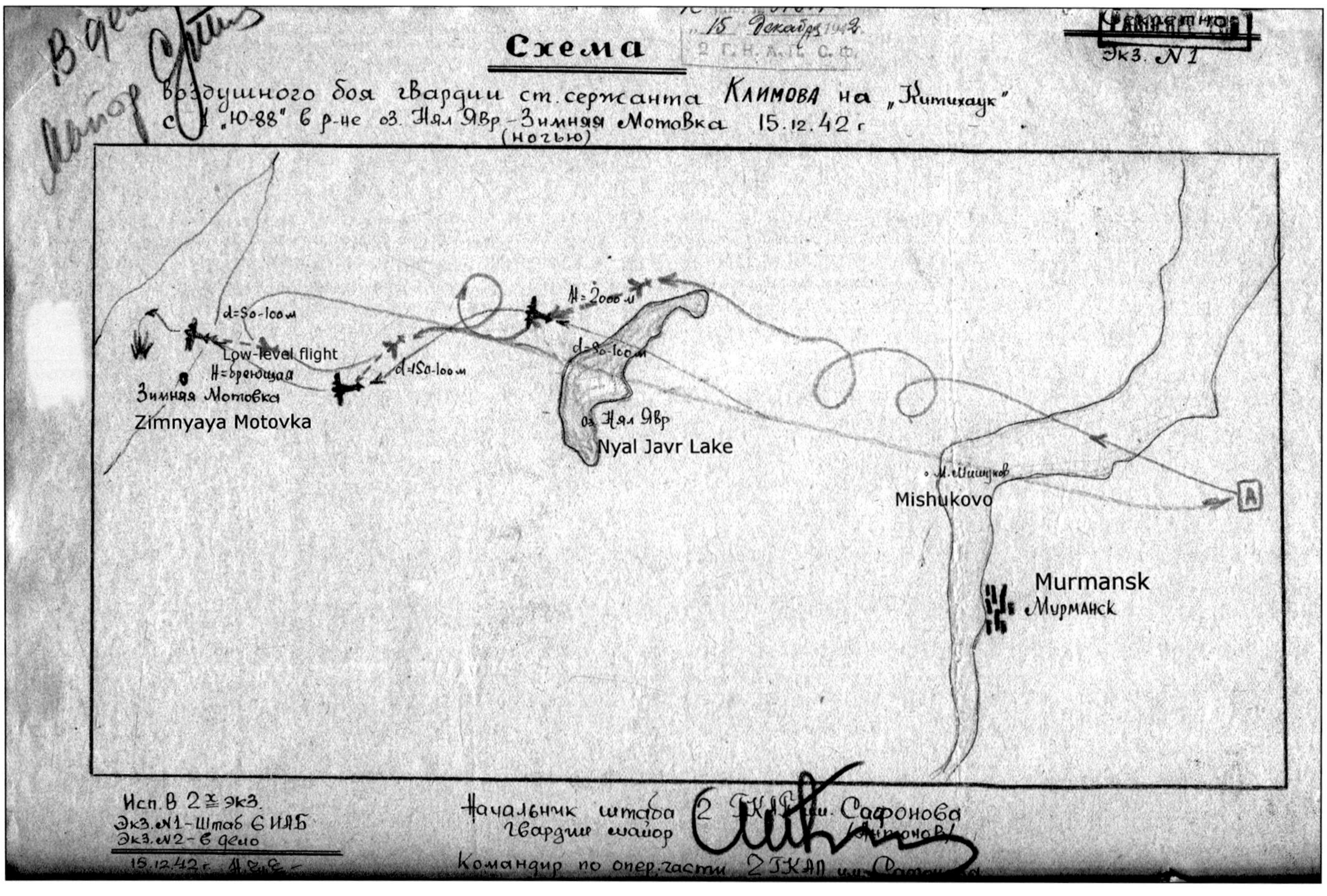

On 26 December the pilots of the 2nd GKAP won the first victory while flying Airacobra fighters. Around 12:40, four Airacobras of the 2nd GKAP encountered a group of Bf 109s and Ju 87s, and after the combat, the Northern Fleet Air Force Headquarters credited one Bf 109 each to Guards Major A.A. Kovalenko and Guards Captain V.P. Pokrovskiy. The only loss of the Northern Fleet Air Force was the Airacobra of Guards Captain D.A. Reutov: it was shot down by anti-aircraft gunners from a British transport ship anchored in Murmansk. Before the Airacobras of the 2nd GKAP approached, four Hurricanes of the 769th IAP engaged the Luftwaffe aircraft. They managed to force the Luftwaffe bombers to drop their bombs without aiming, but lost one aircraft, the pilot of which was killed. According to available German documents, on that day six Bf 109s of the 8. and 9. *Staffeln* of the JG 5 escorted Ju 87s of the I. /StG 5 which were bombing Soviet targets. The pilots of the Bf 109s reported that they fought against the LaGG-3s and shot down one of them. One Bf 109F-4, W.Nr.13086, tactical number 'Black 10', of the 8./JG 5 did not return from this mission. Its pilot, *Feldwebel* Josef Kaiser, survived and was taken prisoner.

On the last day of 1942, the Kittyhawks of the 2nd GKAP scored their last victory of the year and lost their last aircraft. It happened around midday. Four Kittyhawks, which took off at 12:25 on a patrol mission, attacked a group of Luftwaffe aircraft consisting of six Bf 109s and three Ju 87s. From the report of the Guards Senior Sergeant V.M. Grigoriev: "I fired a long burst at a Ju 87 from a distance of 350–70m at 2/4 target aspect ratio. At that moment I was attacked too. According to the report of the ground observation posts, the Ju 87 went down on Ura Lake." At the same time, the pilot of another Kittyhawk, Guards Senior Lieutenant D.G. Sokolov, according to his report, damaged another Ju 87. However, the Luftwaffe fighters were successful as well and managed to shoot down one Kittyhawk, but its pilot, Guards Sergeant V.G. Shvarev, was able to bail out by parachute. The second Kittyhawk, piloted by Guards Senior Lieutenant D.G. Sokolov, was damaged during the air combat, but the pilot managed to land the aircraft at home airfield. At about the same time with the Kittyhawks, five Yak-1s and two LaGG-3s of the 255th IAP, five Airacobras of the 2nd GKAP, 12 Hurricanes of the 78th IAP and three Hurricanes of the 769th IAP fought against the Luftwaffe aircraft. Lieutenant M.I. Kharlamov and Sergeant N.M. Sosnovskiy of the 255th IAP, and Senior Sergeant A.N. Pilipenko of the 78th IAP scored one shot down Bf 109 each. One shot down Ju 87 was credited to Guards Senior Sergeant V.M. Grigoriev of the 2nd GKAP. Three more Bf 109s were indicated as 'presumably shot down' by pilots of the 255th IAP, but the information about these victories is contradictory. The Soviet pilots lost one Kittyhawk s/n 1093 and one Airacobra of the 2nd GKAP whose pilot was killed. The pilots of the 769th IAP were credited with shooting down a Bf 109 and damaging a Ju 87, but one Hurricane made an emergency landing. The pilot was not injured and the aircraft was later repaired. According to available German documents, 23 Bf 109s of the 7., 8. and 9. *Staffeln* of the JG 5 escorted Ju 88 and Ju 87 aircraft on that day to attack targets near Murmansk. The Luftwaffe pilots reported air combats against Kittyhawks and Airacobras, during which they claimed to have shot down five Soviet aircraft. One Bf 109F-4, W.Nr. 13125, tactical number 'White 10', of the 7./JG 5 did not return from this mission. Its pilot, *Unteroffizier* Dietrich Gathmann, abandoned the doomed aircraft by parachute and was taken prisoner.

Two Ju 87s of the I./StG 5 collided after the mission while taxiing, sustaining an estimated 25 percent damage. The collision may have been caused by the damage sustained in the combat with the Kittyhawks. But these aircraft were soon repaired to flying condition.

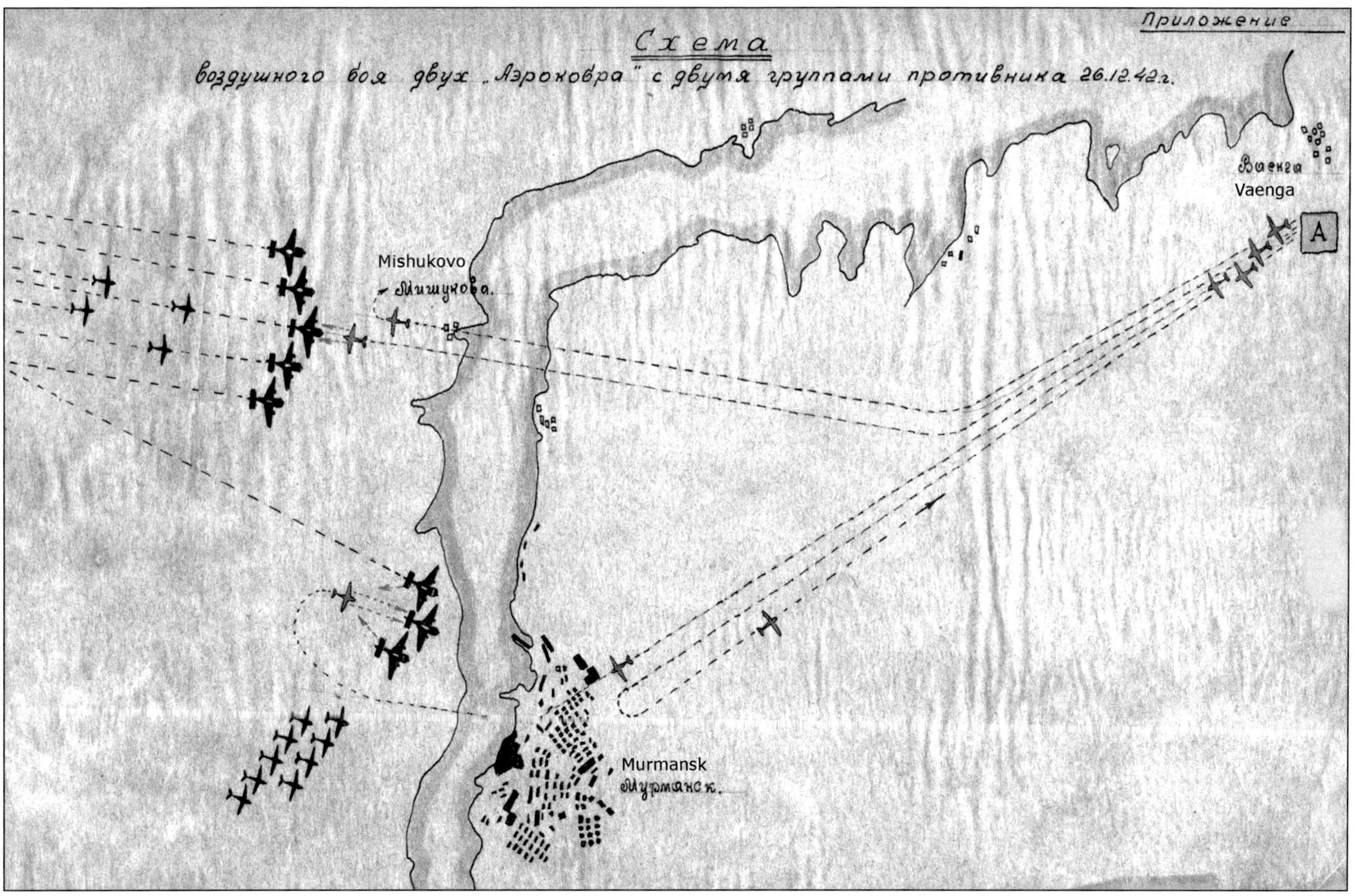

Plan of the air combat of two Airacobras of the 2nd GKAP (piloted by Guards Major A.A. Kovalenko and Guards Captain V.P. Pokrovskiy) against two groups of enemy aircraft on 26 December 1942.

Pilots of the 2nd GKAP awaiting a combat mission.

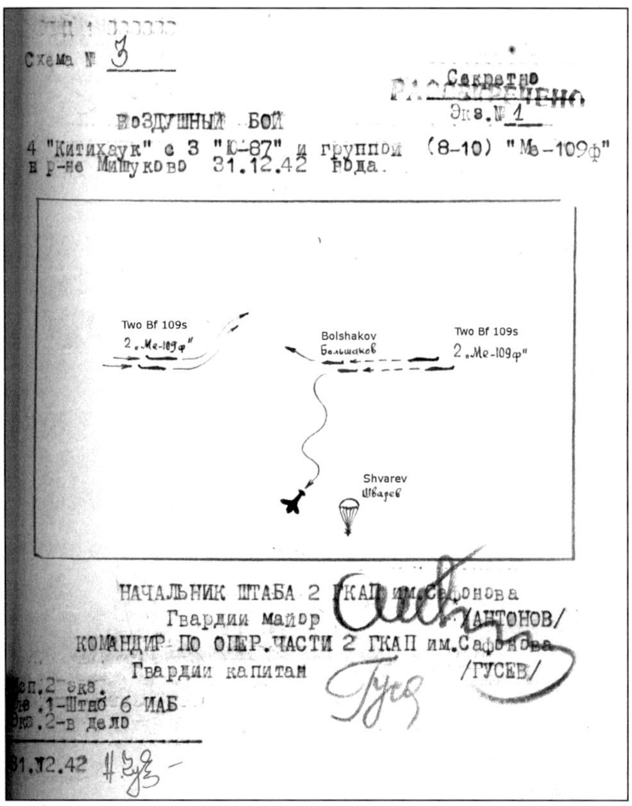

Plan of the air combat of the 2nd GKAP Kittyhawks (piloted by Guards Sergeant Major P.V. Bolshakov and Guards Sergeant V.G. Shvarev) against three Ju 87 and a group of eight–ten Bf 109s in the area of Mishukovo on 31 December 1942.

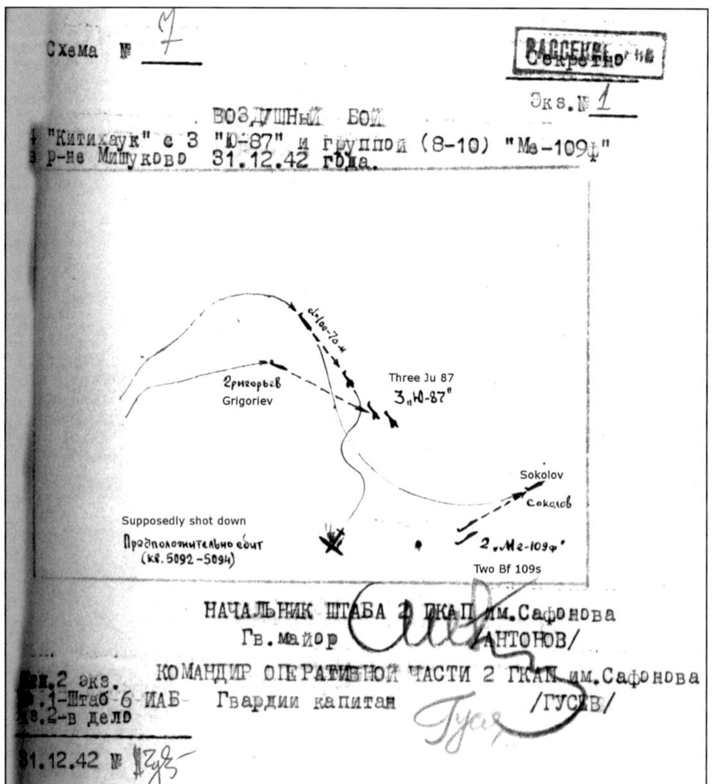

Plan of the air combat of the 2nd GKAP Kittyhawks (piloted by Guards Senior Lieutenant D.G. Sokolov and Guards Senior Sergeant V.M. Grigoriev) against three Ju 87 and a group of eight–ten Bf 109s in the area of Mishukovo on 31 December 1942.

4
KITTYHAWKS IN 1943

As of 1 January 1943, the only regiment armed with Kittyhawks was the 2nd GKAP. It had 16 aircraft of this type, of which only two were serviceable. In addition to Kittyhawks, pilots of the 2nd GKAP flew Airacobras (nine aircraft, of which seven were operational) and Hurricanes (19 aircraft, of which 10 were operational).

A report by the Northern Fleet Air Force gives the following estimate of the Kittyhawk fighter fleet as of 1 January 1943:

> Out of 16 available Kittyhawk aircraft, 10 are without engines, of which four the at the unit location, and six are in the workshops. The aircraft return to operations has been delayed by a lack of serviceable engines. Despite the availability of 12 Allison engines to be repaired, the repair work is delayed by the absence of main bearings. The condition of the aircraft and engine fleet of this type is good. Aircraft remaining service life – 95 per cent, engine service life – 95 per cent.

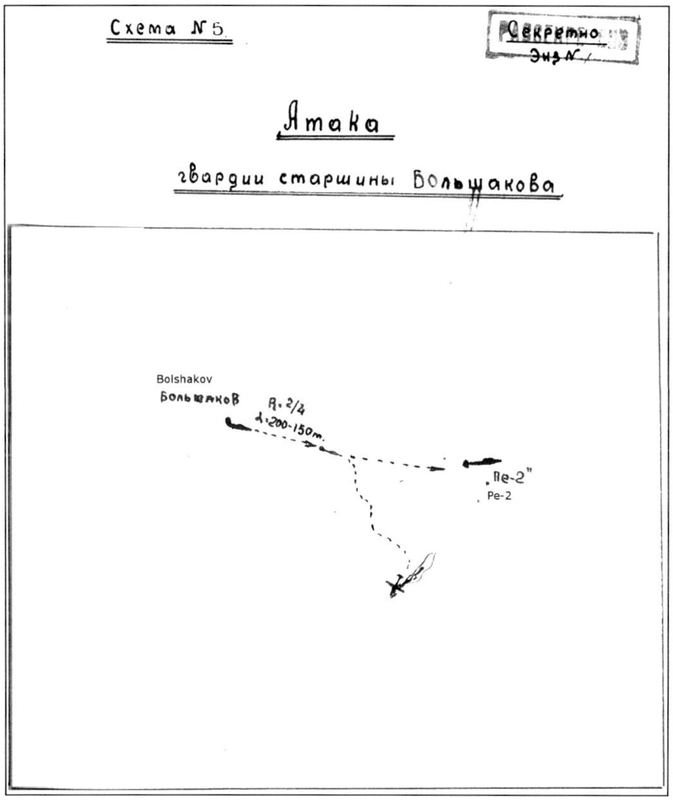

Plan of the air combat of the 2nd GKAP Kittyhawks during the attack on Kirkenes on 10 January 1943. The attack by the Guards Sergeant Major P.V. Bolshakov.

The Kittyhawks won their first victory of the new year on 10 January 1943, while escorting Pe-2 bombers to bomb German transports at Liinahamari.

At 12:30, the 2nd GKAP sent four Airacobras and two Kittyhawks (leader – Guards Captain P.I. Orlov) to cover six Pe-2 bombers of the 29th BAP. The plan was for the bombers to strike Kirkenes, but due to fog they attacked German transports at Liinahamari. According to the available German documents, the attack was unsuccessful. As the bombers approached the target, their formation stretched. At the moment of exiting the dive, at an altitude of 400–450m, Luftwaffe fighters attacked the Soviet aircraft. Soviet fighters counterattacked the Germans. From the report of the Guards Sergeant Major P.V. Bolshakov, pilot of the Kittyhawk of the 2nd GKAP:

> When coming out of a dive I made one attack at a Bf 109F, which was approaching a bomber from its tail; I fired two long bursts from a distance of 200–150m, at target aspect ratio of 2/4, the enemy aircraft went down into a steep dive. Then I was covering a Pe-2 with a damaged engine until it landed three to four kilometres north-east of Shchuk-ozero. Guards Senior Lieutenant Grigoriev did not perform an attack, as he was covering the bombers.

As a result of the air combat, the Northern Fleet Air Force Headquarters credited a total of three victories over the Bf 109s: to Guards Captain P.I. Orlov who piloted the Airacobra, to Guards Sergeant Major P.V. Bolshakov, and to two gunners of the Pe-2 from the 29th BAP – Sergeant F.Z. Yusupov and Junior Sergeant N.E. Khankevich. The Northern Fleet Air Force lost one Pe-2 which was forced to land after being attacked by Luftwaffe fighters and one Airacobra, most probably shot down by anti-aircraft fire. The crew of the dive-bomber survived, while the Airacobra pilot was killed. According to the German documents, Bf 109s of the 9./JG 5 were engaged in combat against Soviet aircraft. Luftwaffe pilots reported five shot down Soviet aircraft with no losses on their part.

However, initial success was followed by failures. The regiment lost two Kittyhawks on 24 January 1943. At 10:05 four Airacobras and two Kittyhawks of the 2nd GKAP took off to escort five Pe-2 dive bombers of the 29th BAP, which were supposed to strike Kirkenes. At about 11:00 the pilots dropped bombs on the German ships at Kirkenes. According to German documents there was no damage from this strike. The raid was repelled by Luftwaffe fighters and anti-aircraft guns. The Soviet pilots did not achieve any victories The losses of the Northern Fleet Air Force on this mission amounted to two Pe-2s and one Kittyhawk. According to the reports of the crews involved in the mission, the Kittyhawk, piloted by Guards Sergeant V.G. Shvarev, was attacked by two Bf 109Fs and left the battle descending towards the Rybachiy Peninsula. Guards Senior Lieutenant Kh.I. Abishev observed a flash on the ground near Skarbeyevskaya Bay. According to German documents, it is now known that two Bf 109s from III./JG 5 repelling the Soviet attack on Kirkenes claimed two Kittyhawks and one Pe-2 without losses of their own. In addition to the fighters, two shot down Pe-2s were claimed by German anti-aircraft gunners. Guards Senior Lieutenant Kh.I. Abishev in the second Kittyhawk landed at 11:35.

Three hours later, the regiment lost a second Kittyhawk under the following circumstances. At 14:28 on 24 January, two Airacobras and two Kittyhawks took off for a mission. The aircraft gained altitude over the airfield. At an altitude of 4,000m, near Shchuk-ozero, Senior Sergeant V.M. Grigoriev spotted a Bf 109F and decided to attack it. Approaching at a distance of 400m, he fired two long machine-gun bursts from the front and below at a 3/4 target aspect ratio. The Bf 109F took a sharp turn and left the sector of fire in a climb. While

Pilot of the 2nd GKAP, Guards Sergeant V.G. Shvarev. He was killed in action on 24 January 1943. The photo was taken during his cadet years.

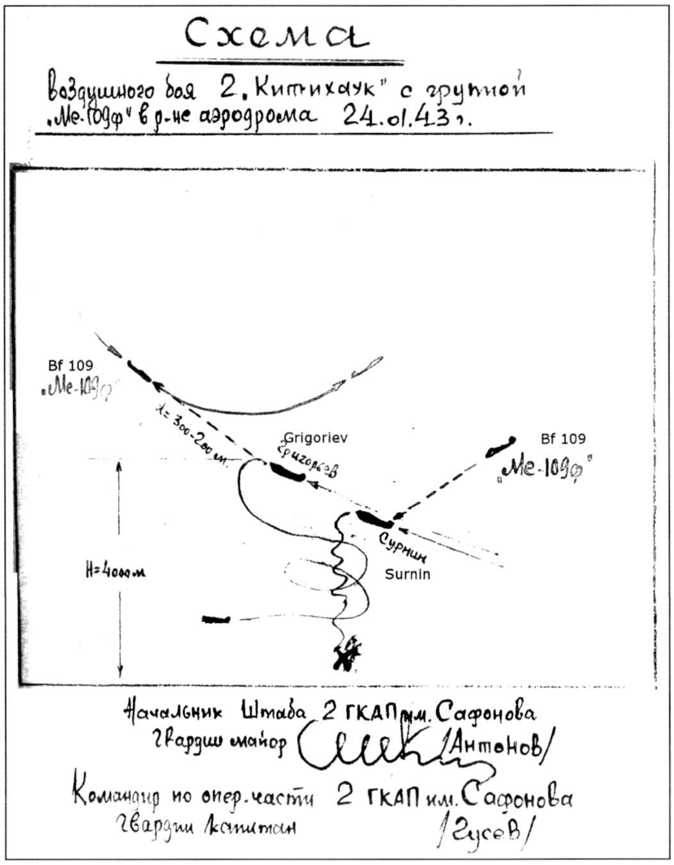

Plan of the air combat of the 2nd GKAP Kittyhawks (piloted by Guards Senior Sergeant V.M. Grigoriev and Guards Sergeant M.M. Surnin) at the area of Vaenga airfield on 24 January 1943.

the leading Bf 109 was under attack, a second Bf 109F (previously unnoticed) attacked and shot down the aircraft of Guards Sergeant M.M. Surnin. His Kittyhawk stalled and crashed near Shchuk-ozero on the slope of Height 174.0. The leader, Guards Senior Sergeant V.M. Grigoriev, noticed the fall of his wingman and accompanied him to the ground, after which he landed on the home airfield. The pilot of the Kittyhawk, Guards Sergeant M.M. Surnin, was killed. Two Airacobras came to the aid of the Kittyhawks, and Guards Sergeant P.D. Romanov shot down one Bf 109. However, German documents give a different interpretation of events. Four Bf 109s of 8./JG 5 were covering the FW 190 fighter-bombers. The Luftwaffe pilots claimed to have shot down two Soviet fighters without sustaining any losses.

The Kittyhawks did not do well in 1943, and their losses were increasing – the next aircraft was lost by 2nd GKAP on 5 February 1943. Around midday six Kittyhawks flew out on a patrol mission. When returning at 13:37, the aircraft of Guards Sergeant V.N. Yemelyanov was attacked by a Bf 109 and shot down. The pilot died. According to German documents, the pilot of 9./JG 5, who was escorting the Luftwaffe bombers during the attack on Murmansk, succeeded in this attack.

The last success of the Kittyhawks of the 2nd GKAP was achieved by Guards Junior Lieutenant N.A. Bokiy. On 13 March 1943 at 20:40 two aircraft flew out on a combat mission to intercept Luftwaffe aircraft at night. From the combat flight log of the 2nd GKAP:

> The mission defined by the Headquarters of the 6th Fighter Aviation Brigade was to detect and destroy enemy aircraft in the area of Kilp Lake, in co-operation with SON-2 gun-laying radar. The task was given to two Kittyhawks piloted by Guards Senior Lieutenant Sokolov and Guards Junior Lieutenant Bokiy. The Kittyhawks were carrying one SAB flare bomb each.
>
> At 19:30 two Kittyhawks took off with a climb and headed to the mission area.
>
> At 20:15 Guards Junior Lieutenant Bokiy, while in the holding area, received an order from the control point of the aviation brigade: 'Drop the bomb'. At 20:15 Guards Junior Lieutenant Bokiy dropped one SAB-55 flare bomb from an altitude of 5,000m and went into a left turn.
>
> It was late twilight at 20:30 and the horizon was also illuminated by the moon, so the effect of the SAB illumination was negligible.
>
> At 20:25, patrolling in his area at 270 degrees heading, the pilot spotted in the light part of the horizon on the upper edge of the cloud cover a silhouette of an aircraft heading 90 degrees towards Murmansk.
>
> He radioed: 'I see an aircraft; I'm going to attack'. After making a left turn, he came onto its tail and fired one long machine-gun burst from a distance of 150–200m. At that moment he heard on the radio: 'I am *Kama-13*, you are shooting at me' (*Kama-13* was a callsign of Guards Senior Lieutenant Sokolov, flying in the same zone at an altitude of 4,000m).
>
> Guards Lieutenant Bokiy radioed: '*Kama 13* – turn on the lights' and on receiving the reply 'Lighted', opened fire at the aircraft in front of him, which was not lighting navigation lights.
>
> He fired two bursts of machine-gun fire at the enemy aircraft from a distance of 150m and, blinded by the tracer fire, lost sight of it.

Kittyhawk of the 2nd GKAP in 1943.

As the enemy aircraft was moving in the dark part of the horizon (with 90 degrees heading), the Guards Junior Lieutenant Bokiy, using a vertical manoeuvre, was unable to spot it and continued patrolling in his area.

At 21:00, he landed normally at the home airfield.

The Northern Fleet Air Force Headquarters credited Guards Junior Lieutenant N.A. Bokiy with one shot down Ju 88. According to historian Alexander Mardanov, a Ju 88A-4 bomber W.Nr. 2298 of the *Stab* I./KG 30 was shot down.

A month later, on 13 April 1943, the 2nd GKAP lost another Kittyhawk. At 18:00 two Airacobras and two Kittyhawks took off on air patrol mission. At 18:15–18:30, two Airacobras and two Kittyhawks were engaged in air combat against four to six FW 190s near the airfield at an altitude of 4,000–3,000m. One Airacobra, piloted by the Guards Junior Lieutenant P.D. Klimov, attacked a FW 190 from behind at 200–150m, and he fired two machine-gun bursts at the enemy. The second attack was made in pursuit, at a low altitude from a distance of 100–150m. The pilot observed one shell exploding in the cockpit. The FW 190 was presumably shot down. According to historian Alexander Mardanov, the FW 190A-3 W.Nr. 2215 was shot down, *Unteroffizier* Kurz Wendler from the 14. *Staffel* was killed. In the course of the combat, another FW 190 attacked and shot down the Kittyhawk piloted by Guards Junior Lieutenant N.I. Zapalenov. The pilot was wounded but managed to abandon the aircraft by parachute. Kittyhawk s/n 751, which had been fighting in the 2nd GKAP since June 1942, was lost. In this air engagement, the Bf 109s of 6./JG 5 fought against the Soviet aircraft. The Luftwaffe pilots claimed two victories with no losses of their own. This ends the story of the Kittyhawks in the 2nd GKAP.

As of 1 May 1943, the 2nd GKAP had nine Kittyhawks (of which one was operational), 21 Airacobras (14 operational), and 10 Hurricanes (four operational) in its strength.

After bitter fighting in May 1943, the regiment was redeployed to the Yagodnik airfield for reformation. Before the regiment was withdrawn from the front, Guards Captain Z.A. Sorokin, piloting an Airacobra, shot down a Bf 109 near Tsyp-Navolok on 24 May 1943. In total, from January till May 1943 the pilots of the regiment shot down 41 enemy aircraft, 10 more were recorded as presumably shot down and three as damaged.

Guards Captain N.A. Bokiy, Hero of the Soviet Union.

The regiment was fully converted to Airacobra fighters and again took part in combat operations starting from March 1944. The

Kittyhawks of the 78th IAP of the Northern Fleet Air Force.

regiment was commanded by Guards Major D.F. Marenko. The first victory after the re-forming was scored on 12 April 1944 by Guards Captain P.L. Kolomiets, who piloted the Airacobra and shot down a Bf 109 to the west of Luostari.

When the 2nd GKAP was being withdrawn for reforming, one Kittyhawk, which had been damaged in combat, was written off, some Kittyhawks were transferred to storage, and several aircraft ended up in the 255th IAP. There the Kittyhawks, although flying combat missions, did not shoot down any Luftwaffe aircraft.

As of 1 July 1943, there was one serviceable Kittyhawk in the 255th IAP, one unserviceable and three in repair shops. They did not suffer any combat losses as part of the 255th IAP activities, but three aircraft were lost in accidents. The first Kittyhawk crashed on 12 September 1943. During a training flight it went down near Varlamovo Bay. The aircraft burned down, the pilot managed to bail out by parachute. The second Kittyhawk was lost in a crash on 23 September 1943. The aircraft, piloted by Junior Lieutenant N.G. Yaglov, fell into Kola Bay in the Vaenga area during a training flight. The aircraft sank, and the pilot perished. Entering a spin was identified as a presumed cause of the crash. As of 1 October 1943, there were nine serviceable Kittyhawks in the 255th IAP, two unserviceable and two in repair shops. The last one, the third Kittyhawk, was written off on 9 October 1943 after an accident, due to the impossibility of repair. Apparently, the Kittyhawk did not take root in the regiment, and by 1 January 1944 there was no such aircraft type in the list of the 255th IAP.

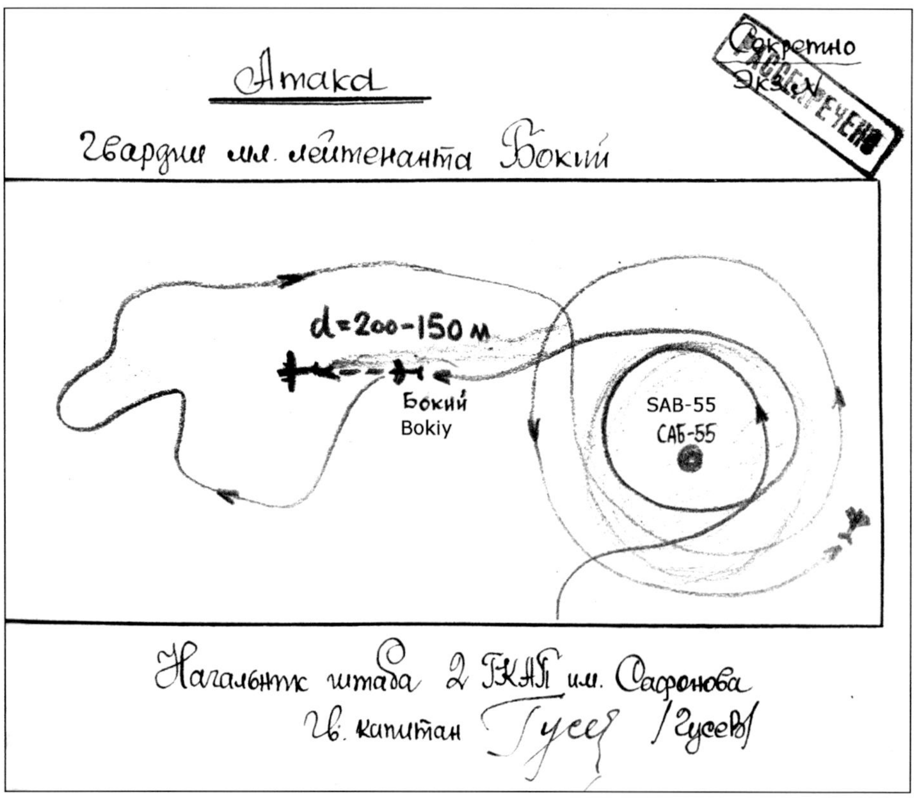

Plan of the air combat of the 2nd GKAP Kittyhawks (pilot – Guards Junior Lieutenant N.A. Bokiy) on 13 March 1943.

In the third quarter of 1943, Kittyhawks were delivered to the 118th RAP. As of 1 October 1943, it had three such aircraft, all in serviceable condition. The regiment was formed in September 1939, and the first commander of the regiment was Lieutenant-Colonel V.N. Vasilyev. The regiment operated different aircraft types, carrying out reconnaissance tasks on the communications and coastal objects of the enemy along the Norway coast. The regimental aircraft also flew to areas where the Northern Fleet Air Force was not engaged in combat operations. For example, their aircraft repeatedly photographed the battleship *Tirpitz* at anchorage. From mid-1943 the main long-range reconnaissance aircraft were the Bostons, while the Kittyhawks, Yak-9s and Spitfires flew at closer ranges. The latter type had the best photographic equipment in the Northern Fleet and, unlike other reconnaissance aircraft, always took good-quality pictures. But one has to pay for everything: the Spitfires carried no weapons. The pilots whose aircraft carried weapons did not hesitate to use them at the opportunity. For example, on 10 October 1944, Lieutenant Yu.F. Aminev, piloting a Boston, shot down a BV 138C-1 seaplane of 1.(F)/SAGr. 130 near Gamwick. The entire crew of the Luftwaffe aircraft, consisting of five men, were killed.

From October 1943, the Kittyhawks of the 118th RAP flew regular reconnaissance missions. The skills of the pilots and the characteristics of the Kittyhawks made it possible for them to avoid heavy losses, although they were not entirely without them.

On 3 November 1943 a pair of Kittyhawks of the 118th RAP took off to search for a large German convoy. At about 16:00 they engaged a Bf 109 of 5./JG 5. The Luftwaffe pilots claimed one victory – the Kittyhawk piloted by Captain A.M. Tishchenko did not return from the sortie. The Northern Fleet Air Force Headquarters credited him with shooting down one Bf 109, which he shot down before being killed, but the available German documents do not clarify the matter.

Almost at the same time as the 118th RAP, Kittyhawks were delivered to the 78th IAP. This regiment was formed in October 1941 and its first commander was Captain B.F. Safonov. Lieutenant D.I. Sinev scored the first victory of the regiment, flying a Hurricane: he shot down a German Bf 109 near Titovka. By the end of 1941 the pilots of the regiment had gained 10 victories. In 1942 the regiment continued to take part in hostilities, engaging in heavy air combat against Luftwaffe aircraft. On 4 January 1942, Sergeant N.A. Bokiy, piloting a Hurricane, shot down a Bf 109 to the west of the Lake Bolshoye Ura-Gubskoe. In total, in 1942 the pilots of the regiment shot down 79 Luftwaffe aircraft plus three victories which were not credited.

The regiment began its third year of the war, 1943, at Vaenga-2 airfield. The unit had 37 Hurricanes in its strength. The first victory in 1943 was scored by Senior Lieutenant P.I. Markov who, on 15 January 1943, flying a Hurricane, shot down a Bf 109 near Rybachiy Peninsula. In 1943 the regiment engaged in heavy air combat against Luftwaffe fighters, providing close cover for Soviet bombers which were attacking German convoys, ports and airfields. In addition to the support of strike aircraft, the Hurricane pilots undertook their first missions as fighter-bombers, attacking enemy's motorboats. But the skills of the pilots could not outweigh the poor characteristics of the Hurricanes, and the regiment increasingly suffered losses in air combat.

In April 1943, the pilots of the regiment shot down one Bf 109, but four Hurricanes did not return from combat missions. In May, the fighters succeeded in shooting down four Luftwaffe aircraft, but lost three Hurricanes. In July, the situation improved, the regiment shot down eight Luftwaffe aircraft while losing four Hurricanes. In August, in nine air combats, it shot down 18 Luftwaffe aircraft but lost 11 Hurricanes. September ended in complete failure: four Luftwaffe aircraft were shot down while seven Hurricanes were lost.

The time of Hurricanes was over, and in October 1943 the regiment departed for reforming.

From September 1943 the regiment was commanded by Major V.I. Babernov. It was under his command that the pilots of the regiment were converted to Kittyhawks. In addition to air combat skills, the pilots were also trained to attack surface targets, and as a result the regiment was able to inflict significant losses on German and Norwegian vessels in 1944. From the combat flight log of the 78th IAP: "On 10 October 1943 the regiment was re-formed and converted to the new aircraft type, Kittyhawk, at Kekhta airfield near Arkhangelsk."

Pilot of the 118th RAP, Captain A.M. Tishchenko. He was killed in action on 3 November 1943.

Three Kittyhawks arrived at the regiment on 12 October 1943 from the 255th IAP, and the personnel began to master the new fighter. However, these aircraft were subsequently transferred to the 27th IAP. The conversion training was not without incident. On 20 November 1943, Lieutenant A.Y. Shvailakh, piloting a Kittyhawk during take-off from Kekhta airfield, deviated to the left by 35–40 degrees, stalled and crashed. The aircraft was written off, the pilot left the crash site unharmed.

In October 1943, the 27th IAP was the last to receive Kittyhawks. This regiment was created on the basis of two squadrons of the 2nd GKAP in March 1942. The first commander of the regiment was Major N.I. Khryashkov. The pilots of the regiment shot down their first enemy aircraft on 4 April 1942, when Senior Lieutenant I.A. Volovodov, piloting a I-153, shot down a Ju 88 over the Yokanga. Despite the obsolete fleet that included I-15bis, I-153 and I-16 fighters, the pilots of the regiment managed to shoot down 27 Luftwaffe aircraft by the end of 1942.

As of 1 January 1943, the regiment had 31 aircraft on its strength and was based at Vaenga-2 airfield. In March 1943 the regiment received its first Hurricane fighters, but this did little to solve the problem of obsolete types in service. However, the first victory in 1943 was achieved on 22 May, when Captain V.A. Ageichev, flying a Hurricane, shot down a FW 190 near Ustoyarvi Lake. In May the regiment removed from service its last I-15bis aircraft, becoming probably the last regiment in the Red Army Air Force to use them in combat. In June the last I-153s were also taken off the regiment's lists followed by the I-16s in September, thus the unit fully converted to Hurricanes. Performance of the regiment remained poor, with only 13 Luftwaffe aircraft shot down (plus five presumables) in total in 1943. It was attempted to rectify the situation by transferring Kittyhawk fighters to the regiment.

In October 1943 the 27th IAP received eight Kittyhawks from the 255th IAP, in November three Kittyhawks of the 78th IAP, while the pilots of the regiment continued to operate Hurricanes. According to the aircraft list, the Kittyhawks s/ns 1001, 1098, 1112, 1844, 1847, 1885 and 1976 were the first to arrive at the regiment. The first three had been in service in 2nd GKAP, the others arrived in 1943. According to the aircraft register of the regiment, all these Kittyhawks were armed with two ShVAK cannon and six heavy machine guns. It hasn't yet been possible to find in the documents as to when and where these aircraft were fitted with ShVAK cannon. In the meantime, the powerful armament prompted the command of the 6th IAD to use these aircraft as fighter-bombers.

As of 1 November 1943, the regiment had 11 Kittyhawks and 20 Hurricanes in service. In November the regiment lost five Kittyhawks and failed to shoot down a single enemy aircraft. The first loss was related to a technical malfunction – on 19 November 1943, the engine of the Kittyhawk, piloted by Junior Lieutenant N.M. Ivanov, failed on take-off. The aircraft was seriously damaged, but the pilot was not hurt. Considerable losses for the 27th IAP were inflicted during the attack on the Luostari airfield on 25 November. An attempt by naval aviation to strike the airfield in the morning ended in failure due to bad weather. The command of the Northern Fleet Air Force then ordered the unit to to repeat the strike. According to the plan of the Headquarters, the airfield was to be attacked by two groups of aircraft. The first group included eight Il-2s of the 46th Ground-attack Aviation Regiment (ShAP, *Shturmovoy Aviatsionniy Polk*) led by Senior Lieutenant P.A. Yevdokimov, eight Yak fighters of the 20th IAP (leader – Lieutenant Colonel I.M. Umanskiy), six Hurricane fighters of the 27th IAP (leader – Junior Lieutenant V.I. Laptev). The second group consisted of eight Il-2s of the 46th ShAP (leader – Senior Lieutenant S.A. Gulyaev), six Kittyhawk fighters of the 27th IAP (leader – Senior Lieutenant A.P. Anuchin), and six Yak fighters of the 20th IAP (leader – Captain A.P. Shipov). The plan was for the Kittyhawks and Hurricanes to provide direct cover for the attack aircraft, while the Yaks were to act as an air combat team. The plan was good, but it ended in disaster for the Kittyhawks of 27th IAP. At 13:09, five Kittyhawks of the 27th IAP (Senior Lieutenant A.P. Anuchin acting as a leader, Lieutenant P.M. Demikov, Junior Lieutenant N.G. Nesterov, I.D. Rylshchikov, E.M. Kolykhaev) took off from Vaenga-2 airfield. Lieutenant P.M. Demikov's aircraft began developing engine problems and the pilot had to return. The other four Kittyhawks did not return from the mission. The first mistake was made by the Kittyhawks' leader. His aircraft joined the first group of attack aircraft. The second mistake was made by the 6th IAD command. They ordered the Kittyhawks to attack German anti-aircraft artillery positions near the Luostari airfield. And they followed the order. From the combat flight log of the 6th IAD for the fourth quarter of 1943:

> On 25 November 1943, while escorting the Il-2 aircraft on a bombing/ground-attack mission on the Luostari airfield, the Kittyhawk group (together with the leader of the ground-attack aircraft group) was tasked with suppressing enemy anti-aircraft positions at the Luostari airfield. As a result of the attack, four Kittyhawk aircraft failed to return from their mission. Three pilots were killed, one pilot – Senior Lieutenant A.P. Anuchin, was shot down by enemy anti-aircraft fire and made a forced landing near the Luostari airfield, the pilot returned to his unit four days later. The results of the attack have not been established.

The Kittyhawks attacking the anti-aircraft batteries most likely failed to gain altitude and were shot down by Luftwaffe fighters. The German fighter pilots claimed eight Kittyhawks that they shot down south-east and south-west of Petsamo. Lieutenant A.P. Anuchin managed to reach Soviet positions, while Lieutenants N.G. Nesterov, E.M. Kolykhaev, I.D. Rylshchikov did not return from the mission. Serial numbers of the aircraft that failed to return were 1112, 1847, 1976, and 1885. At 13:50, at the same time as the Kittyhawks, the attack aircraft struck the Luostari airfield. According to German documents there was damage and personnel loss at the airfield. However, after the attack, the Germans brought up all of the Bf 109 fighters and the FW 190 fighter-bombers of III./JG 5. The Luftwaffe fighters totalled about thirty aircraft. Then, for some unknown reason, eight Yak aircraft of the 20th IAP, which were to act as a 'combat group' for the first group of attack aircraft, departed for their airfield. The remaining six Hurricanes of the 27th IAP were defending the attack aircraft of the first group, and the Northern Fleet Air Force Headquarters credited one presumably shot down Bf 109 to the leading pilot, Lieutenant V.I. Laptev. As a result of the air combat, one Hurricane (pilot Junior Lieutenant P.V. Bogdanov) made an emergency landing at his home airfield. The aircraft went to a repair shop and the pilot was unharmed. Two more Hurricanes were damaged, but repaired by the regiment's technicians. The attack aircraft of the first group were even less successful. Three Il-2s were

Pilot of the 2nd GKAP, Guards Senior Sergeant V.M. Grigoriev. The photo was taken during his cadet years.

shot down by fighters and anti-aircraft artillery, and their crews were killed.

Six Yaks of the 20th IAP covering the second group of attack aircraft claimed eight victories over Luftwaffe fighters, losing one fighter. However, three Il-2s of the second group did not return to their airfields and two more made forced landings.

The Soviet pilots and crews were credited by the Northern Fleet Air Force Headquarters with a total of 13 shot down aircraft and one presumably shot down Bf 109, but this was little consolation. There is no reason to be surprised at this outcome of the combat. The Yaks of Lieutenant Colonel I.M. Umanskiy did not take part in the air engagement; the Kittyhawks were lost while carrying out the attack on anti-aircraft batteries. As a result, the attack aircraft were actually covered by twelve fighters, while the number of Luftwaffe fighters were about thirty. In addition, the German anti-aircraft batteries located around the airfield were a serious threat. They probably managed to shoot down some of the lost Soviet aircraft, and inflict damage on the attacking Kittyhawks and Il-2s. According to available German documents, the Bf 109s of the 7., 8. and 9. *Staffeln* of JG 5 took part in the air combat. In addition to them, the FW 190 fighter-bombers of 14./JG 5 participated in the battle. The Luftwaffe pilots at first claimed to have shot down 30 Soviet aircraft, but later the number of victories was reduced to 24. The Luftwaffe known losses to date are one Bf 109G, tactical number 'White 10', of the 7./JG 5.

Following the strike at Luostari, the 27th Aviation Regiment was permanently assigned to support the combat operations of the 46th ShAP, with the task of providing direct cover for the attack aircraft, while the 20th IAP was also permanently assigned to the 46th ShAP with the task of allocating an air combat group for the attacking aircraft.

In December, the 27th IAP received two Kittyhawks from the Northern Fleet Air Force Supply Department; the aircraft, according to the aircraft registry, had been produced by American factories in October 1943.

Due to bad weather, the Northern Fleet Air Force had almost no combat operations before the beginning of 1944.

5
KITTYHAWKS, JANUARY-MAY 1944

January and February 1944

By early 1944, the Kittyhawks were being used by the 27th IAP and the 118th RAP. The 27th IAP continued conversion from Hurricanes to Kittyhawks. As of 1 January 1944, the regiment had eight Kittyhawks (of which seven were serviceable) and 18 Hurricanes (including 13 serviceable). The regiment was based at the Kildin airfield, but occasionally flew combat missions from the Vaenga-2 and Pummanki airfields. In January 1944, the aircraft of the 27th IAP flew a total of 79 combat missions. During the month, the unit did not shoot down a single aircraft, but did not lose any of their own. Bad weather in January and February hampered combat operations. In February, the regiment flew 173 combat missions, there were still no combat losses, but one aircraft was lost in a crash.

On 29 February at 9:07 a wing of Kittyhawks took off to cover transports and convoys in the Kola Bay. During take-off Junior Lieutenant N.P. Poduzhaylo made a piloting error, as a result of which the aircraft crashed and the pilot was killed. This happened 1.5km south-east of Vaenga-2 airfield. There is a version that the pilot tried to show off for the girls from the canteen and performed an aerobatic manoeuvre, but an altitude was not sufficient. This accident had no effect on the conversion process, and in January–February the regiment received 26 Kittyhawks from the supply depots of the Northern Fleet Air Force. Judging by the Allison-V-1710-99 power plant and the armament of six large-calibre machine guns, as well as the production date (from October to December 1943), these were the P-40N-20 version or later.

As of 1 March 1944, the 27th IAP had 33 Kittyhawks and seven Hurricanes in its strength. The pilots of the regiment underwent training on dive-bombing technique in the first quarter of 1944. From the Combat flight log of the Northern Fleet Air Force for the first quarter of 1944: "Personnel of the 27th IAP underwent the dive-bombing training on Kittyhawk aircraft. Systematic training for 1.5 months made it possible to use the Kittyhawk aircraft as light bombers against enemy naval vessels." Unfortunately, as future events will show, the pilots were not trained well enough.

As of 1 January 1944, the 118th RAP had 33 aircraft (27 serviceable), including two Kittyhawks (both in serviceable condition). The reconnaissance aircraft of the regiment, when the weather permitted, flew daily reconnaissance missions of ports, convoys and ships at sea.

In addition to reconnaissance, the Kittyhawk pilots didn't hesitate to fire their machine guns. On 2 February one Kittyhawk fired at two motorboats near Hamningberg, but no results were observed, and nine days later another Kittyhawk attacked a German convoy on the Sredniy Peninsula. In March, the Northern Fleet Air Force and its Kittyhawk pilots faced serious difficulties fighting against German convoys.

March 1944

March brought the first serious combats between the Northern Fleet Air Force and the German convoys. Kittyhawk fighters escorted the attack aircraft without losing any of the Il-2s they covered, while the fighter-bomber version struck the convoys themselves. The Kittyhawks also acted as 'free hunters' against coastal ships and vessels, but no serious results were achieved here.

As of 1 March 1944, the 27th IAP fleet numbered 33 Kittyhawks and seven Hurricanes. In all, during March the regiment's aircraft conducted 249 combat missions, including 28 bombing strikes on enemy ships and transports. In March the Kittyhawk pilots scored eight shot down Luftwaffe aircraft. The regiment lost six Kittyhawks, and three were sent to repair shops. The regiment received two new Kittyhawks from the Northern Fleet Air Force supply depots. Meanwhile, another regiment of the 6th IAD – the 78th IAP, was completing its conversion to Kittyhawk aircraft. The regiment received 31 of them; according to the register of the Northern Fleet aircraft, they were P-40Ns. The regiment lost two Kittyhawks in a month for non-combat-related reasons.

After completing its conversion, the regiment arrived at Vaenga-2 airfield on 15 March 1944. On 30 March 1944 it made its first combat mission to cover the airfields.

2 March

At 11:15, two Kittyhawks of the 1st Squadron, 78th IAP, piloted by Captain M.N. Veryovkin and Junior Lieutenant N.T. Pavlichenko, took off from the Ponoy airfield to intercept Ju 88 bombers. Almost immediately after take-off, Captain Veryovkin developed aircraft engine problems and returned to the airfield. What happened next is written in his combat flight log: "Pavlichenko took off after me and as there was no visibility, he did not see me and after making two circles near the airfield he hit a heavy snow squall, lost his spatial orientation and crashed into a lake six kilometres from the airfield. The aircraft was destroyed, its pilot, Junior Lieutenant Pavlichenko died." The lost Kittyhawk s/n 35875 was manufactured in September 1942.

3 March

At 8:10 a Pe-3 crew of the 118th RAP took off to carry out reconnaissance of enemy communications off the coast of northern Norway. The pilot, Junior Lieutenant V.V. Makarov, and the navigator, Junior Lieutenant G.G. Pavlov, were looking for German shipping. At 9:00 they discovered an enemy convoy in the Pers Fjord and transmitted a radiogram about their discovery. This was convoy Rp.108.Ki consisting of a gunboat K-3, a M-306 minesweeper, patrol ships V-6111, V-6113, V-6115, V-5911, V-5916, submarine hunters UJ-1208, UJ-1212, UJ-1219, UJ-1220, transports *Sabine Howaldt* (5,958grt), *Welheim* (5,455grt), *Phoenicia* (4,124grt), *Patagonia* (5,898grt), tankers *Else* (638grt) and *Utsire* (468grt). The convoy left Reppe Fjord on 2 March 1944 for Kirkenes. Based on the situation analysis, the Northern Fleet Air Force command decided to launch a combined attack against the convoy by attack aircraft and torpedo bombers in the area of Eckerö Cape. The Kittyhawks of the 27th IAP and the 118th RAP took part in the operation. The fighters of the 27th IAP were to perform two tasks:

1. Provide direct cover for attack aircraft of the 46th ShAP when striking the convoy.
2. Send a distraction group to the Luostari airfield area in order to divert Luftwaffe fighters from the convoy.

A Kittyhawk reconnaissance aircraft of the 118th RAP was to provide tracking of the convoy. At 11:20 the Kittyhawk of the 118th RAP came to replace the Pe-3 reconnaissance aircraft and radioed: "Head of convoy at Kramvik Cape, end of convoy at Kibergnes Cape. The convoy composition: four transports, six destroyers, two minesweepers, four patrol boats, covered by two Bf 109s."

At 12:05, six Il-2s of the 46th ShAP (leader – Captain D.V. Osyka) took off from Vaenga-2 airfield under cover of eight Yak-9s of the 20th IAP (leader – Captain A.A. Malinovskiy) and six Kittyhawks of the 27th IAP (leader – Senior Lieutenant M.I. Boychenko). The Kittyhawks acted as fighters of direct cover, while the Yaks performed as an air combat group. After take-off, the attack aircraft and Yaks of the 20th IAP formed a group and flew towards the target. After seven to eight minutes, six Kittyhawks of the 27th IAP joined the group on the traverse of Set-Navolok Cape, thus fully assembling the force. At 12:53 near Lille-Eckerö Island, the attack aircraft struck the enemy convoy in a dive, exiting from the clouds. The attack resulted in a bomb hitting the *Sabine Howaldt* transport, but there was no explosion, and the submarine hunter UJ-1220 was lightly damaged by cannon and machine-gun fire. Although the patrol boat V-6115 claimed to have shot down one Il-2 aircraft, the attack aircraft group suffered no casualties. Almost simultaneously, at 13:01, the convoy was attacked by four Boston torpedo bombers of the 9th GMTAP (leader – Guards Captain G.F. Shebanov) under cover of eight Airacobras of the 255th IAP (leader – Captain P.A. Rassadkin). The torpedo bombers missed the target and the German anti-aircraft gunners shot down the Boston of Guards Captain G.F. Shebanov. Luftwaffe fighters arrived late and attempted to intercept the Soviet aircraft. The Soviet attack aircraft and escort fighters spotted the attacking Bf 109s in advance and repulsed all of their attacks without losses.

From the combat flight log of 6th IAD: "At 12:58, two Kittyhawks were engaged in an air combat with one Bf 109 at an altitude of 600m near Eckerö. As a result of the combat, Senior Lieutenant Boychenko shot down one Bf 109. The enemy aircraft fell into the water two to five kilometres south-east of Eckerö." The Northern Fleet Air Force Headquarters credited one shot down Bf 109 each to the combat record of the Kittyhawk pilot of the 27th IAP, Senior Lieutenant M.I. Boychenko, and to the Yak-9 pilot of the 20th IAP, Junior Lieutenant A.D. Vasiltsov. It was the first victory on this aircraft type for 27th IAP, and it was the first victory for this regiment in 1944.

The group of torpedo bombers was also attacked by Luftwaffe fighters. In the air combat, Captain P.A. Rassadkin and Junior Lieutenant L.I. Smirnov of the 255th IAP shot down one Bf 109 each. The Luftwaffe fighters succeeded in shooting down an Airacobra of the 255th IAP, its pilot, Junior Lieutenant G.N. Gerasimenko, was killed.

According to the available data, the Bf 109s of the 8. *Staffel* and *Stab* II./JG 5 were involved in the air combat over the convoy. The Luftwaffe pilots scored three victories with no losses of their own.

At the same time as the first success of Kittyhawks in the fighter role, the 27th IAP lost two aircraft. This was due to pilots' error. At 12:23, four Kittyhawks of the 27th IAP (leader – Senior Lieutenant I.S. Yedush) flew to the Luostari airfield to carry out demonstrative actions to distract Luftwaffe fighters. What happened next is recorded in the report on the aircraft's loss: "During the flight over the enemy territory, the aircraft were met by two Bf 109s passing below and were exposed to the enemy's anti-aircraft artillery fire. While evading fire and focusing the attention on the enemy's fighters, the leader of the second pair [Junior Lieutenant Nadolinskiy – *Author's note*] abruptly manoeuvred and collided with the wingman of the first pair [Junior Lieutenant Rodionov – *Author's note*]. One of the pilots bailed out with parachute from an altitude of 3,000m, the second – Rodionov – landed within enemy territory". Both pilots, Junior Lieutenants V.P. Nadolinskiy and I.K. Rodionov, were taken prisoner. The two remaining Kittyhawks landed safely at Kildin airfield at 13:35.

5 March

As early as the evening of 4 March, reconnaissance aircraft of the 118th RAP spotted a German convoy in the Brei Sund Strait. However, due to the darkness, the reconnaissance mission had to be interrupted. In the morning, the reconnaissance aircraft again managed to track the convoy. The convoy discovered by the reconnaissance aircraft was called Rp.109.Ki; it left Reppa Fjord for Kirkenes on 4 March 1944. The convoy consisted of a gunboat K-1, patrol ships V-5912, V-5913, V-5914, NH-03, submarine hunters UJ-1207, UJ-1212, UJ-1219, UJ-1220, minesweeper M274, steamers *Ilse Fritzen* (4,883grt), *Theda Fritzen* (2,882grt), *Irmtraut Cords* (2,843grt) and *Falkenfels* (6,318grt). Having received a report of the convoy sighting, the Northern Fleet Air Force command began to prepare strike teams. The same as two days earlier, the plan was to strike with attack aircraft and torpedo bombers near Eckerö. To divert Luftwaffe fighters for the duration of the attack on the convoy, distraction groups of fighters were assigned for action at the Luostari

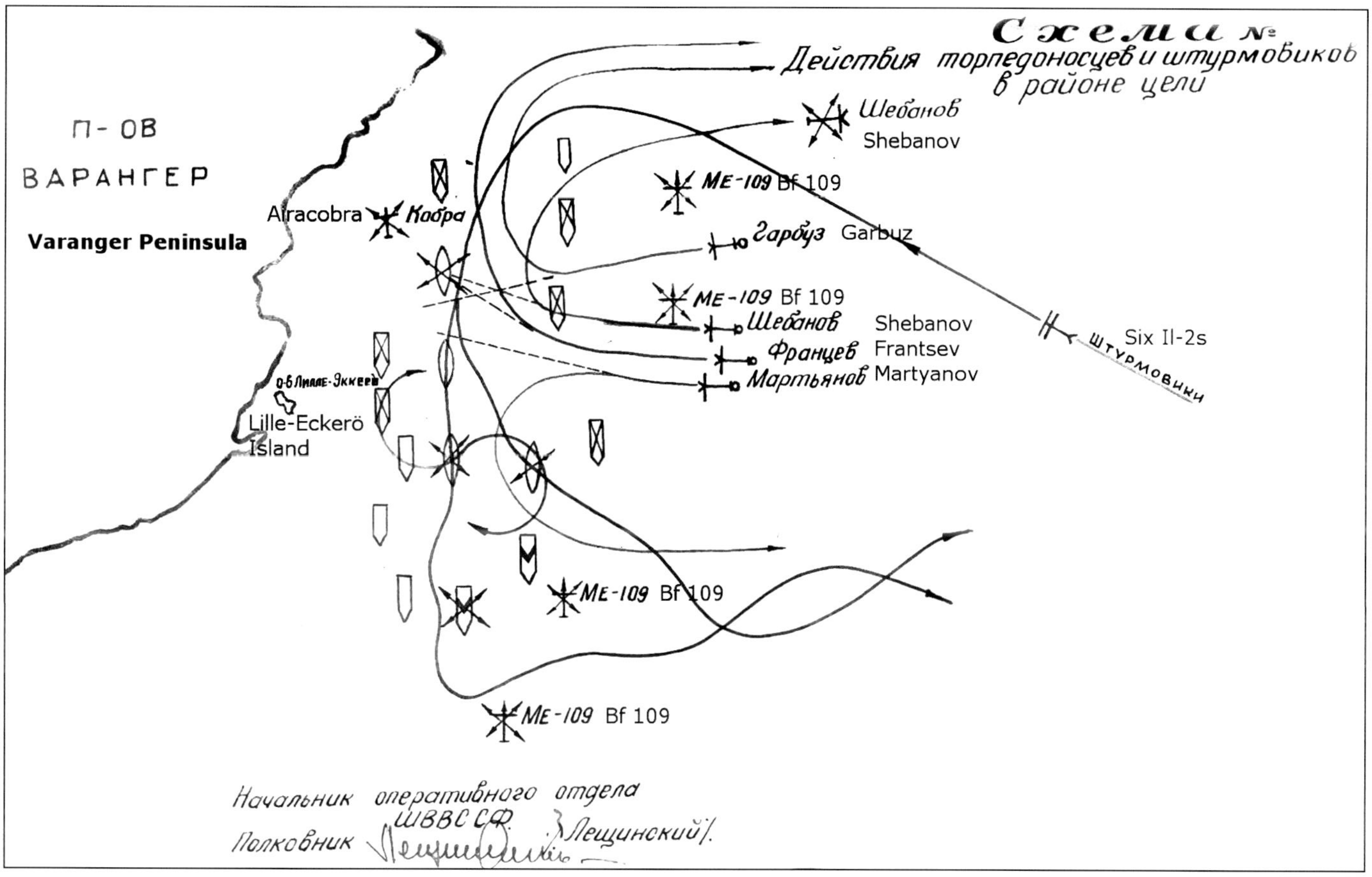

Plan of attack on the German convoy Rp.108.Ki by the aircraft of the Northern Fleet Air Force on 3 March 1944.

Airacobra of the Northern Fleet Air Force.

and Svartnes airfields. The Kittyhawks involved in this operation had three objectives:

1. Kittyhawk reconnaissance aircraft of the 118th RAP provided convoy tracking and monitoring of strike results.
2. Six Kittyhawk fighters of the 27th IAP were to fly a distraction mission around the port of Vardö and the passage of a convoy.
3. Six Kittyhawk fighters of the 27th IAP were assigned to accompany the attack aircraft. They provided direct cover for the attack aircraft, while the Yaks of the 20th IAP functioned as an 'air combat group'.

The operation against the convoy was initiated by the groups assigned for distraction. At 13:32, six Kittyhawks of the 27th IAP (leader – Senior Lieutenant V.I. Zorin) took off from the Kildin airfield and flew at high altitude across the Rybachiy Peninsula to the Svartnes airfield, the Luftwaffe fighter base. Almost simultaneously with them a distraction group of four Yak-1s of the 20th IAP flew to the Luostari airfield.

The distraction groups fulfilled their tasks. According to radio reconnaissance data, Luftwaffe fighters received orders to hold at their airfields and the attack on the convoy was repelled only by the fighters on patrol over the convoy. The Luftwaffe fighters, which had stayed near their airfields, appeared over the convoy only after the

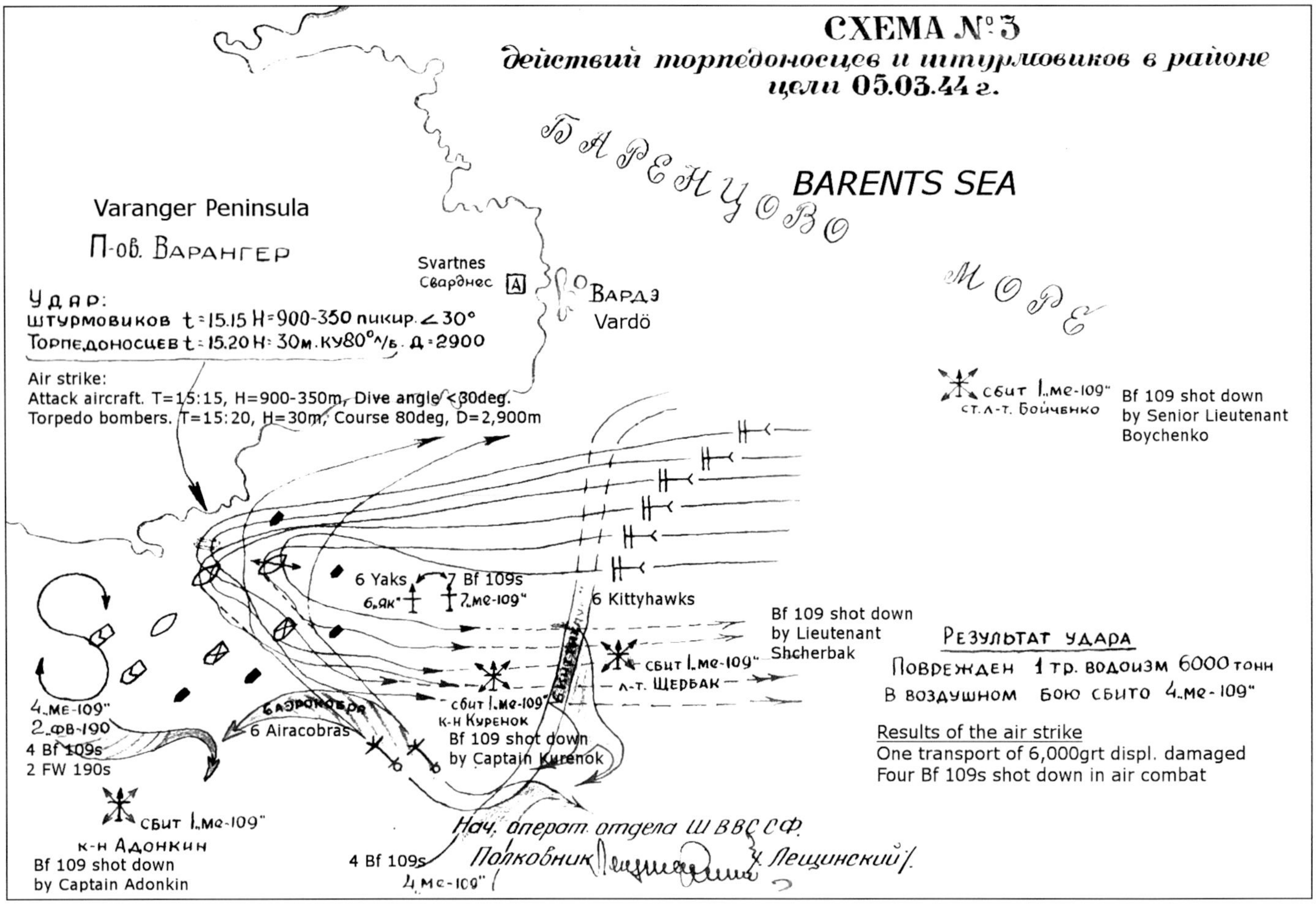

Plan of attack on the German convoy Rp.109.Ki by the aircraft of the Northern Fleet Air Force on 5 March 1944.

Pilot of the 27th IAP, Senior Lieutenant M.I. Boychenko.

attack aircraft and torpedo bombers completed their strike. This time there was no trouble for the Soviet side, and all aircraft of the distraction groups returned without loss or damage.

At 14:25 six Il-2s of the 46th ShAP (leader – Senior Lieutenant I.B. Katunin) took off from the Vaenga-2 airfield followed by eight Yaks of the 20th IAP (leader – Captain A.A. Malinovskiy). In an organised manner, a group of attack aircraft gathered over the airfield and flew to the convoy. On the traverse of Set-Navolok Cape they were joined by six Kittyhawks of the 27th IAP (leader – Senior Lieutenant M.I. Boychenko). The group's route: Vaenga-2 – Shchuk-ozero – Set-Navolok – Tsyp-Navolok – Vaitolahti lighthouse – target. In the vicinity of the Eckerö Peninsula, the group spotted a convoy. While approaching the convoy, the Soviet aircraft were attacked by four Bf 109s, but the attack was repulsed by the aircraft gunners and fighter aircraft. While repulsing the Luftwaffe attack, Senior Lieutenant M.I. Boychenko, piloting a Kittyhawk of the 27th IAP, shot down one enemy fighter. From the combat flight log of the 6th IAD for the first quarter of 1944:

> At 15:10, on approach to the target at an altitude of 1,000m, the attack aircraft rearranged into a stretched right echelon. The Kittyhawks moved to the right flank and accordingly stretched deep into the Il-2s formation, ensuring their successful approach and attack on the enemy transport and convoy ships. At 15:14 Senior Lieutenant Boychenko, diving with his wingman Junior Lieutenant Dyogtev, noticed two Bf 109s in close proximity to the leading Il-2 from below and at the front, trying to attack the Il-2s. Boychenko turned his aircraft and fired one burst of machine-gun fire

at them from a 600–400m distance. He continued to track them down and attacked again as the two Bf 109s turned left and tried to shoot down the wingman Junior Lieutenant Dyogtev. Having been repulsed, the enemy aircraft went away with a climb, but Senior Lieutenant Boychenko, having a large reserve of speed, banked left, overtook the enemy aircraft which were completing the climb, and attacked from below and from the side at a distance of 200–250m, at the moment of the beginning of their horizontal flight. As a result of two aimed machine-gun bursts, the leading Bf 109 overturned and plunged into the water two to three miles north of the convoy ships, while the wingman's Bf 109 climbed upwards. Junior Lieutenant Dyogtev manoeuvred and supported his leader's action with machine-gun fire. He attacked one Bf 109 that was attempting to tail Senior Lieutenant Boychenko and, following in pairs, interacting with the lead, ensured that he successfully attacked and destroyed one Bf 109. Providing cover for the Il-2s during the attack and seeing no further direct threat to the attack aircraft, Senior Lieutenant Boychenko and his wingman followed the Il-2s and continued to accompany them while they were flying away from the target. At 15:14, at 700–800m altitude, Lieutenant Vashchenko with his wingman, Junior Lieutenant Cherednichenko, spotted two Bf 109s gaining altitude with the aim of engaging the rear attack aircraft when exiting the strike. The enemy's plan was recognised, and Lieutenant Vashchenko immediately turned with his wingman to the right and opened fire at the enemy from a distance of 400–300m. The enemy aircraft split one down and the other upwards with a sharp climb. Subsequently, returning to the Il-2s, Junior Lieutenant Cherednichenko and Lieutenant Vashchenko once again attacked one Bf 109, which was pursuing our aircraft and was seen approaching from behind and from above. During the attack, the enemy aircraft went down and disappeared at a low altitude. At 15:14, Lieutenant Anuchin and his wingman Junior Lieutenant Demikov covered the attacking Il-2s at low altitude, tacking over them at the 90 degrees angle. There were no encounters with the enemy. All of our aircraft continued to cover the attack aircraft.

It should be noted that the fall of the Bf 109 shot down by Senior Lieutenant M.I. Boychenko was recorded in the reports of the attack aircraft crews. It is very likely that it was he who shot down the only Bf 109 whose destruction in that combat is confirmed by German archive documents.

At 15:15, the Il-2 aircraft attacked the convoy. As a result of cannon and machine-gun fire, the steamship *Irmtraut Cords* (2,843grt) caught fire, two crew members were wounded. Simultaneously with the attack aircraft, two Boston torpedo bombers of the 9th GMTAP (lead – Guards Captain L.I. Markov), under cover of six Airacobras of the 255th IAP (lead – Guards Captain V.S. Adonkin) attacked the convoy. All the torpedoes missed the German ships, but machine-gun fire from the torpedo bombers caused a small fire on the UJ-1220 submarine hunter: a depth charge caught fire, and two sailors were injured.

When exiting the strike, the Soviet aircraft were again attacked by the Bf 109s, but after losing three aircraft (according to Soviet data), the Germans retreated. The victories over the Luftwaffe fighters were credited to Captain V.S. Adonkin of the 255th IAP, Captain N.K. Kurenok, and Lieutenant I.Z. Shcherbak of the 20th IAP.

German documents show that the Bf 109s of the 8. *Staffel* of the JG 5 were engaged in air combat over the convoy. The Germans claimed to have shot down two Soviet aircraft, which is not confirmed by Soviet documents, and admitted the loss of one fighter – the Bf 109, W.Nr. 13800; its pilot, *Unteroffizier* Heinz Finzsch, went missing. When attacking the convoy, four Il-2s were damaged, but no Soviet aircraft were shot down.

14 March

Improved weather and the absence of large enemy convoys enabled the Northern Fleet Air Force Headquarters to begin strikes against enemy coastal ships. Coastal ships include small vessels (up to 300–400 tonnes) that provide shipping of both military and civilian cargoes along the coastline. Apart from Kirkenes, the Norwegian ports of Vadsø and Vardö were their main points of their deployment, so these ports became targets for Soviet air strikes. The first strikes in 1944 were rather tentative in nature, but by the end of the year they had developed into massive attacks, causing serious damage to German warehouses, port facilities, and ships anchored in ports.

Four Il-2 aircraft (leader – Senior Lieutenant I.B. Katunin) under cover of six Yak-9s of the 20th IAP (leader – Senior Lieutenant V.V. Nuzhin) and four Kittyhawks of the 27th IAP (leader – Senior Lieutenant M.I. Boychenko) conducted a bombing attack on the concentration of enemy small vessels in the port of Vadsø at 15:45–15:50 of 14 March. The escort Yak-9 and Kittyhawks fighters, due to the absence of an airborne enemy, decided not to stand aside and also took part in the attack on the motorboats, firing cannons and machine guns at them.

German sources noted damage to the motorboat *Liv Asbjorg* from a Soviet aircraft attack before the strike on the port of Vadsø. One soldier of the *Festungs-Bataillon* 665 was killed on the motorboat and four soldiers from other units were wounded. In Vadsø harbour itself, one motorboat was destroyed by a direct bomb hit, while another was sunk at sea. Another motorboat was attacked by a single aircraft, which drove it to the island, but it was unharmed. One prisoner of war and two Norwegians were killed in the raid, while three Germans were wounded.

The Northern Fleet Air Force Headquarters credited the pilots of the 27th IAP with two sunken and one damaged vessels. It was probably during this flight that the Kittyhawks opened the count of ships destroyed in 1944. This was the first notable raid on Vadsø in 1944. Soon they would become regular. The attacks of Soviet aircraft forced the naval commander of Kirkenes to think that if they were repeated, the movement of single ships under 300grt would have to be halted, as there was nothing to escort them. In addition, the anti-aircraft defences of Vadsø had to be strengthened, as at the time of Soviet raid on 14 March, the port air defence consisted of a single 20mm anti-aircraft gun.

17 March

At 7:11, a Boston reconnaissance aircraft of the 118th RAP (pilot – Junior Lieutenant M.Y. Sologubov) spotted another convoy in Kongs Fjord. This was the convoy Rp.110.Ki which left Lo Fjord on 16 March 1944 for Kirkenes. It consisted of a gunboat K-3, minesweepers M-364, M-272, M-273, M-306, patrol ships V-5911, V-5912, V-5914, V-6110, NKI-11, submarine hunters UJ-1206, UJ-1207, UJ-1208, UJ-1219, NH03, NH06, steamers *Boltenhof* (3,307grt), *Sevre* (4,585grt) and *Knute Nelson* (5,748grt), tankers *Algol* (972grt) and *Binz* (715grt), and a tug boat *Arngast* (729grt). Having received information about the convoy, the Northern Fleet Air Force Headquarters decided to attack it in three groups at the

Hamningberg – Vardö leg. The first to attack the convoy were the Kittyhawk fighter-bombers of the 27th IAP, followed after 30 minutes by the attack aircraft of the 46th GKAP and, finally, by the torpedo bombers of the 9th GMTAP. On their return, all the aircraft were to prepare for a second attack at the Vardö –Kirkenes leg. This time the Kittyhawks of the 27th IAP had two tasks:

a. Twelve Kittyhawks were to dive bomb the convoy under cover of six Airacobras of the 2nd GKAP.
b. Six Kittyhawks were to provide direct escort for the Il-2s. Since the attack aircraft were to strike from Pummanki airfield, the Kittyhawks were to be relocated there.

At 10:45, a Kittyhawk reconnaissance aircraft of the 118th RAP, piloted by Junior Lieutenant A.V. Bystrov, spotted a convoy near Bos Fjord. The pilot discovered that the convoy had slowed down and reported this to Fleet Headquarters. The Headquarters decided to postpone the start time of the convoy attack by half an hour.

At 11:40, twelve Kittyhawk fighter-bombers of the 27th IAP (leader – Major A.J. Dizhevskiy) took off from the Kildin airfield. They were joined by six Airacobras of the 2nd GKAP (leader – Guards Major D.F. Marenko) which had taken off from Vaenga-2 five minutes earlier, and the first strike groups began to move towards the convoy. The group flew to Vaitolahti at a low altitude, and then gained an altitude of 3,000m proceeding to their destination. In addition to the bomb strike, this group was also tasked with distracting enemy fighters. From documents of the Northern Fleet Air Force Headquarters: "The first to strike is the Kittyhawk group, which, in addition to causing damage to the convoy, diverts and exhausts enemy fighter aviation, thus ensuring subsequent strikes by attack aircraft and torpedo bombers." From documents of 6th IAD:

> At 12:20–12:25 fighter-bombers spotted in the Havningsberg area an enemy convoy consisting of three transport ships, four destroyers, from eight to ten minesweepers. At 12:25, a group of our aircraft, having approached from the sun, bombed transports of the enemy, having dropped 24 FAB-100s from dive. The attack was carried out in fours, against the direction of the convoy move, in a dive from 3,000–2,500m to 600–1,100m. Bomb dropping altitude was 800–1,500m. During the approach to the target, the second and third fours of the Kittyhawks stretched to a distance of 800–1,000m and began to dive early at a low angle (45–50 degrees). The fighter-bombers dropped bombs on the three largest convoy transports – *Boltenhof, Sevre, Knute Nelson*. [Despite the report of one transport being hit by an FAB-100, no hits were achieved – *Author's note*]. When exiting the dive, Major Dizhevskiy fired at one patrol ship, expending 550 rounds of Colt-Browning machine gun, no result of the firing was observed. During the attack, the enemy created a powerful anti-aircraft barrage by firing machine guns and automatic cannon from the transports and escort ships. The retreat from the target and exiting the dive was made in the direction of the smallest concentration of the escort ships. The entire group gathered after the attack in three to four minutes north-west of the convoy. The enemy aircraft covering the convoy (two Bf 109s and one He 115) did not take up air combat and went under the cover of their ships' anti-aircraft artillery.

Thus, the attack of the 27th IAP fighter-bombers ended in a draw – neither Soviet side nor the Germans suffered any losses. Alas, the task of diverting enemy fighters was not accomplished. From the combat flight log: "The 12 Kittyhawks, striking the enemy convoy half an hour before the approach of the attack groups, were unable to divert and exhaust the enemy fighters. This could have happened for two main reasons: either the enemy was late in taking off, or they had figured out the plan." The most unpleasant thing started next. In the half-hour interval between the raids the Germans, apparently, called in additional fighters. This could probably have been countered if the attack aircraft and torpedo bombers had acted according to the plan. However, this was not the case. Instead of attack aircraft, torpedo bombers were the first to strike at 12:58. A group of four Bostons of the 9th GMTAP (leader – Captain L.I. Markov) and eight Airacobras of the 255th IAP (leader – Captain P.A. Rassadkin) took off around noon and assembled in an orderly manner over the Vaenga-1 airfield, after which they proceeded to their target along the route: east of Tsyp-Navolok – north of the Rybachiy Peninsula – north of Vardö and, on leaving the Pers Fjord, they eventually spotted an enemy convoy. At 12:55, near Pers Fjord, the group detected a convoy covered by a large group of Luftwaffe fighters. The leader of torpedo bombers radioed: "Convoy on the left", and commanded the leader of the fighters of the strike group to move forward. Captain Markov made a mistake… From the documents of the Northern Fleet Air Force Headquarters: "Given the opportunity to strike directly behind the Il-2s because the latter, being on approach to the target, were in the sight of the torpedo bombers, and the commander of the fighters suggested that Captain Markov should manoeuvre and let the Il-2 group move ahead, the commander of the torpedo bombers did not perform as suggested, thus attracting all enemy fighters to his group."

From the documents of the 255th IAP:

> Captain Rassadkin, the leader of the strike group, understood the command and gave the command himself: 'To the close cover group – stay with the torpedo bombers', while he and his group began to move forward, gaining altitude. Looking back, he noticed a group of enemy fighters of two flights of four aircraft each was approaching the torpedo bombers from behind. Captain Rassadkin radioed to the torpedo-bomber leader that he noticed the enemy fighters, turned around, and entered into a fight with them. The torpedo bombers with the close cover group continued moving forward to the enemy convoy, and the strike group engaged in a fight against eight Bf 109s. The combat lasted about 10 minutes from 12:55 to 13:05 at altitudes of 200m and lower, 20–15km from the enemy convoy. Captain Rassadkin successfully attacked one Bf 109 from below and behind, and shot it down. The enemy aircraft fell into the water. Lieutenant Vlasov attacked one Bf 109 on a left turn and shot it down. At this time another Bf 109 approached the aircraft of Junior Lieutenant N.G. Tsibizov from behind, attacked and shot him down. Lieutenant Vlasov himself was engaged in the fight against the enemy and did not have time to repulse the attack of the enemy on Junior Lieutenant Tsibizov. The close cover group went further to the target along with the torpedo bombers. The torpedo bombers were flanked by Major Chertov and Senior Lieutenant Burmatov on the left, and Senior Lieutenant Samarkov and Junior Lieutenant Vasin on the right. On the approach to the convoy, about 10–15km short of it, the group of torpedo bombers was attacked from behind by enemy fighters. The left torpedo bomber was shot down and fell into the water, the third bomber on the left with the starboard engine knocked

P-40E s/n 41-13531 of the 2nd Guards SAP flown by Guards Lieutenant Colonel B.F. Safonov, May 1942.

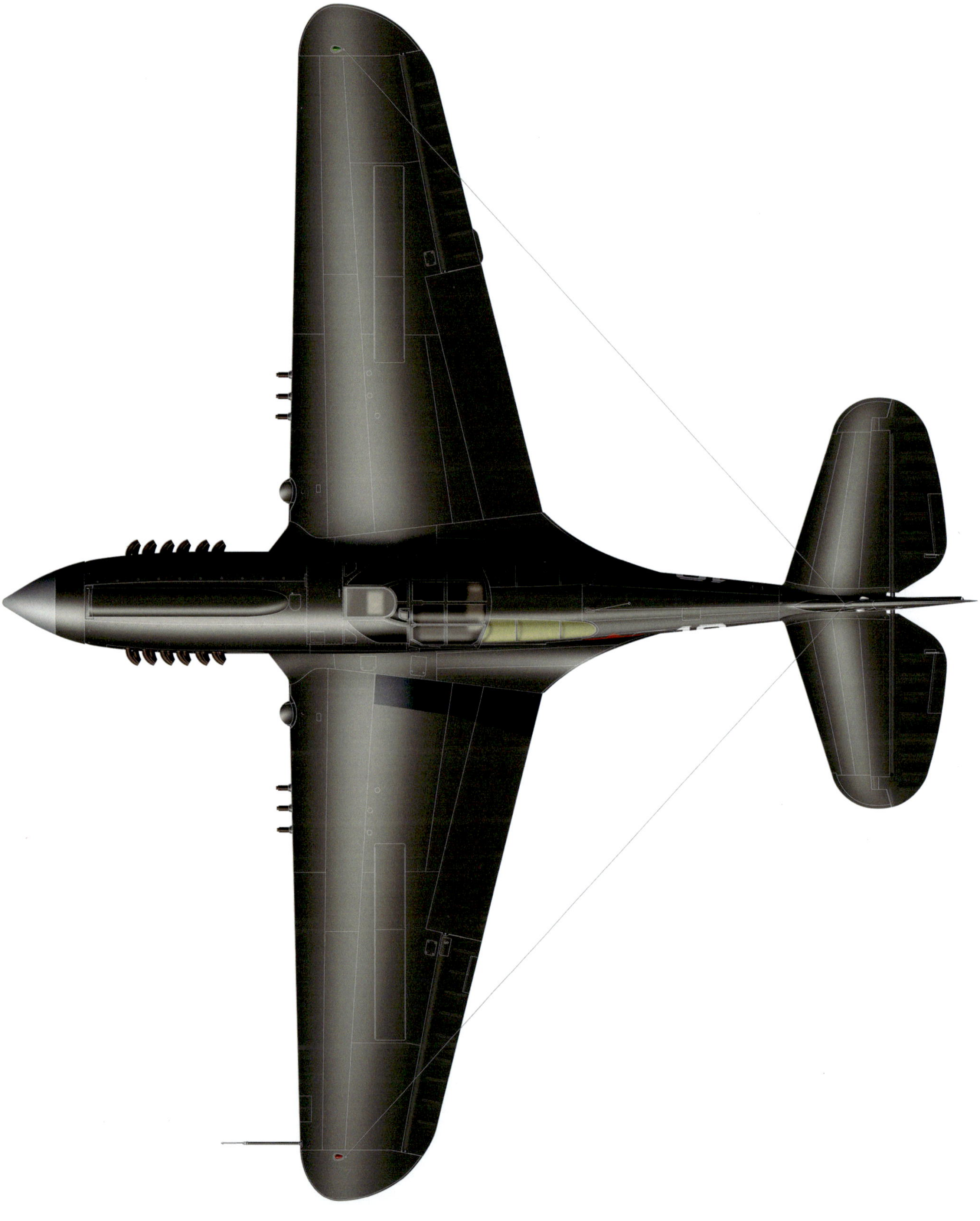

P-40E s/n 41-13531 of the 2nd Guards SAP flown by Guards Lieutenant Colonel B.F. Safonov, May 1942.

P-40E-1 presumably of the 2nd Guards SAP, 1942.

Hurricane IIB of the 78th IAP, autumn 1941.

P-400 Airacobra Mk.I of the 2nd GIAP, Murmansk, winter 1942–1943.

P-39D-2 of the 2nd GIAP, Vaenga airfield, summer 1943.

A-20B of the 9th GMTAP, winter 1943–1944.

> out and with black smoke kept moving towards the target. The second bomber on the left entered the area of anti-aircraft fire, suffered a direct hit of shell in the fuselage, lost its tail, turned over on its back and fell into the water in an upside-down position. At this time, the close cover group was tied up by the enemy fighters in cover. The left-hand pair, Major Chertov and Senior Lieutenant Burmatov, was attacked from behind by three Bf 109s. Major Chertov and Senior Lieutenant Burmatov took a left turn, while the enemy also took a left turn. Major Chertov began to change from the left to the right turn and at this time Senior Lieutenant Burmatov, being pursued by the enemy, lost sight of Major Chertov, made four left turns himself and exited from the enemy's attack. [The commander of 255th IAP Major N.G. Chertov did not return from the combat mission – *Author's note*.] The right-hand pair of direct cover aircraft was attacked and engaged in combat by four enemy fighters, and when this pair repelled the attack, the torpedo bombers were no longer in the target area.

The torpedo bombers, despite their losses, tried hard to make their way to the transports. But a large number of Luftwaffe fighters and heavy anti-aircraft fire barrage led to the defeat of the torpedo bombing group. All four torpedo bombers were shot down, their crews were killed.

At 12:40, a group of attack aircraft took off from Pummanki airfield. The group consisted of seven Il-2s of the 46th ShAP (leader – Lieutenant A.N. Sinitsyn), five Kittyhawks of the 27th IAP (leader – Senior Lieutenant M.I. Boychenko) and eight Yaks of the 20th IAP (leader – Senior Lieutenant V.V. Nuzhin). The fighters were divided into two groups: Yaks in the strike group and Kittyhawks in the close cover group. At about 13:00, the group of attack aircraft spotted a German convoy in the Pers Fjord area. The group was attacked by Luftwaffe fighters while approaching the target, and two Yak-9s were shot down in an air combat. Their pilots, Lieutenant I.Z. Shcherbak and Junior Lieutenant A.V. Vasiltsov, were killed.

At 13:05 the attack aircraft struck the convoy from a dive. One crew member on the *Knute Nelson* (5,748grt) steamship was wounded due to close explosions and machine-gun fire. In addition to the steamer, the M-364 and M-306 minesweepers were also hit by machine-gun fire, and five sailors were wounded. On the UJ-1208 submarine hunter, one man was killed and three wounded among the members of the 88mm gun crew. However, the Il-2 flying over the ship did not fire at it: the nature of the wounds made it clear that all the sailors had been hit by anti-aircraft fire from the guard ships and transports. One of the wounded men later died in the infirmary.

Meanwhile, the escort fighters engaged in heavy air combat against twelve Bf 109s of the *Stab* III./JG 5, 8. and 9. *Staffeln* of the JG 5. From the combat flight log of the 6th IAD:

> At 13:32, about 15km north-east of Bludstuden Peninsula, at an altitude of 1,000m, six Kittyhawks were engaged in combat with two Bf 109s. As a result of the combat, Junior Lieutenant Demikov shot down one Bf 109. It fell 15km north of the convoy. Lieutenant Anuchin shot down one Bf 109. The Bf 109 caught fire, ditched and sank 10km north of the convoy.

The Luftwaffe pilots reported after the combat that they had shot down 16 Soviet aircraft. This time they had much to be proud of. The losses of the Soviet side in this attack included four Bostons of the 9th GMTAP, two Airacobras of the 255th IAP, and two Yak-9s of the 20th IAP. Apart from one or two torpedo bombers, they were all shot down by Luftwaffe fighters. The Germans lost one Bf 109 (a black 'nine') of the 8. *Staffel* – it crashed during an emergency landing at Skogerre Island. Its pilot, *Feldwebel* Josef Kunz, survived. The Soviet pilots claimed nine shot down Luftwaffe fighters; one Bf 109 each was credited to the Kittyhawks pilots of the 27th IAP – Lieutenant P.M. Demikov and Lieutenant A.P. Anuchin. After the landing of all attacking groups, the Northern Fleet Air Force command was forced to change the assignment of forces for a second attack on the German convoy. The second attack was supposed to take place at Eckerö Cape. The Kittyhawks of the 27th IAP were assigned two tasks:

a) Eight Kittyhawk fighter-bombers were to bomb the convoy together with Boston torpedo bombers of the 9th GMTAP under the cover of Airacobras of the 255th IAP.
b) Six Kittyhawk fighters were to provide close cover for a group of attack aircraft of the 46th ShAP striking from Pummanki airfield.

At 16:00, a Kittyhawk reconnaissance aircraft of the 118th RAP, piloted by Lieutenant S.I. Pankrashin, radioed: "Convoy at Kibergnes Cape". Its data was transmitted to the Soviet aircraft preparing to take off.

At 17:00, four Il-2s (leader – Captain V.M. Skopintsev) and seven Yaks of the 20th IAP (leader – Captain A.P. Shipov) took off from Pummanki airfield. They were joined by six Kittyhawks of the 27th IAP (leader – Lieutenant A.P. Anuchin), which had taken off from the Kildin airfield fifteen minutes earlier. The group assembled over the airfield and set a course for the target.

At 17:23, the attack aircraft struck the convoy at Eckerö. They were countered by Luftwaffe fighters and also were exposed to heavy anti-aircraft fire. None of the bombs dropped by the Il-2s hit their targets, but machine-gun fire added two casualties on the gunboat K-3 and three casualties on the UJ-1208 submarine hunter. The fact that this was the result of the strike by the attack aircraft of the 46th GKAP can be assumed based on the position of both ships in the convoy's order. They were both at the head of the convoy, which, according to the plan of the 27th IAP attacks, was not targeted by Kittyhawk fighter-bombers. The fighters covering the attack aircraft engaged the Luftwaffe fighters and scored six victories. From the combat flight log of 6th IAD:

> At 17:40, near Volokovaya mountain, at an altitude of 600m, six Kittyhawks in the course of the second flight fought against four Bf 109s. As a result of the combat, Lieutenant Yermilin shot down a Bf 109 which fell into the water between the Heinesaari Island and Sredniy Peninsula. Junior Lieutenant Ivanov shot down a Bf 109 which went down burning at Musto-Kalio Cape.

The Soviet fighters lost two aircraft. Both were damaged in the air engagement and attempted to land at Pummanki airfield. The first was a Yak-9 of the 20th IAP – the aircraft was seriously damaged and the pilot was trying to land. The Luftwaffe fighter shot him down on approach. The pilot, Junior Lieutenant V.P. Goncharov, was killed. The second was a Kittyhawk of the 27th IAP. From the accident report on the loss of the aircraft:

> While covering the attacking aircraft, the leader of the second flight of six Kittyhawks [Junior Lieutenant V.K. Vashchenko – *Author's note*] was attacked by four FW 190 aircraft. The wingman of the pair fell behind, fought on his own, and could

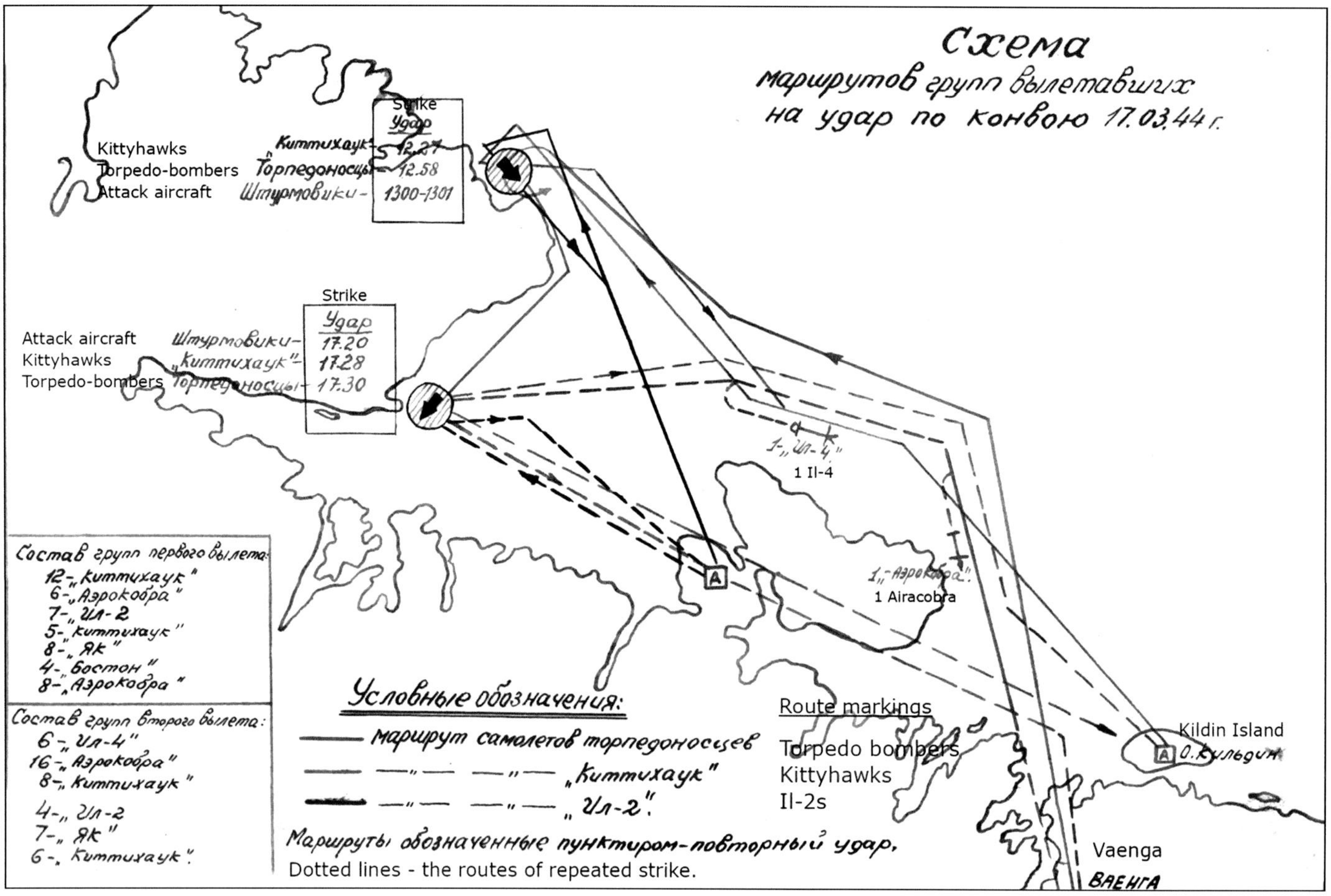

Plan of attack on the German convoy Rp.110.Ki by the aircraft of the Northern Fleet Air Force on 17 March 1944.
Compositions of groups of the first sortie: 12 – Kittyhawks; 6 – Airacobras; 7 – Il-2s; 5 – Kittyhawks; 8 – Yaks; 4 – Bostons; 8 – Airacobras.
Compositions of groups of the second sortie: 6 – Il-4s; 16 – Airacobras; 8 – Kittyhawks; 4 – Il-2s; 7 – Yaks; 6 – Kittyhawks.

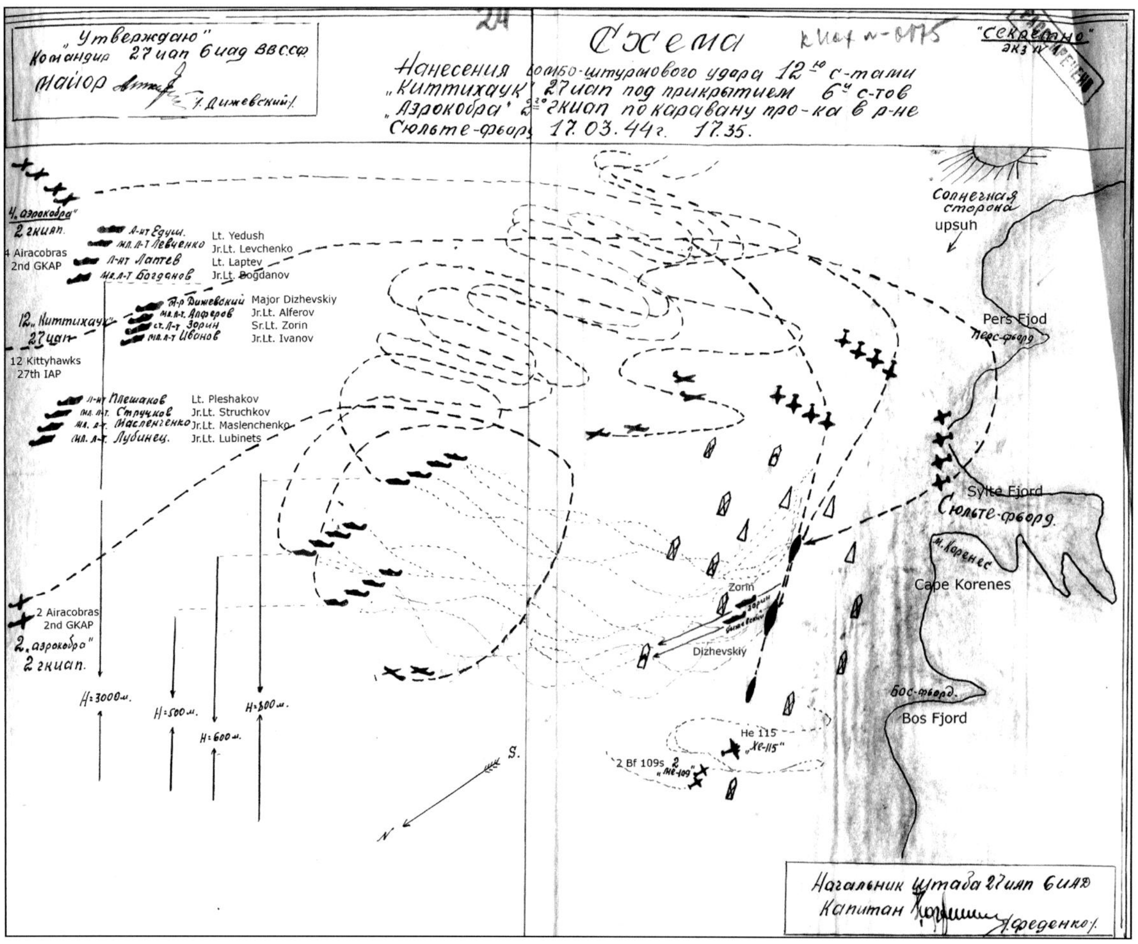

Plan of attack on the German convoy Rp.110.Ki by the Kittyhawks of the 27th IAP on 17 March 1944. Timing – 12:25 (the scheme indicates incorrect timing).

not get any help from the combat group because they were tied up in the fight. As a result, one FW 190 was shot down by him and, having been hit himself, made a forced landing near the Pummanki airfield – giving the opportunity for the Il-2s to land at their home airfield. The aircraft burned, the pilot received minor facial burns.

During the evening attack on convoy Rp.110.Ki, three Kittyhawk pilots, Lieutenant A.I. Yermolin, Junior Lieutenants N.M. Ivanov and V.K. Vashchenko, each scored one victory over the Bf 109s. Three more Bf 109 fighters were scored by pilots of the 20th IAP. The available German data indicate the loss of one Bf 109G-2, W.Nr. 14068, of the III./JG 5, which crashed in Petsamo-Fjord. Its pilot, *Leutnant* Bernhard von Hermann, was killed.

The groups of torpedo bombers and fighter-bombers joined the attack. At 16:34, six Il-4 torpedo bombers of the 9th GMTAP took off from Vaenga-1 (leader – Guards Major A.N. Voloshin), followed by eight Airacobras of the 255th IAP (leader – Captain V.S. Adonkin) and eight Airacobras of the 2nd GKAP (leader – Guards Captain S.M. Loginov). The aircraft gathered over the Vaenga-1 airfield and set course for Kildin Island, the home base of the 27th IAP. By the time they approached Kildin Island, eight Kittyhawk fighter-bombers of the 27th IAP (leader – Senior Lieutenant V.I. Zorin) had taken off and joined the group. From there, the group flew through Tsyp-Navolok Cape, then followed 15–20km seaward of Rybachiy Peninsula and reached Eckerö Cape where they found the convoy. One Il-4 returned from a mission from the Varanger Fjord area due to a torpedo problem. Technical malfunctions, this time with the engine, forced one Airacobra of the 255th IAP to return as well. From the combat flight log of the 6th IAD:

Commander of the 27th IAP, Major A.Ya. Dizhevskiy.

> At 17:30, flying at an altitude of 3,000m and at a distance of 15km, the group spotted the enemy convoy moving on a course of 210–215 degrees: three transport ships covered by up to 17 other vessels. Kittyhawks were the first to attack. They approached the target from the west along the course of the convoy at a 45 degrees angle from the starboard. At 17:35, they consistently, in groups of four aircraft, in right echelon formation from an altitude of 3,200m, turning to the left, performed bombing from a dive. Sixteen FAB-100 bombs were dropped from altitudes of 1,000–1,300m, with exiting from a dive at altitudes of 600–800m. All pilots witnessed explosions of bombs in the immediate vicinity of enemy transports, in the radius of five to fifteen metres. [According to German documents, transport *Knute Nelson* and patrol ship NH-03 were hit, but they were not damaged and had no casualties – *Author's note*]. When diving and exiting from the target, all pilots used a counterfire evasive manoeuvre. The enemy's air defence barrage over the target was dense. The bursts were exactly at the aircraft altitude with undershoot on the right and on the left. The enemy fighters, up to eight Bf 109s and FW 190s showed no activity, stayed aside and hunted for our single aircraft, which had broken away from the formation. On the return route, while retreating from the target and up to the Rybachiy Peninsula, the Kittyhawks were pursued by a group of enemy aircraft up to four Bf 109s. There was no air combat. Our aircraft had no losses or damage. Due to a heavy snow storm passing over Kildin Island, the aircraft landed at Vaenga-2 airfield.

At 17:30, the high-altitude torpedo bombers dropped torpedoes on the convoy from an altitude of 3,000m. In this case they achieved no result. All the torpedoes failed to hit their targets.

In the air combat, the pilots of the 2nd GKAP and 255th IAP did not claim any victories; however, they lost one Airacobra of the 255th IAP. Its pilot, Captain V.S. Adonkin, was killed. However, some documents claim that his aircraft was hit by a snow squall before approaching the convoy, after which no other crews saw his Airacobra. Meanwhile, the fighters covering both strike groups were engaged in heavy air combat with the Bf 109s of the *Stab* III./JG 5, the 7., 8., and 9. *Staffeln* of the JG 5. On returning to the base, the Luftwaffe fighters claimed to have shot down 14 Soviet aircraft. According to Soviet records, one Yak-9 of the 20th IAP, one Kittyhawk of the 27th IAP, and one Airacobra of the 255th IAP did not return from the evening attack on the convoy.

20 March

On this day the 78th IAP lost its second Kittyhawk in March for non-combat reasons. Junior Lieutenant A.M. Kovalenko was forced to land due to an engine failure during a training flight. During the landing the aircraft was damaged, the pilot only sustained bruises. It is known that this aircraft had serial number 2365 and was rolled out in the USA on 9 October 1943.

24 March

On this day, the Kittyhawks of the 27th IAP flew two 'free hunting' missions against minor enemy shipping. However, both flights ended in the loss of aircraft while bringing no success. It was one of the regiment's worst days.

At 5:40, four Kittyhawks (leader – Senior Lieutenant Yu.Kh. Gryaznov) took off on a 'free hunting' mission with FAB-50 bombs in the Vardö – Vadsø area, with the task of destroying all small enemy ships. The group passed Zubovka and flew along the coastline of the Rybachiy Peninsula in a low-level flight (20–30m altitude). At 6:00, Lieutenant Pleshakov, the leader of the second pair, perished when his aircraft hit a hill in the area six to seven kilometres south-west of May-Navolok Cape, flying below the leader of the group. The remaining three aircraft, after flying for three to five minutes and encountering deteriorating weather conditions, returned to the home airfield. The bombs were dropped at sea; one aircraft did this at the Kildin Island range. These aircraft landed at 6:28.

At 5:52, following the first four aircraft, a wing of Kittyhawks (leader – Senior Lieutenant M.I. Boychenko) with underwing fuel tanks and AO-15 bombs flew out for a 'free hunting' mission in the Vardö area to Nordkapp and through all the fjords with the task of destroying small enemy shipping. This group did not find any targets as far as Berlevåg. On reaching Tana Fjord they encountered a sharp deterioration in the weather (powerful winds, low overcast cloud) and turned back. On the way back, at 7:20, they bombed eight to ten schooners in the port of Makkaur, approaching from the north-west, from an altitude of 150m. At 7:20–7:25, while attacking the schooners, the Kittyhawks were attacked by four Bf 109s (two from above and two from below). Lieutenant N.G. Alferov, leading the second pair, repelling the attack from the top two Bf 109s on the first pair of Kittyhawks, shot down one Bf 109. The enemy aircraft went down in the Makkaur area. Soviet aircraft were met by heavy anti-aircraft fire in the port area. At 7:30, Senior Lieutenant M.I. Boychenko attacked a schooner at Korenes Mountain in two approaches from a low-altitude flight. Two Kittyhawks, piloted by Junior Lieutenants N.G. Alferov and K.N. Cherednichenko, did not return from the combat mission for unknown reasons. The aircraft of Junior Lieutenant N.M. Ivanov had 25 bullet and splinter holes.

German documents give the following interpretation of the events: "From 06:38 to 07:30, four Il-2 aircraft attacked a Kiberg battery. The attack was repulsed by 363 rounds of 2cm and 193 rounds of 4cm, well targeted. The bombs were dropped in the water, Vardö battery maintained defence with 8.8cm, 20 rounds. One aircraft emitted smoke followed by a powerful explosion at sea. Nothing else was observed as the aircraft disappeared into the haze." German documents also state that their fighters took off at 6:46, but the Luftwaffe pilots did not claim victories, and there is no information about their losses. The accident report clarifies the circumstances of the losses: "During an air strike on the Makkaur berth, the aircraft entered the enemy anti-aircraft artillery barrage and were simultaneously attacked by four Bf 109 fighters. The group left the area of anti-aircraft fire by performing a left turn and lost visual and radio contact with the group leader. The leading pair left the anti-aircraft fire zone by making a right turn and entering a snow squall. Loss of the crews was not observed." Based on German and Soviet documents, it appears that the two Kittyhawks collided under poor visibility conditions. Junior Lieutenants N.G. Alferov and K.N. Cherednichenko did not return from the combat mission. The two remaining Kittyhawks landed safely at 8:10 on the Kildin airfield. That was the tragic end of one of the first missions to hunt for small ships. The only positive outcome was the conclusion of the command of the 6th IAD: "For performing the air strikes, it is necessary to send Kittyhawks under the cover of faster fighters". This conclusion indicates that the command had no illusions about the capabilities of the Kittyhawk in air combat, so this would become a guide to action that would help avoid many losses in the future.

April 1944

In April, after a long period of conversion from Hurricanes to Kittyhawks, the 78th IAP went into action. The regiment was based at Vaenga-2 airfield with 27 operational and one unserviceable Kittyhawk. During April 1944, the 78th IAP flew 201 combat missions, but did not perform any attack on enemy shipping. During the month the regiment lost four Kittyhawks and three pilots. The Northern Fleet Air Force Headquarters credited the regiment pilots with two shot-down Bf 109s.

The 27th IAP continued to fight as well. It has in its strength 26 Kittyhawks (including two unserviceable) and five Hurricanes (one serviceable and four under repair). In addition, the regiment had in its list one training two-seat Hurricane and a U-2. Curiously enough, two Hurricanes of the regiment were used as cargo aircraft. The regiment was based at Vaenga-1 and Kildin Island airfields. In April, the 27th IAP flew 145 combat missions, 56 of which were against ships and convoys. In addition, the regiment aircraft flew 32 missions to attack enemy coastal artillery batteries. The regiment lost one Kittyhawk and one pilot. The Northern Fleet Air Force Headquarters credited the regiment pilots with three shot-down Bf 109s.

In the reconnaissance regiment, the 118th RAP, the number of Kittyhawks increased. As of 1 April 1944, the 118th RAP operated 31 aircraft (26 of which were serviceable), including six Kittyhawks (five serviceable). Since the beginning of the year the regiment had not lost a single Kittyhawk, despite intensive use of these aircraft.

7 April

The Kittyhawk reconnaissance aircraft of the 118th RAP piloted by Junior Lieutenant S.I. Pankrashin was the first to encounter the German convoys in April 1944. At 5:00 the pilot detected the enemy in Kobbholm Fjord and reported to the Northern Fleet Air Force command post: "Convoy, course 270 degrees, speed seven to eight knots, two transports and 14 warships". The Northern Fleet Air Force command decided to carry out an air strike on the caravan using attack aircraft from Pummanki airfield under the cover of fighters. Six Kittyhawks of the 27th IAP were to join the close cover group. The Kittyhawk reconnaissance aircraft of the 118th RAP, piloted by Junior Lieutenant A.V. Bystrov, flew out to reconnoitre the convoy at 6:40 and examined Beck Fjord in detail, but did not find any convoy. The Germans had gone into the fog that covered the northern part of the fjord. Having spotted nothing, the reconnaissance pilot turned north and at 6:50 found another convoy off Kibergnes Cape. He radioed a report of the discovery of the convoy. In fact, Lieutenant A.V. Bystrov discovered the convoy Ki.114.Rp consisting of patrol ships V-5911, V-5912, submarine hunters UJ-1212, UJ-1219, NH-03 and the steamer *La France* (616grt) pulled by the tug boat *Gulosenfjord*. The convoy left Kirkenes on 7 April 1944 and proceeded to Reppa Fjord. Meanwhile at 6:20 the Soviet attack aircraft took off from Pummanki airfield. They were joined by the air cover fighters, and the group set off towards the target. The group consisted of six Il-2s of the 64th ShAP (leader – Lieutenant S.P. Sheikin), six Kittyhawk fighters of the 27th IAP (leader – Senior Lieutenant A.P. Anuchin), six Yaks of the 20th IAP (leader – Lieutenant I.P. Kuzhanov), and six Airacobras of the 2nd GKAP (leader – Guards Captain P.L. Kolomiets). The Yaks acted as a strike group, while the remaining fighters acted as close escort group. As the message of Lieutenant A.V. Bystrov was not delivered to the attack aircraft group of Lieutenant S.P. Sheikin, the group flew to Kobbholm Fjord and did not find the convoy, but the leader decided to go to Kibergnes and search there. At 7:02 a group of attack aircraft spotted the convoy and carried out the strike at 7:04.

According to German documents, there were no casualties from the Soviet attack – only a few holes from bomb splinters and cannon/machine-gun fire on one of the steamers. Luftwaffe Bf 109 fighters of 9./JG 5 engaged Soviet aircraft and claimed five victories without their own losses, but did not actually inflict any losses on the Soviet aircraft. From the combat flight log of the 6th IAD: "At 6:55, near Kibergnes, at an altitude of 800–1,200m, six Kittyhawks engaged in air combat with four to six Bf 109s. As a result of the combat, Senior Lieutenant Anuchin shot down one Bf 109. The enemy aircraft fell into the water in the vicinity of the convoy." Based on the results of the air combat, the Northern Fleet Air Force Headquarters credited Lieutenant L.P. Lapin and Junior Lieutenant G.A. Dmitrik of the 20th IAP with one Bf 109 each. Senior Lieutenant A.P. Anuchin of the 27th IAP scored the presumed victory over a Bf 109.

While the attack aircraft were striking the convoy, the Northern Fleet Air Force command decided to make a repeated attack. But in order to do so, another reconnaissance mission had to be carried out. The Kittyhawk reconnaissance aircraft of the 118th RAP performed this task – at 8:50 the convoy was discovered by Junior Lieutenant G.S. Dzhulaev. He corrected the data about the enemy's position and transmitted it to the Northern Fleet Air Force Headquarters. Having received information about the convoy, the second strike group took off. At 9:34 six Il-4 high-altitude torpedo bombers of the 9th GMTAP (leader – Guards Major A.N. Voloshin) and 16 Airacobras of the 255th IAP (leader – Captain P.A. Rassadkin) took off from the Vaenga-1 airfield. Having gathered over the airfield, they followed to the airfield on Kildin Island, where they were joined by eight Kittyhawk fighter-bombers of the 27th IAP (leader – Captain Yu.Kh. Gryaznov). Meanwhile, at 10:00 the convoy was discovered by a Spitfire reconnaissance aircraft of the 118th RAP piloted by Senior Lieutenant K.V. Popovich. He reported the discovery of a convoy in the Sylte Fjord area. A pair of Luftwaffe FW 190s attempted to pursue the reconnaissance aircraft, but Popovich managed to escape. At 10:43 the second strike group spotted the convoy in the Sylte Fjord area. The Kittyhawks were the first to drop the bombs from dives on the German ships, followed by the torpedoes launched from the Il-4s. According to available German documents, the convoy sustained no damage. One Il-4 was hit by anti-aircraft artillery fire from German ships, and its port engine was damaged. Despite serious damage, the torpedo bomber managed to reach the Pummanki airfield. The Luftwaffe fighters of 7./JG 5, engaged the Soviet aircraft and claimed one victory without their losses. From the combat flight log of the 6th IAD:

> After a bombing raid in cooperation with Airacobras of the 255th IAP, eight Kittyhawks were engaged in air combat with 10–12 Bf 109s. As a result of the air combat, Senior Lieutenant Zorin shot down one Bf 109, which crashed near the convoy. Lieutenant Yedush and Captain Gryaznov hit one Bf 109 each in the air combat.

Based on the results of the air combat, the Northern Fleet Air Force Headquarters credited the pilots of the 255th IAP, Captains D.F. Amosov and P.A. Rassadkin, and the pilot of the 27th IAP, Senior Lieutenant V.I. Zorin, with one Bf 109 shot down each. Four pilots – two of the 255th IAP (Senior Lieutenants V.A. Burmatov and F.E. Samarkov) and two of the 27th IAP (Captain Yu.Kh. Gryaznov and Lieutenant I.S. Yedush) scored presumably one shot down Bf 109 each.

While torpedo bombers and fighter-bombers were attacking the convoy, a group of attack aircraft flew out to conduct a second attack on the convoy. According to the plan of the Northern Fleet Air Force Headquarters, it was to consist of three Il-2s of the 46th ShAP (leader – Senior Lieutenant S.S. Rolbin), eight Airacobras of the 20th IAP (leader – Senior Lieutenant A.K. Tarasov), and six Kittyhawk fighters of the 27th IAP (leader – Senior Lieutenant A.P. Anuchin). The Airacobras were to act as the 'air combat group' and the Kittyhawks as the 'close cover group'. At 10:54 Airacobras of the 20th IAP approached the Pummanki airfield and were joined by three Il-2s of the 46th ShAP, so all headed towards the target. The Kittyhawk fighters were prevented from taking off from the Pummanki airfield by the Il-4 torpedo bomber, which was performing a force landing due to the damage sustained in the battle with the convoy. Only 16 minutes later, the runway was cleared, and the Kittyhawks took off, attempting to catch up with the attack aircraft. After reaching Sylte Fjord and finding no one, they turned to their home airfield on Kildin Island. At 11:50 the attack aircraft and fighters of the 20th IAP spotted the convoy in the Makkaur area. At 11:53 a dive attack took place, and once again the strike was unsuccessful.

Luftwaffe Bf 109 fighters of the 8. and 9. *Staffeln* of the JG 5 attempted to attack the Soviet aircraft, but despite the incomplete number of escort fighters, the attacking group did not suffer losses, while the Luftwaffe pilots reported four shot down Soviet aircraft. The Soviet pilots did not claim to have shot down any enemy aircraft.

The last strike against the convoy was again carried out by torpedo bombers. This group consisted of a pair of Boston torpedo bombers of the 9th GMTAP (leader – Guards Captain P.P. Gusev) and was covered by two groups of fighters: eight Airacobras of the 255th IAP and four Airacobras of the 2nd GKAP. At 13:50 the aircraft gathered over Vaenga-1 airfield and set off to attack the convoy in the area of Tana Fjord. At 14:39 the crews spotted the enemy and at 14:41 attacked the ships. Torpedoes missed the targets and the only damage was caused by gunfire from the Soviet aircraft: the German crews had to plug small bullet holes with wedges. The Luftwaffe fighters did not show themselves in any way and did not claim any victories. The Soviet pilots had no successes either. The battle for the Ki.114.Rp convoy essentially ended in a draw. The German ships and Luftwaffe aircraft suffered no losses, nor did the Northern Fleet Air Force.

10 April

The operation, which was a major success for the Northern Fleet Air Force, was preceded by the competent work of three types of reconnaissance. The first to report on the large number of German ships assembled near Kirkenes were the 'soldiers of the invisible front'. These men, whose names remain unknown to this day, passed the information through the intelligence agents to the Northern Fleet Air Force Headquarters. The second valuable input was achieved through the excellent service of the radio reconnaissance personnel. They established that the Bf 109s based at Luostari airfield were ferried to Rovaniemi airfield. According to the book of Eric Mombeek, III./JG 5 flew to Pontsalenjoki at 14:00 on 9 April. Three days later, on 12 April, the entire group returned to Luostari. Based on these data, the Northern Fleet Air Force Headquarters concluded that the air cover over the German ships would either be non-existent or weak. The third type of reconnaissance, which ensured the success of the operation, was the work of reconnaissance aviation. Pilots of the 20th IAP flew over the Luostari airfield and found that there were indeed no Luftwaffe aircraft on it. Around the same time, the reconnaissance aircraft of the 118th RAP took photographs of the Kirkenes area. After processing the photos, the Northern Fleet Air Force Headquarters counted 21 transports of 1,500–15,000 tonnes, two destroyers, two minesweepers, eight patrol ships and six patrol boats there.

The Northern Fleet Air Force command decided to attack German ships and vessels with torpedo bombers of the 5th Mine-Torpedo Aviation Division (MTAD, *Minno-Torpednaya Aviatsionnaya Diviziya*), attack aircraft of the 14th Composite Aviation Division (SAD, *Smeshannaya Aviatsionnaya Diviziya*) and fighter-bombers of the 6th IAD. Naturally, Kittyhawk aircraft also took part in the operation. They were assigned with the following tasks:

1. Two groups of six Kittyhawks each of the 78th IAP – to provide close cover for two Il-2 attack groups of the 46th ShAP;
2. One group of six Kittyhawks of the 27th IAP – to provide close cover for a group of attack aircraft from Pummanki airfield;
3. Eight Kittyhawks of the 27th IAP – to carry out a dive-bombing attack on ships and vessels in Kirkenes;
4. Kittyhawk reconnaissance aircraft of the 118th RAP – to provide monitoring over the attack results.

This operation was the first of a series of successful strikes conducted by the Northern Fleet Air Force in 1944 against German ships and vessels in Kirkenes.

Since the main success of the operation came from the strike by three groups of attack aircraft, there is no point in describing in detail the attacks of the 46th ShAP. The Kittyhawk fighter-bomber group which took part in the attack did not achieve any success. At 18:07, eight Kittyhawk fighter-bombers of the 27th IAP (leader – Captain Yu. Kh. Gryaznov) took off from the Ura-Guba airfield. An escort of eight Airacobras of the 2nd GKAP (leader – Guards Captain S.M. Loginov), which took off from the Kildin airfield, was waiting for them. The group assembled over the Kildin airfield and proceeded to target along the route Pummanki – Bek Fjord – the target. At 18:47 the Kittyhawks dropped bombs on the transports from a dive, from altitude of 700m. According to the pilots' reports, there were no direct hits, the bombs exploded 10–30m away from the ships. Considering that it was the FAB-100 bombs, the absence of any result is obvious. The reports of radio reconnaissance were correct: not a single Luftwaffe fighter appeared over the German ships under attack. As a result of the strike, the attack aircraft of the 46th ShAP managed to achieve the first major success in attacking naval targets in the Northern Fleet. The steamships *Markobrunner* (8,140grt) and *Boltenhof* (3,307grt) were severely damaged. Both had to be grounded by the Germans. The first was not repaired until July and left Kirkenes on 3 August 1944 with convoy Ki.125.Lf. The second was repaired a month earlier and departed Kirkenes on 29 June 1944 with convoy Ki.122.Rp. In addition to the steamers, the gunboat K-1 was lightly damaged by the gunfire of the attackers. There were three wounded crew members on board. Three hours after the strike, the German ships were attacked by torpedo bombers of the 9th GMTAP, but all the torpedoes missed the targets. The last to take part in the attack were five DB-3f bombers of the 9th GMTAP, with the task of laying mines. They performed this task successfully and without incident.

The day of 10 April 1944 became the first day of that year when the Northern Fleet Air Force were able to inflict serious damage on enemy ships. Further and more successful strikes would soon follow.

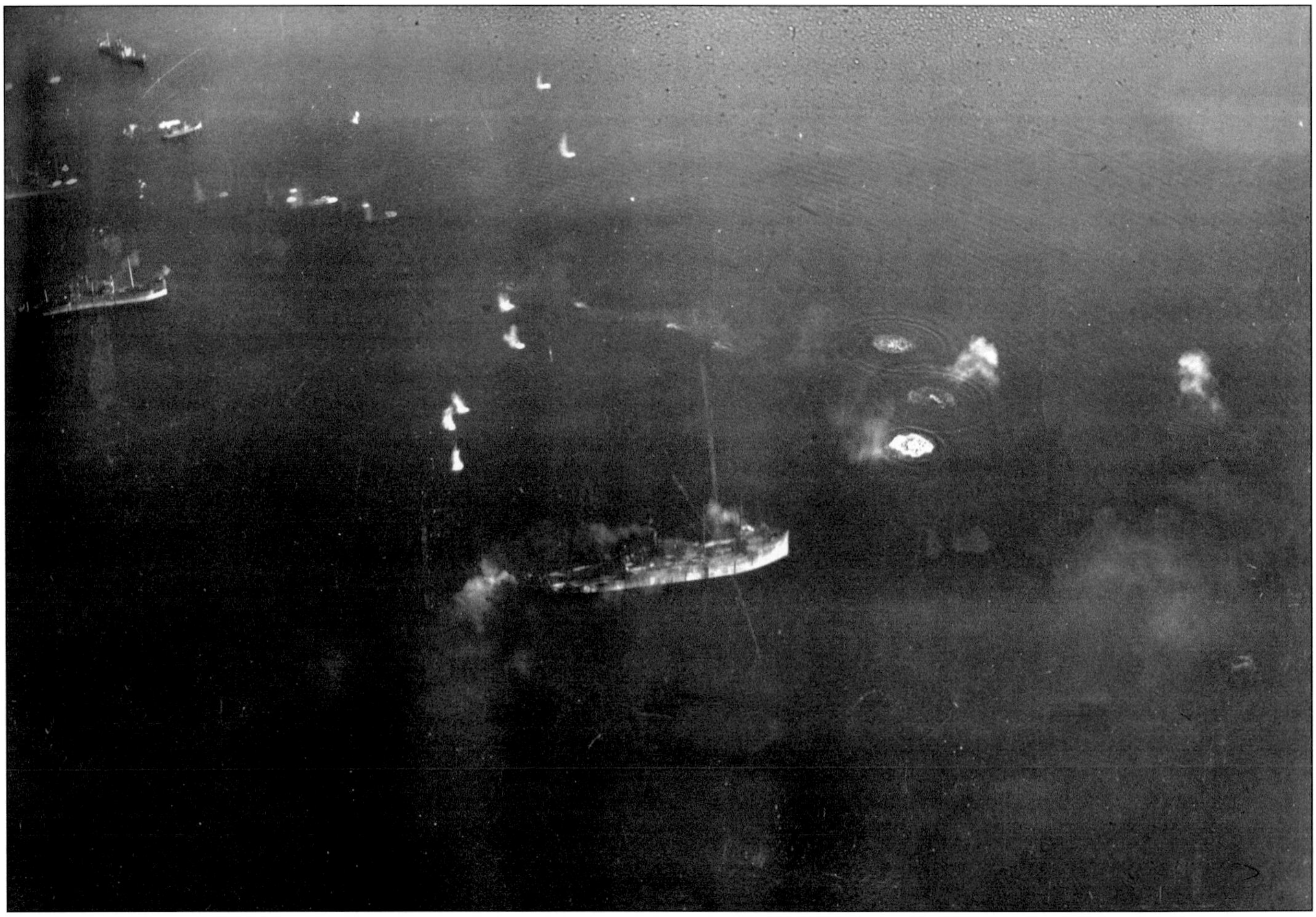

German transports in Kirkenes under attack by aircraft of the Northern Fleet Air Force, 10 April 1944.

14 April

The Soviet fighter-bombers achieved success on this day, but the northern weather managed to inflict damage where the Germans failed, and the Northern Fleet Air Force again suffered losses. A group of four Airacobras of the 2nd GKAP (leader – Guards Senior Lieutenant N.M. Didenko) and a pair of Kittyhawks of the 27th IAP departed on a mission: "To assist the submarines at Makkaur Cape. Attack small vessels". At 19:15 two Kittyhawks of the 27th IAP (pilots Junior Lieutenant V.T. Lubenets and A.A. Maslichenko) took off. They joined a group of four Airacobras of the 2nd GKAP and headed for the target, Makkaur Cape. None of the aircraft in the group carried bombs, and the combat mission was supposed to be achieved by fighter's cannon and machine guns. According to pilots' reports, at 20:15 these six Soviet fighters attacked several schooners off Makkaur Cape. Fleet Air Force Headquarters credited the sinking of two schooners to the 2nd GKAP and one schooner to the 27th IAP. According to German documents, five Russian aircraft near Makkaur fired at motorboats transporting the 210. *Infanterie-Division*. As a result of the Soviet attack, the motorboat *Vesper* (120grt), loaded with food, mail and ammunition, caught fire, drifted into the sea and eventually sank. The following motorboat *Solveig* (it was being towed for repairs with a broken engine) was towed to Bos Fjord in a damaged condition by the Norwegians, but was not repaired. In addition, 10 minutes after the first attack, Soviet pilots unsuccessfully fired at the motorboat *Boelken* that belonged to the Havningsberg coastal battery, and at a nearby lighthouse. In both cases, the 20mm anti-aircraft guns from batteries (Makkaur and Havningsberg, respectively) were firing at the attacking aircraft, with one aircraft supposedly set on fire. But more dangerous than the German anti-aircraft gunners was the northern weather. On the way back the Soviet fighters were caught in a snowstorm. From the report on the forced landing of Airacobra of 2nd GKAP, piloted by Guards Senior Lieutenant N.M. Didenko:

> There was no engagement with fighters or anti-aircraft artillery. The pilot made a forced landing due to bad weather conditions on the return route. The crews navigated in difficult weather conditions with visibility down to 50m. It was impossible to avoid the snow squalls as the area to the south-east and south-west and the sea was completely off-limits. When the aircraft reached the land, the flight became even more challenging, as the snow cover merged with the background, so the aircraft lost sight of each other. The pilot followed the shoreline and reached Sayda Guba, where he was forced to land.

Three Airacobras of the 2nd GKAP, piloted by Guards Lieutenant N.G. Kashcheev and Guards Junior Lieutenants Yu.I. Boychenko and A.I. Podrez, were missing because of the snowfall. The fate of the pilots was clarified during the search operation – they were found dead. One Kittyhawk of the 27th IAP went missing along with the Airacobras. From the accident report on the loss of the Kittyhawk: "On returning from the mission, weather conditions deteriorated sharply. Under the circumstances of dusk, low cloud cover, and visibility down to one to three kilometres, wingman Junior Lieutenant V.T. Lubinets fell behind the formation during the turn. Continuing on his own with an attempt to reach the airfield, he crashed on the Rybachiy Peninsula. The aircraft was destroyed. The pilot was killed." Junior Lieutenant A.A. Maslenchenko, pilot of the 27th IAP, was the only one of the six Soviet aircraft to land at home airfield. His aircraft landed at 21:36.

23 April

Another convoy was attacked, and the first German warship was sunk in 1944 by the Northern Fleet Air Force. The battle with the convoy was started by the Kittyhawk reconnaissance aircraft. At 8:45 the Kittyhawk of the 118th RAP, piloted by Junior Lieutenant A.V. Bystrov, spotted the German convoy near Eckerö Cape. This was the Ki.117.Rp convoy that left Kirkenes for Reppa Fjord at 6:45 on 23 April 1944. The convoy included minesweepers M-251, M-202, M-31, M-35, M-154, patrol ships V-6109, V-6110, V-5911, V-5914, UJ-1209, UJ-1212, UJ-1219, UJ-1220, NH-03, motor minesweeper R-157, gunboat K-1, motor minesweeper *Weser*, steamers *Muhlheim Ruhr* (5,350grt), *Sivas* (3,832grt), *Knute Nelson* (5,748grt), *Moshill* (2,959grt), *Vale* (5,981grt), *Sevre* (4,585grt), *Arna* (4,390grt), *Hanna Cords* (1,891grt), tankers *Gerdmor* (761grt), *Grete* (638grt), *Unkas* (499grt). *Oleum* (476grt), *Utsire* (468grt) and *Movenriff* (465grt). The Northern Fleet Air Force command decided to launch a massive attack on the convoy using attack aircraft of the 46th ShAP and low-altitude torpedo bombers of the 9th GMTAP.

The Kittyhawks of the 78th and 27th IAPs were assigned the task of covering the attack aircraft of the 46th ShAP in the close cover groups. The Kittyhawk reconnaissance aircraft of the 118th RAP traditionally conducted reconnaissance and monitored the results of the strike.

Having armed the bombs and received the necessary orders from the commanders, the attack groups took off. The first to take off from Vaenga-2 at 10:37 was a group of eight Il-2s of the 46th ShAP (leader – Captain I.B. Katunin), and at 10:45 it was to be joined by eight Kittyhawk fighters of the 78th IAP (leader – Captain M.N. Veryovkin), but in fact only four of them took part in accompanying this group. At 10:52, six Airacobras of the 20th IAP (leader – Senior Lieutenant A.K. Tarasov) also took off. Half an hour later, at 11:18, a second group of four Il-2s of the 46th ShAP (leader – Lieutenant N.N. Surovov) took off from Pummanki airfield, covered by four Yak-9s of the 20th IAP (leader – Lieutenant I.P. Kuzhanov) and six Kittyhawks of the 27th IAP (leader – Senior Lieutenant A.P. Anuchin). Both striking groups were met by the Luftwaffe even before they reached their target. The Kittyhawks of the 27th and 78th IAPs and the Yaks of the 20th IAP joined the combat to repel enemy fighters' attacks.

Captain M.N. Veryovkin's group of the 78th IAP, consisting of eight Kittyhawks, split into two before the air battle began. One group of four Kittyhawks, headed by the leader, joined the attack aircraft group from Pummanki airfield (the second attack aircraft group); the second group of four Kittyhawks, commanded by Lieutenant Kravchenko, continued to provide close cover for the attack aircraft group from Vaenga-2 airfield (the first attack aircraft group). From the documents of 78th IAP:

> Captain Veryovkin with his group of four aircraft spotted six Bf 109 aircraft flying to seven kilometres away from the target, four of them on the left and two on the right, trying to attack Il-2 aircraft from behind. He repulsed the attack of the right Bf 109s with barrage fire from a distance of 400–500m. Then Captain Veryovkin turned around and went in a head-on attack going to the left Bf 109s; enemy aircraft could not stand the attack, turned away and went into the clouds. While diving, the group led by Lieutenant Kravchenko spotted a pair of Bf 109s trying to attack Il-2 aircraft from below and from the front. Lieutenant Kravchenko opened fire and attacked from above and from the front at 2/4 target aspect ratio, from 200–150m. He fired two short bursts and began a combat on

> turns. At this point, two Airacobras approached and engaged in combat, while Kravchenko withdrew from the battle and joined the exiting group of attack aircraft. During the battle Junior Lieutenant Komashko [in a Kittyhawk – *Author's note*] spotted four Bf 109s approaching the Il-2s, attacked the leader of the first pair, fired two short and one long bursts at target aspect ratio of 2/4 from behind, from a distance of 50m. The fire intersected the cockpit, pieces flew off the aircraft and it fell into the water. Junior Lieutenants Dzyuba and Komashko observed the fall. Komashko made a turn out of the attack towards Vardö, but on the turn his aircraft stalled at 700–800m altitude. When coming out of his dive he was attacked by two Bf 109s, the enemy fire was passing on the left and right sides of the fuselage. He sideslipped out of the attack, went into a turn with gaining altitude and attacked one Bf 109 at 3/4 target aspect ratio from a distance of 70–50m, no results observed.

At 11:30–11:34, both attack groups almost simultaneously struck the convoy near Vardö. The attackers came in from the starboard of the convoy, so the transports and escort ships in the rear of the convoy came under attack. The gunner of one of the attack aircraft, N.I. Lidin shot down a Luftwaffe He 115 seaplane during the strike. The Germans claimed that there were no direct bomb hits, but the steamer *Arna*, which was the last ship in the left-hand line of the transports, was damaged by cannon and machine-gun fire, and two men were injured, one seriously and one lightly. In addition to the steamer, one sailor was lightly wounded, but the other died of his wounds on the submarine hunter UJ-1209. In addition, the attack aircraft fired cannon and machine guns at the anti-aircraft battery in Vardö, but without causing any damage. The battery fired back and scored two shot down Soviet attack aircraft, though not confirmed by Soviet documents. Anti-aircraft fire from German ships was fatal for the leading attack aircraft of the first group. Unfortunately, the crew perished along with the aircraft. All the other attack aircraft, though being attacked by fighters and anti-aircraft fire and sustaining damage, managed to return home.

The Germans continued to attack Soviet aircraft as they retreated from their target. Two groups of Bf 109s took part in the air battle on the enemy side (10 aircraft of the 7. and 9. *Staffeln* in the first group and 11 aircraft of *Stab* III./JG 5 and the 8. *Staffel* in the second group). From the documents of the 78th IAP:

> At this moment the Il-2 aircraft were moving away from the target. After four to five minutes on the reverse course, Lieutenant Pavlov's pair was attacked from behind on the right by four Bf 109s. Captain Veryovkin noticed the attack and warned Pavlov by radio, then turned and fired a barrage burst from a distance of 400m; the enemy aircraft descended and disappeared. In three to four minutes the same group of four aircraft appeared and again tried to attack our aircraft from two directions. Captain Veryovkin repulsed the attack of those coming from the left, the pair coming from the right was attacked by Lieutenant Pavlov, who engaged in a turning fight with them, the latter went out of the attack by climbing. After that Lieutenant Pavlov did not see Veryovkin's pair. In one to two minutes one Bf 109 attacked the aircraft of Junior Lieutenant Zinchenko from behind on the left from distance of 100–80m, the latter was hit and headed for the Rybachiy Peninsula, but was attacked at that time. Lieutenant Pavlov repulsed the attack with long bursts from distance of 100–80m at 0/4 target aspect ratio from behind, the enemy aircraft disappeared in clouds in a zooming climb. Pavlov set a course to Pummanki and did not see the aircraft of Junior Lieutenant Zinchenko again, but he saw one burning aircraft crashed on the shore near Vaitolahti. As Captain Veryovkin was approaching Vaitolahti, he saw two Bf 109s behind him at 1,000m distance trying to approach him from tail. Having turned at 180 degrees, he went into a head-on attack and opened fire from 300–200m distance; one enemy aircraft caught fire, rolled back to the left, went into a dive and crashed near Vaitolahti. The crash was confirmed by Junior Lieutenants Dzyuba and air observation posts. Junior Lieutenant Dzyuba attacked the wingman of the two Bf 109s from behind and fired a long burst from a distance of 120–100m. The enemy's aircraft went off on 45 degrees heading while emitting smoke. After the attack, Dzyuba joined his leader Captain Veryovkin and they directed to home airfield. When leaving the target and 30km away from Vaitolahti, Kravchenko spotted up to nine Bf 109s approaching a group of attack aircraft, so he decided to attack the leader of the group; the latter noticed the approach of our fighters, turned away from the Il-2s and attacked Kravchenko. One Bf 109 attacked his wingman – Junior Lieutenant Shiryaev from a distance of 100m at zero degrees aspect angle. He fired a long burst; Shiryaev went sharply down and fell into the water. Lieutenant Kravchenko attacked the Bf 109 from a distance of 400m at a 4/4 target aspect ratio. At this time, two Bf 109s attacked the aircraft of Junior Lieutenant Kozhevnikov from behind and from below. Lieutenant Kravchenko noticed the danger to Junior Lieutenant Kozhevnikov and attacked the leading aircraft of the Bf 109 pair from behind at zero degrees aspect angle, from distance of 50m. After two bursts, the enemy aircraft abruptly went down and the wingman went up in a climb. Lieutenant Kravchenko did not see the aircraft of Junior Lieutenant Kozhevnikov after this attack. There were no Airacobra aircraft in this engagement. While fighting, Kravchenko tried to draw the enemy to his territory (Rybachiy Peninsula).

The records of the 27th IAP do not contain such a detailed description of this air battle. Some details have been found only in the combat flight log of the 6th IAD:

> At 11:30, an air battle against four Bf 109s was fought over an enemy convoy at an altitude of 300m. As a result of the air engagement Lieutenant Anuchin shot down one Bf 109. The enemy aircraft fell in the water in the area of the convoy. At 11:43 while returning to Vaitolahti, at an altitude of 700m they were engaged in an air battle with six Bf 109s. As a result of the combat, Lieutenant Yermilin shot down one Bf 109. The enemy aircraft crashed on the northern cape of Vaitolahti.

Two victories over the Bf 109 each were credited by the Northern Fleet Air Force Headquarters to the pilots of the 78th and 27th IAPs and two victories to the gunners of the 46th ShAP. Lieutenants A.P. Anuchin and B.G. Yermilin of the 27th IAP, Captain M.N. Veryovkin, Junior Lieutenant Komashko of the 78th IAP, navigator Lieutenant M.S. Nitsak and air gunner N.A. Grigoriev of the 46th ShAP increased their kill counts. It is now known that the Germans lost a Bf 109G-6, W.Nr. 412110, tactical number 'White 5', which was piloted by *Feldwebel* Peter Rohde of the 7./JG 5 during the morning battle. It crashed in the sea. Another Bf 109G-2, W.Nr. 13473, tactical number 'Black 5' flown by *Unteroffizier* Günther Gorgas of the 8. *Staffel* crashed while landing on the shore. Both Luftwaffe pilots were killed. The Luftwaffe pilots scored a total of 28 (!!!) victories, but in fact the Northern Fleet Air Force lost three Kittyhawks of the 78th IAP in the air battle. The pilots of two aircraft, Junior Lieutenants A.I. Zinchenko and V.P. Shiryaev, were killed. Junior Lieutenant N.F. Kozhevnikov was wounded, but after recovery returned to the regiment. All the fighters of the 27th IAP and the 20th IAP managed to return to their home airfields.

At 10:35 six Boston torpedo bombers of the 9th GMTAP (leader – Captain P.P. Gusev) took off from the Vaenga-1 airfield under the cover of 16 Airacobras of the 255th IAP (leader – Major A.E. Tulskiy). At 12:15, on leaving Busse-Sund (north of Vardö), the Fs attacked the convoy. Torpedoes were aimed at the transports, and one of them hit the patrol ship V-6109. The torpedo hit the central part, closer to the bow of the ship. Sixteen crew members and one passenger were killed. The bow of the ship broke off, but the patrol boat stubbornly stayed afloat. Seeing that the ship was not sinking, the convoy commander ordered the minesweeper M-154 and the patrol boat V-6110 to tow it to the shore. Anti-aircraft fire from German ships led to the loss of the Boston torpedo bomber piloted by Junior Lieutenant V.S. Garbuz and the Airacobra fighter piloted by Junior Lieutenant T.F. Chistov. The Boston crew and the Airacobra pilot were killed. There was essentially no air combat. From the documents of the 255th IAP:

> At 12:15, two Bf 110s were encountered in the area of the convoy; they tried to attack the torpedo bombers but were repulsed and did not appear in the target area again. When the torpedo bombers were exiting the attack, Junior Lieutenant Yegorov attacked a Do 24 enemy aircraft performing an antisubmarine defence of the convoy and shot it down from a distance of 50m.

The Northern Fleet Air Force Headquarters credited the victory over the seaplane to Junior Lieutenant D.I. Yegorov of the 255th IAP.

At 13:50, the Northern Fleet Air Force Commander ordered a second attack on the convoy. For this purpose, six attack aircraft of the 46th ShAP were ferried to the Pummanki airfield. In addition, two decoy groups took off. At 14.55, two fighter decoy groups were sent out: one, consisting of four Kittyhawks, to the Luostari airfield area, and the other, of two Kittyhawks, to the Vaitolahti area. According to radio reconnaissance, these groups managed to draw attention of some of the Luftwaffe fighters. At 14:40 six Il-4 torpedo bombers of the 9th GMTAP took off from Vaenga-1(leader – Captain K.F. Shkaruba) under cover of twelve Airacobras of the 255th IAP (leader – Captain P.A. Rassadkin). Having gathered over the airfield, the group proceeded to Kongs Fjord. At 15:40 the attacks on the convoy began, but this time luck favoured the Germans. All torpedoes missed the ships and vessels of the convoy. The Germans were more accurate and shot down the Airacobra of the 255th IAP with anti-aircraft fire. Its pilot, V.S. Kurlakov, was killed. As the group of torpedo bombers were retreating from the target, they were attacked by Luftwaffe fighters. From the documents of the 255th IAP:

> There were no enemy fighters over the convoy when we were approaching the target and during the torpedo attack. After the attack on the convoy, on the retreat from the target a group of four to six enemy fighters was spotted on the right behind our torpedo bombers. The enemy fighters tried to catch up and attack our torpedo bombers, but were spotted by our fighters at a long distance and were not allowed to approach the torpedo bombers. In the air battle that followed two enemy Bf 109s were shot down. Lieutenant Rossiychuk attacked the leader of the Bf 109 pair and shot it down from behind from a distance of 50m. Lieutenant Bogdanov shot down the second Bf 109. The remaining enemy fighters did not attack anymore and withdrew from the battle. All torpedo bombers returned to their airfield unharmed. As a result of the air combat, one Airacobra of Junior Lieutenant Zaitsev was damaged, but landed safely.

The Northern Fleet Air Force Headquarters credited one shot down Bf 109 to Lieutenant P.D. Bogdanov and Lieutenant I.I. Rossiychuk each.

At 15:26, a group of seven Il-2s of the 46th ShAP (leader – Captain S.A. Gulyaev) took off from Pummanki airfield under cover of six Kittyhawk fighters of the 78th IAP (leader – Lieutenant V.G. Mitrofanov) and four Yak-9s of the 20th IAP (leader – Lieutenant L.P. Lapin). Some sources erroneously assume that the Kittyhawks carried bombs on this mission, but the documents of the 6th IAD do not confirm this. The group did not find the convoy because it had gone into a bad weather area, but spotted a group of ships towing the damaged patrol ship V-6109 to the shore. At 15:45, Soviet crews saw a small group of German ships heading towards Vardö and attacked them. The Luftwaffe fighters, hiding in the clouds and occasionally attacking our aircraft, did not cause much trouble for the attacking aircraft. In fact, according to German data, only one Soviet aircraft attacked the M-154 minesweeper, while the others concentrated their efforts on bombing the patrol ship V-6110 which was towing the wrecked V-6109. From the report of the fighter pilot of the 78th IAP Lieutenant V.G. Mitrofanov: "The bombs exploded near the large transport. I did not observe any direct hits. The large transport was smoking when it retreated". According to German documents, the engine room bulkhead on the damaged patrol ship V-6109 collapsed due to bomb explosions, and the ship sank. In response, the German anti-aircraft gunners were able to shoot down two Il-2s, one of which crashed when exiting the attack, and the other, having sustained damage, was forced to land near the Sredniy Peninsula. Unfortunately, the losses of the Northern Fleet Air Force were not limited to two attack aircraft. According to the report of Lieutenant A.N. Nour, the Kittyhawk of his wingman, Junior Lieutenant B.G. Fedurakin, exploded in the air after a direct hit by an anti-aircraft shell. The accident report on the loss of the aircraft says: "The crews retreated using an anti-aircraft-fire manoeuvre. During the retreat the ships opened barrage fire. At a distance of four to six kilometres, after entering the anti-aircraft fire barrage, the aircraft was shot down by a direct hit of anti-aircraft shell."

The Soviet torpedo bombers and attack aircraft were opposed by fighters of the 8./JG 5, who claimed a total of 10 victories but actually only managed to damage one Soviet aircraft. On the enemy side the victim of this battle was a Bf 109G-2, W.Nr. 13727, tactical number 'Black 12', of the 8. *Staffel*. The wounded pilot, *Unteroffizier* Karl-Heinz Witt, was able to make a forced landing at Liinahamari. Whether this Bf 109 was later restored to flying condition is not known.

All in all, the pilots of the JG 5 who fought over the convoy that day scored 39 victories, of which only three were confirmed by Soviet documents. On the other hand, according to documents of the JG 5, that day two more Bf 109s (including the one flown by Karl Witt) were forced to land in addition to two Bf 109s lost in the morning fights, and three more Bf 109s sustained damage of unknown severity and made emergency landings at their home airfield. Soviet pilots and air gunners were credited with seven victories over the Bf 109s on that day.

A convoy under attack by torpedo bombers of the Northern Fleet Air Force.

Attack aircraft of the 46th ShAP of the Northern Fleet Air Force in flight.

May 1944

The Kittyhawk fighter-bombers became also more active in May. The 78th IAP, under the leadership of Captain F.S. Plotko, mastered the skip-bombing method. In the course of one month the pilots of the 78th IAP sank a transport and a submarine hunter using the new method of bombing attack. In May, the 78th IAP flew 280 combat missions, 75 of which were strikes against ships and convoys. In addition, 14 bombing missions were conducted against enemy bases and 10 against enemy airfields. In May, the Northern Fleet Air Force Headquarters credited 10 Bf 109s, one Bf 110, and one FW 190 to the pilots of the regiment. The losses of the 78th IAP during this period included eight Kittyhawks due to enemy action and two crashed in accidents, with nine pilots killed in total.

The 27th IAP was also engaged in combat operations. In May, the regiment flew 186 combat missions, 54 of which were strikes against ships and convoys, 19 missions were flown to bomb enemy airfields, 12 against artillery batteries, and four on the enemy bases. The Northern Fleet Air Force Headquarters credited one shot down Bf 109 to the pilots of the regiment. The losses of the 27th IAP included two Kittyhawks, of which one was due to enemy actions. One pilot was killed during a training flight.

The reconnaissance aircraft of the 118th RAP continued to search for German ships and vessels. They succeeded in their task while suffering no casualties. It should be noted that two Kittyhawk pilots of the regiment scored one shot down Bf 109 each during the battle over the convoy on 25 May 1944.

9 May

Strikes against coastal shipping and basing ports, which had begun as early as March 1944, continued to intensify. Based on air reconnaissance data, the Northern Fleet Air Force carried out a series of strikes against Vadsø. The first to attack were the Kittyhawk fighter-bombers of the 27th IAP. At 14:06, six Kittyhawks of the 27th IAP (leader – Senior Lieutenant I.S. Yedush) took off from Kildin airfield, joined by four Airacobras of the 20th IAP (leader – Lieutenant K.V. Boychenko) which provided air cover, and flew for the mission of hunting small ships at Berlevåg. At 15:18, the fighter-bombers attacked four motorboats near Vadsø. A German anti-aircraft battery attempted to counterattack unsuccessfully. The attack resulted in sinking the motorboat *Maliblomsten*. Two of its crew were killed, six were seriously wounded and three slightly wounded.

Two hours later, the strike on Vadsø was repeated. The strike involved fighter- bombers of the 27th and 78th IAPs and attack aircraft of the 46th GKAP. At 16:44, four Kittyhawk fighter-bombers of the 27th IAP (leader – Senior Lieutenant I.S. Yedush) took off, 11 minutes later followed by six Kittyhawk fighter-bombers of the 78th IAP (leader – Senior Lieutenant V.P. Strelnikov). Their air cover was provided by six Airacobras of the 2nd GIAP. At about the same time, six Il-2s of the 46th ShAP (leader – Captain A.N. Sinitsyn) took off to attack Vadsø, covered by six Yak-9s of the 20th IAP (leader – Captain A.A. Malinovskiy) and six Kittyhawks of the 78th IAP (leader – Captain M.N. Veryovkin). The attack aircraft struck at 17:30, the fighter-bombers of both regiments – at 17:43. According to German documents, Soviet air strikes were carried out against the battery, the settlement and two motorboats near Kiberg. One army *Obergefreiter* was killed, one army official was seriously wounded, and two sailors were wounded. One army barrack was lightly damaged as well as the city water supply.

10 May

The day before, on 9 May, Luftwaffe aircraft had conducted several attacks on Soviet ships in the Kola Bay.

First two FW 190s carrying out armed reconnaissance at 12:24 attacked the minesweeper No.39 which was on patrol, and six minutes later attacked the submarine L-20 which was going out for combat training and a boat with soldiers near Tsyp-Navolok Cape. The Germans mistook the minesweeper for a merchant vessel, believing that they had set it on fire. On the minesweeper, one sailor was killed and eight were wounded. The Germans also managed to hit the submarine and wounded its commander, Captain 3rd Class Alekseev. The submarine was damaged. Then at 14:10–14:15 another pair of FW 190s dropped bombs on Kuvshinskaya Salma. As a result, the Northern Fleet lost four 27-ton small hunters: MO-435,

Vadsø under attack by Soviet aircraft on 9 May 1944.

MO-437, MO-439, MO-443, which were either sunk or sustained so much damage that they could not be recovered. Heavy damage was sustained by the big hunter BO-207, which sank but was later repaired, and light damage was sustained by the torpedo boat TKA-238. Twenty-three sailors lost their lives. At the same time a third pair of FW 190s attacked the convoy IK-9 in the Kola Bay. A direct hit by a bomb resulted in sinking the minesweeper No.31, killing 62 sailors. Other ships were able to remove 74 men from the sinking minesweeper, of whom 23 were wounded. The second victim of the attack was the tanker *Yukagir*. One bomb hit the bow of the tanker, broke through its top deck, exited the starboard side one metre above the waterline, and exploded five metres off the side of the ship. The blast damaged the navigation and engine instruments; the tanker's commander and three sailors were wounded. Despite the damage, the *Yukagir* reached Murmansk on its own. The eight Kittyhawks of the 78th IAP and eight Airacobras of the 2nd GKAP, which were covering the convoy, reacted a little late; however, the Airacobras still managed to shoot down one FW 190, another was shot down by the anti-aircraft fire from the ships. These were the last ships lost to enemy aviation by the Northern Fleet during the war. The raid was conducted by FW 190 attack aircraft of the 4./JG 5. It is not known which of the Luftwaffe pilots succeeded, while their losses on 9 May amounted to one aircraft. Naturally, such events led to an immediate reaction by the Northern Fleet Headquarters. An order was given to the commander of the Northern Fleet Air Force to attack enemy airfields on the night of 9–10 May in order to destroy aircraft and infrastructure. According to the Northern Fleet Headquarters, the main targets of the strikes were to be the Luostari, Hebugten and Salmijärvi airfields.

The Northern Fleet Air Force Headquarters, having received the order, planned an operation to strike the airfields, which was to be carried out as surprise attack with reliable fighter cover. The plan was strike Luostari with three groups of attack aircraft:

- the first – six Il-2s, six Kittyhawks, six Airacobras were to make a strike at 2:00 approaching the target from the north-east and exiting to the left;
- the second – eight Il-2s, six Kittyhawks, six Airacobras were to strike at 2:02 approaching the target from the south-east and exiting to the left;
- the third – six Il-2s, six Kittyhawks, six Yaks were to strike at 2:05 approaching from the north-west and exiting to the left.

At 2:20, 14 Kittyhawks and eight Airacobras were to attack the Hebugten airfield from the north.

The Salmijärvi airfield was to be attacked by 12 Kittyhawks and eight Airacobras from the south at 2:15. Ten Airacobras were to remain in reserve to cut off any Luftwaffe fighters who would pursue the attacking groups after the strikes. They were to fly out on a separate signal from the Northern Fleet Air Force command post.

Having planned the operation, the Northern Fleet Air Force Headquarters issued the following orders:

a) To the commander of the 6th IAD – prepare fighters to escort attack aircraft and fighter-bombers to strike the airfields.
b) To the commander of the 5th MTAD – to prepare 18 Airacobras, including eight with jettisonable fuel tanks to accompany attack aircraft.
c) To the commander of the 46th ShAP – to prepare 20 Il-2s for attacking the Luostari airfield.
d) To Major Klimov, Pummanki Air Task Group Commander, to prepare six Il-2s, six Kittyhawks and six Yak fighters to attack the Luostari airfield.

In order to better understand the combat mission, all unit commanders were gathered at the Northern Fleet Air Force Command Post where the order for the operation and detailed instructions for its execution were given. The Pummanki Air Task Group received the instructions on the combat mission by telephone.

The group under the command of Captain S.A. Gulyaev was the first to reach the target. The group consisted of eight Il-2s of the 46th ShAP (leader – Captain S.A. Gulyaev), six Kittyhawks of the 78th IAP (leader – Senior Lieutenant V.P. Strelnikov), four Airacobras and two Yak fighters of the 20th IAP (leader – Senior Lieutenant A.K. Tarasov). At 1:23 the group took off from Vaenga-2 airfield, gathered over the airfield and followed the route Vaenga-2 – Set-Navolok – Korabelny Cape – Motka Bay – Luostari. The attack on the Luostari airfield was carried out at 2:01. The attacking aircraft were flying at ground level and struck the north-eastern part of the airfield with bombs, rocket projectiles, and cannon and machine-gun fire. Aircraft parking areas, hangars, workshops and anti-aircraft artillery posts were hit. The crews observed explosions near the aircraft parking areas, in one hangar and in a workshop. The escort fighters, without encountering the enemy in the air, took part in the attack on the airfield, burned a fuel truck and suppressed several anti-aircraft artillery firing positions. The Kittyhawk, piloted by Lieutenant A.S. Pavlov, had to make a forced landing at Vaenga-2 airfield due to damage caused by anti-aircraft fire. The aircraft was sent for repairs and the pilot was unharmed.

The second to strike the Luostari airfield was a group of attack aircraft that took off from Pummanki. The plan was for it to be the third, but it turned out to be the second. Lieutenant N.N. Surovov of the 46th ShAP led this group. It consisted of six Il-2s of the 46th ShAP, six Kittyhawks of the 78th IAP (leader – Captain M.N. Veryovkin) and six Yak fighters of the 20th IAP (leader – Lieutenant L.P. Lapin). At 1:51 the group took off from the Pummanki airfield and, gathering above the airfield, took the Pummanki – Ristiniemi Cape – Luostari route. The attack aircraft approached the target at ground level and at 2:08 attacked the aircraft parking areas in the south-east and west parts of the airfield, dropping bombs, firing rocket projectiles, cannons and machine guns at the targets. The crews observed several fires, a bomb hitting a hangar, and two explosions. On the way back one Kittyhawk was shot down by anti-aircraft fire. From the accident report on the aircraft loss: "In the target area of the Luostari airfield the aircraft were exposed to anti-aircraft artillery fire. While retreating, near Titovka, the aircraft was hit by anti-aircraft fire." The pilot of the Kittyhawk, Junior Lieutenant I.A. Kondratyev, was killed. German documents show that five aircraft flew at 02:35 at low level over the Hausberg stronghold heading south-east, came under fire, and one went down with a large pillar of smoke south of Riffelmassiv [it is not clear what place is meant – *Author's note*].

The third group went under the worst conditions; the group struck the Luostari airfield and consisted of eight Il-2s of the 46th ShAP (leader – Major G.V. Pavlov), covered by six Kittyhawks of the 78th IAP (leader – Major V.I. Babernov) and six Airacobras of the 2nd GKAP (leader – Guards Captain P.L. Kolomiets). According to the mission plan, the group was to strike after the group of Captain A. Gulyaev, but from the outset it was plagued by trouble. The ground technical staff took a long time to prepare the aircraft, and the group began to take off late, at 1:41. At 2:09, the attack aircraft made a single approach striking the enemy aircraft parking positions at the south-eastern part of the airfield. After dropping bombs and firing rocket projectiles, the crews counted up to 10 fires at the parking positions. The Kittyhawk escort fighters were not left behind and fired machine guns at anti-aircraft artillery positions, fuel trucks, vehicles and offices. The Kittyhawk flown by Junior Lieutenant A.S. Volkov was damaged by anti aircraft fire, but he was able to return safely to home airfield. The most unpleasant thing happened next. The leader of the whole group, Major G.V. Pavlov, exited the attack to the left, only two attack aircraft followed him, and this group returned home safely. The leader of the second four aircraft, Lieutenant S. Burmistrov, and with him the crews of Lieutenant I.V. Maksimenko, and Junior Lieutenants V. S. Lopukhin and L.I. Mamporia went to the right. At that time Bf 109 fighters of the 8./JG 5 approached the airfield and attacked the Soviet aircraft. The Germans claim to have shot down one Il-2 and four Airacobras without any losses of their own. In turn, the Soviet fighters claimed to have shot down two Luftwaffe aircraft and two more presumably, including one victory credited by the Northern Fleet Air Force Headquarters to Lieutenant V.I. Kirichenko, Kittyhawk pilot of the 78th IAP. From the combat flight log of the 6th IAD: "At 02:35 during retreat from the target at an altitude of 100–25m, we engaged in air combat with two Bf 109s. As a result of the combat, Lieutenant Kirichenko shot down a Bf 109. The enemy aircraft crashed three to five kilometres south of Luostari." One attack aircraft, piloted by Junior Lieutenant V.I. Markovskiy, was attacked by enemy fighters during retreat, was hit and made a forced landing near the front line on the Soviet territory near Ura-Guba. The pilot was slightly wounded, the gunner was unharmed. None of the four attack aircraft that followed Lieutenant S.V. Burmistrov, returned to the home airfield. The Northern Fleet Air Force documents indicate that en route to the base the leader of this group passed through the Titovka area, which was saturated with anti-aircraft artillery. It was soon discovered that all four attack aircraft had been damaged by anti-aircraft fire. Two crews were killed, two managed to reach Soviet positions. From the records in German documents: "At 02:15, 10–12 enemy aircraft flew over the Russkiy camp. After opening anti-aircraft artillery fire, one aircraft fell down burning 1.5km north of the 21st Kilometre point, two men bailed out with parachutes and descended in a north-easterly direction, a patrol was sent after them. At 09:45, 19km northward of the Russkaya road, the patrol of the *schwere Batterie 1./Flak-Regiment 47* caught two pilots who had bailed out of the Il-2 shot down at the 21st Kilometre point. The pilots resisted and were killed in action." According to Soviet documents, Lieutenant S.V. Burmistrov and air gunner Junior Sergeant A.D. Akulov were killed in the combat with the German soldiers, as the second perished crew was killed near Petsamo. The German records then say: "One aircraft went down burning near the Titovka infirmary." It was the lost Kittyhawk. S.V. Burmistrov's group was joined by a number of fighters. One Kittyhawk was shot down by anti-aircraft artillery near the front line. From the accident report about the loss of the aircraft: "On approach to Luostari airfield, Junior Lieutenant Mzokov was repelling the attack a of Bf 109, diverting the enemy from his leader and was attacked simultaneously, then he lost sight of his group and joined the other group, which deviated from planned route and went through the area with strong anti-aircraft artillery. The aircraft was shot down by anti-aircraft fire." The pilot, Junior Lieutenant K.K. Mzokov, was killed. According to German records, as the result of Soviet strike on the Luostari airfield, four barracks were damaged, one soldier wounded.

At the time when the tragic events were unfolding over Luostari, two groups of fighter-bombers were approaching their targets.

The Hoybuktmoen airfield was attacked by a group of 14 Kittyhawk fighter-bombers of the 27th IAP (leader – Captain Yu. Kh. Gryaznov) under the cover of eight Airacobras of the 255th IAP (leader – Captain I.P. Konev). At 2:20, they carried out a dive-bombing strike, dropping bombs on the Luftwaffe aircraft parks. As a result, three explosions with thick black smoke were observed in the south-western part of the airfield. Four Kittyhawks fired machine guns at the anti-aircraft battery at the south end of the airfield. Near the airfield, two Airacobras of the 255th IAP engaged in combat with Bf 109s of the 9./JG 5 and lost one Airacobra, whose pilot, Junior Lieutenant V.E. Kochetkov, was killed. His aircraft was seen crashing at 02:45 near Jacobselv. The Germans credited two victories to their pilots; the pilot of the 255th IAP scored one presumed victory. The following is known from the German documents: "01:55–02:08. Twenty attack aircraft and fighters attacked Kirkenes airfield. There were two approaches, eight bombs dropped, cannon and machine guns fired. Five barracks were badly damaged. One female of the Luftwaffe auxiliary service was wounded."

The raid on the Salmijärvi airfield went according to plan. Twelve Kittyhawk fighter-bombers of the 78th IAP (leader – Major A.V. Polkovnikov) covered by eight Airacobras of the 255th IAP (leader – Captain D.I. Sinev) dropped bombs on the airfield and conducted an air strike at 2:35. The pilots observed their bombs hitting the hangar, one caponier was destroyed, and four anti-aircraft positions were suppressed. There were no encounters with Luftwaffe fighters and all aircraft returned home safe.

The Northern Fleet Air Force Headquarters considered the operation a success, except for the actions of Major G.V. Pavlov's group.

Despite the successes and losses, the war continued, so in the evening fighter-bombers struck Vadsø. At 20:40 a group of eight Kittyhawk fighter-bombers and two reconnaissance Kittyhawks of the 78th IAP (leader – Captain F.S. Plotko) and six Airacobras of the 2nd GKAP (leader – Guards Senior Lieutenant P.D. Romanov) took off from Vaenga-2 airfield to strike at the ships and coastal facilities at Vadsø. At 21:10 the fighter-bombers dropped their bombs and fired at the German machine-gun positions. The targets were chosen by pilots independently. According to the records of the 6th IAD, skip bombing was used for the first time in the Northern Fleet. The pilots of the 78th IAP chose, according to their reports, the following targets:

> Captain Plotko dropped bombs on the western pier of the port, observed explosions north of the pier among residential buildings – one was destroyed.
>
> Senior Lieutenant Batrakov struck at the northern pier of Store-Vadsø Island, with no results observed.
>
> Lieutenant Antonov struck at a transport near the western pier; the former sank from a direct hit. Junior Lieutenant Vasilyev dropped bombs on the warehouses at the eastern end of the main pier, causing an explosion and fire, presumably blowing up a fuel depot.
>
> Junior Lieutenant Guguev dropped bombs on a motorboat near the northern pier of Store-Vadsø Island. He observed a direct hit on the motorboat, which sank.

The German documents state the following:

> At 21:25, seven bombers accompanied by fighter cover dropped about 15–20 50-kg bombs. Mainly the camps I and II were attacked, three barracks of *Artillerie Abteilung* 112

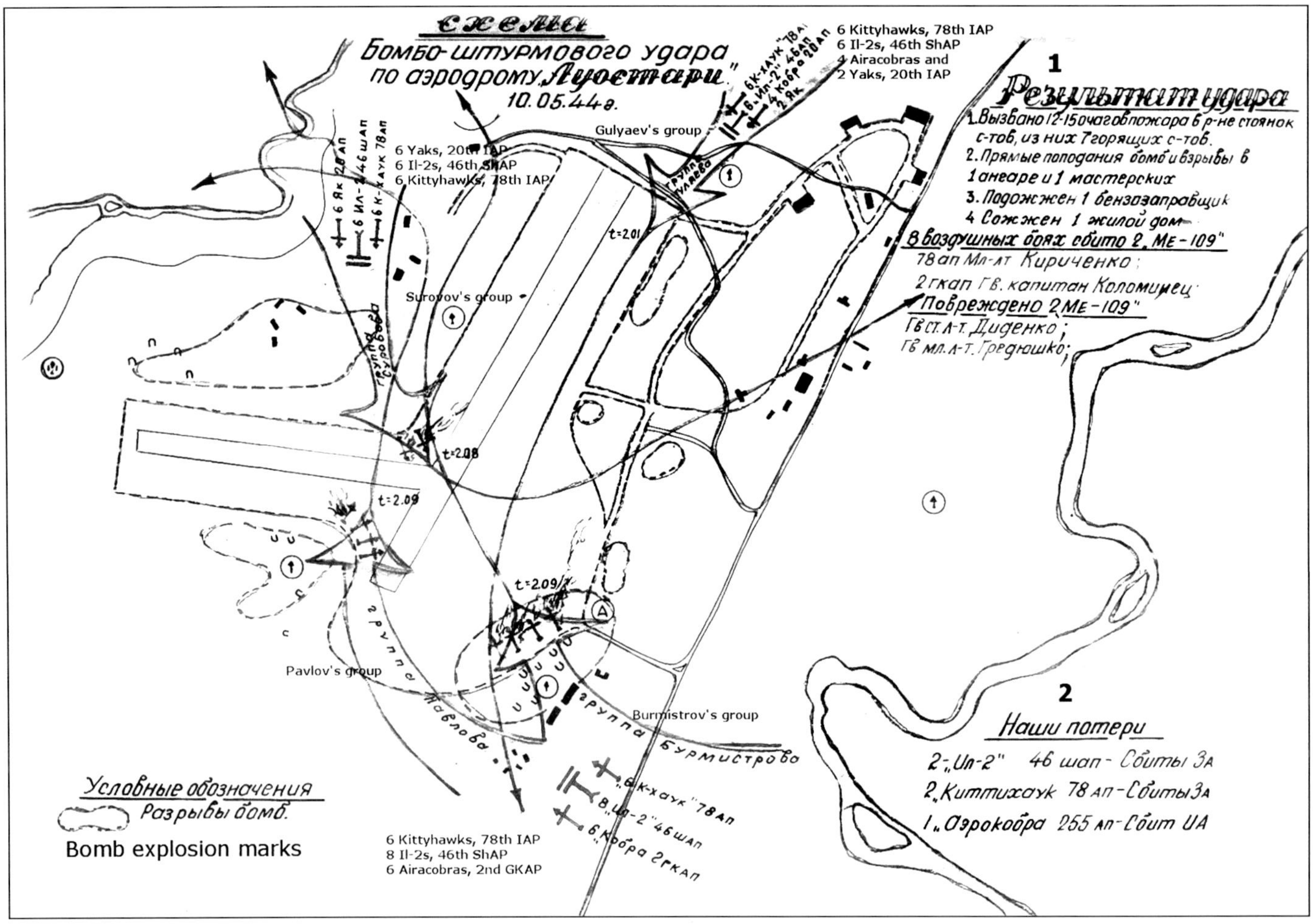

Plan of the air strike on Luostari airfield, 10 May 1944.
1. Results of the air strike:
1. At the aircraft parking area, 12-15 spots of fire were caused, including 7 aircraft on fire.
2. Direct hits and explosions in a hangar and in a workshop.
3. One fuel truck was set on fire.
4. One apartment house burnt down.
Two Bf 109s shot down in air battles
– Junior Lieutenant Kirichenko of the 78th IAP;
– Guards Captain Kolomiets of the 2nd GKAP
Two Bf 109s damaged
– Guards Senior Lieutenant Didenko;
– Guards Junior Lieutenant Gredyushko.
2.
Our losses
Two Il-2s of the 46th ShAP – shot down by anti-aircraft artillery.
Two Kittyhawks of the 78th IAP – shot down by anti-aircraft artillery.
One Airacobra of the 255th IAP – shot down by fighter aviation.

> were severely damaged, 14 soldiers were wounded (of them 13 men from artillery crews). One aircraft was shot down by the 2cm anti-aircraft gun fire of the *Festungs-Bataillon* 663. The aircraft was found burnt three kilometres north-east of Vadsø, the pilot perished with it. The Headquarters of the Harbour Guard Flotilla and the Headquarters platoon had to temporarily move to the barracks camp of the 210. *Infanterie-Division* because of the damage to the barracks.

The German report corresponds with the actual situation. One Kittyhawk of the 78th IAP was shot down. From the accident report about the loss of the aircraft: "When approaching for a bombing run from a low-level flight, at the moment of coming out from a dive at an altitude of 100m, the aircraft was set on fire by a shell and fell one to two kilometres north of Vadsø when approaching the target." The pilot of the aircraft, Junior Lieutenant N.N. Yelanskiy, was killed.

11 May

A Pe-3 reconnaissance aircraft of the 118th RAP flew on the evening of 10 May to reconnoitre enemy communication routes. At 18:40 the crew spotted a large German convoy and a radiogram was sent to the Air Force Headquarters. Soon another battle with a large German convoy followed. This was convoy Rp.118.Ki, which left Lo Fjord on 10 May 1944 and was en route to Kirkenes. The convoy consisted of floating base *Bali*, patrol boats V-6111, V-6113, V-6115, Nki-08, Nki-12, submarine hunters UJ-1209, UJ-1210, UJ-1211, UJ-1219, UJ-1220, minesweepers M-31, M-154, M-202, M-251, M-252, motor minesweeper R-159, high-speed landing barges F-216, F-226, F-232, artillery barge AF-25, steamers *Nordlicht* (2,491grt), *Vulkan* (998grt), *Pernambuco* (4,121grt), *Bugsee* (2,307grt), *Leba* (1,586grt), *Belpamela* (3,165grt), *Activ* (506grt), tankers *Grete* (638grt), *Tripp* (364grt), *Gerdmoor* (761grt), *Amrum* (671grt), tugboat *Jason* (296grt). By the time the attack started the steamer *Activ* and the motor minesweeper R-159 left the convoy; the high-speed landing barges sailed astern of the convoy, about eight miles away, as they could not keep up with it.

The attack on the convoy was supposed to be a combined high-altitude and low-altitude torpedo-bombing attack by the 5th MTAD, in co-operation with the fighter-bombers of the 6th IAD. Kittyhawk fighter-bombers of the 27th and 78th IAPs were to strike the escort ships to ensure the attack by torpedo bombers, for which two FAB-100 bombs were to be suspended under each aircraft. After the torpedo bombers attack, the Kittyhawks were tasked with providing the fighter cover. After the convoy had entered the flight range of the attack aircraft, the aircraft from the Pummanki airfield were supposed to conduct another strike. However, in this case the ships were to be struck by the attack aircraft only, while the Kittyhawks acted as fighter cover. It should be noted that they performed this task brilliantly.

After the attacking aircraft had returned to their airfields, the Northern Fleet Air Force Headquarters planned to launch a second attack. The operation to destroy the convoy had been planned and communicated to all participants. All that remained to be done was to wait for the convoy to come within a distance that would allow the fighters to escort the strike aircraft.

The first to attack was a group of high-altitude torpedo bombers headed by Guards Major A.N. Voloshin. It consisted of six Il-4 torpedo bombers of the 9th GMTAP, seven Kittyhawk fighter-bombers of the 27th IAP (leader – Captain Yu.Kh. Gryaznov) and five Airacobras of the 255th IAP (leader – Captain I.P. Konev). Captain Yu.Kh. Gryaznov's group of Kittyhawks fell behind the torpedo bombers and managed to catch up with them closer to the target. Having detected the convoy near Kongs Fjord around 1:25, the fighter-bombers started attacking the transports and German warships, which were on the left, near the end of the convoy. Two Kittyhawks bombed from horizontal flight from an altitude of 2,800m due to engine problems. The others made a diving attack, dropping bombs from an altitude of 1,000m, and opened fire at the German escort ships when exiting the strike. According to the combat log of the Kriegsmarine 5th Minesweepers Flotilla, the bombs exploded around the M-251 minesweeper, flooding the ship with fountains of water. According to the Kittyhawk pilots' reports, the transport ship *Belpamela* (3,165grt) must have also been hit, but the German documents do not mention this. When exiting the attack the Kittyhawks, according to reports from their pilots, fired machine guns at the escort ships that were heading to the right of the convoy. According to German sources, the patrol ship V-6115 and the minesweeper M-252 were hit, several persons were wounded. Two Luftwaffe Bf 109 fighters of the 8./JG 5, initially preferred to hide in the clouds, but attempted to pursue the retreating Soviet aircraft. At Sharapov Cape the Kittyhawk pilots of the 27th IAP, Captain Yu.Kh. Gryaznov and Junior Lieutenant V.G. Levchenko, apparently engaged this very pair of Bf 109s. As a result, Captain Yu.Kh. Gryaznov scored one shot down Bf 109, while the Luftwaffe fighters shot down the Kittyhawk of Junior Lieutenant V.G. Levchenko. From the accident report on the loss of the Kittyhawk: "Two Kittyhawks were attacked by four Bf 109s from above and behind. Junior Lieutenant Levchenko warned about the attack by radio. Both aircraft turned around and fought one by one. The battle was fought at ground level, mainly on head-on attacks. After the third attack Levchenko was hit and landed on Rybachiy Peninsula. The pilot was wounded, the aircraft was destroyed".

Following the fighter-bombers, the high-altitude torpedo bombers of Guards Major A.N. Voloshin attacked. At 1:30 they dropped torpedoes from 3,000m altitude. The Germans reported the dropping of high-altitude torpedoes which fell between the minesweeper M-31, the patrol ship V-6113 and the transports *Amrum* and *Pernambuco*. Two high-altitude torpedoes hit the patrol ship V-6113. The ship quickly sank, taking 10 persons with it. One of the gunners/radio operators of the torpedo bombers of the 9th GMTAP described the ship's sinking: "The torpedoes entered the water well, I saw two explosions against one transport… I saw the transport completely sunk; the ships were conducting heavy anti-aircraft artillery fire. After leaving the attack I gave a radiogram: mission accomplished, I am coming back."

As planned by the Northern Fleet Air Force Headquarters, a group of low-altitude torpedo bombers under the command of Guards Major S.K. Litvinov followed the high-altitude torpedo bombers into the attack. The group consisted of five Bostons of the 9th GMTAP, six Kittyhawk fighter-bombers of the 27th IAP (leader – Senior Lieutenant L.M. Semyonov) and 10 Airacobras of the 255th IAP (leader – Captain V.A. Burmatov). At 1:33, low-altitude torpedo bombers dropped torpedoes on the convoy. According to German documents, the ships were not hit. The Kittyhawk fighter-bombers, part of the low-altitude torpedo bomber group, did not achieve more success. The two fighter-bombers, piloted by Junior Lieutenants N.M. Ivanov and I.F. Popov, had engine problems and chose to return before reaching the convoy. The remaining four Kittyhawks dropped bombs on the German escort ships at 1:40. Their bombs exploded near the ships of the Kriegsmarine 12th Submarine Hunters Flotilla, but did no damage. On the way out of the attack, the Kittyhawks fired machine guns at the high-speed landing barges behind the convoy. According to German documents, several sailors on the high-speed landing barge F-214 were wounded.

The Soviet aircraft withdrew, and it was time for the Germans to count their losses. The patrol boat V-6115, the minesweeper M-252 and the high-speed landing barge F-214 approached the floating base *Bali* one by one. In total, one dead, five seriously wounded and two lightly wounded sailors were transferred to the floating base, which had a doctor on board. One of the wounded died at the floating base. Attacks by Kittyhawk fighter-bombers of the 27th IAP in the early morning of 11 May 1944 were considered unsuccessful.

In order to cut off Luftwaffe fighters from the returning Soviet aircraft after attacking the convoy, six Airacobras of the 2nd GKAP were sent. They did not encounter any enemy aircraft, but on the way back one of the Airacobras fell into the water. Its pilot, Guards Junior Lieutenant I.I. Kharkevich was killed. In some documents he is listed as missed in action while escorting torpedo bombers, but probably this is a mistake, as the torpedo bombers were escorted by fighters of the 27th and 255th IAPs.

At 2:10 a reconnaissance Kittyhawk of the 118th RAP found a convoy in Bos Fjord and reported seeing 27 German ships and vessels, whereas the previous reconnaissance aircraft had reported 28. Thus, one German ship was lost. The convoy entered the flight radius of the attack aircraft from Pummanki airfield, and the aircraft under the command of Senior Lieutenant S.S. Rolbin took off for a strike. This group consisted of six Il-2s of the 46th ShAP (leader – Senior Lieutenant S.S. Rolbin), six Yak fighters of the 20th IAP (leader – Lieutenant L.P. Lapin) and six Kittyhawks of the 78th IAP (leader – Captain M.N. Veryovkin). At 4:02 near Sylte Fjord, the attack aircraft dropped bombs from dive and fired cannons and machine guns at the escort ships. As a result of the attack, the submarine hunter UJ-1209 was taken out of action with a damaged anti-aircraft gun and six wounded crew members (including personnel of the 88mm gun). In addition to the hunter, the minesweeper M-251 suffered casualties, with four crew members wounded. After attacking the convoy, the S.S. Rolbin's group was attacked by 10 Bf 109s of the 7. and 8. *Staffeln* of the JG 5. The information about what happened next can be found in the documents of the 78th IAP:

> On the traverse of Vardö Cape the crews spotted enemy aircraft including six Bf 109s and two FW 190s attacking Il-2 aircraft. A signal that enemy aircraft had appeared was immediately given to all aircraft. The close cover group repelled the attacks of enemy aircraft on the Il-2s on the crossing courses. The enemy aircraft, coming from the right and from behind, were

trying to break the battle formation of our aircraft, to distract the fighter aircraft of the cover groups, because at this time the combat group consisting of six Yak-9s had already been engaged in combat against FW 190s and Bf 109s flying above the enemy aircraft of the first group. While repulsing the attacks of the FW 190s, Lieutenant Pavlov attacked one FW 190 which was attacking an Il-2, gave a barrage burst from a distance of 300m at target aspect ratio of 3/4, the enemy aircraft turned to the right and repeated the attack. At that time Lieutenant Mitrofanov attacked the leading FW 190 at a 1/4 target aspect ratio, fired two machine-gun bursts from the front, from 200–150m range, the enemy aircraft turned to the right. Lieutenant Mitrofanov turned his aircraft and repeated the attack from the tail at 0/4–1/4 target aspect ratio. He fired two long machine-gun bursts from a distance of 60m, the enemy aircraft rolled over and crashed into the sea. The wingman's FW 190 turned to the right with climbing. At that time four Bf 109s appeared from the front on the left which had been trying to attack the (Soviet) attack aircraft. Lieutenant Pavlov beat off the attack of enemy aircraft, the Bf 109s turned to the right, Pavlov steered the aircraft and approached the leading Bf 109 from the tail. Pavlov fired two machine gun bursts from 40–20m distance at 0/4 target aspect ratio, the enemy aircraft fell into the sea 10–12km north-west of Vaitolahti. During the leader's attack, the wingman's Bf 109 tried to attack Lieutenant Pavlov but after one burst of barrage fire changed his attack to Il-2 aircraft. The pilot of the Il-2 fired one or two bursts at the Bf 109. No further results were observed, as the Il-2 gunner fired a flare towards the direction of the newly appeared two Bf 109s and Lieutenant Pavlov turned sharply on them. Lieutenant Pavlov's wingman Junior Lieutenant Dzyuba attacked the wingman's Bf 109 from 100m distance at 1/4 target aspect ratio, the enemy's aircraft was hit. Junior Lieutenant Dzyuba pursuing the enemy fired short bursts, forcing the Bf 109 pilot to land. The Bf 109 pilot landed at Vaida-Guba, the pilot was taken prisoner.

As a result of the battle, the Luftwaffe pilots claimed seven victories, but none of these were confirmed by Soviet documents. Three victories over the Bf 109s were credited to Soviet pilots: Lieutenant I.P. Kuzhanov of the 20th IAP, Lieutenant A.S. Pavlov, and Junior Lieutenant D.P. Dzyuba of the 78th IAP. The German documents available in the archives confirm the loss of two fighters: a Bf 109G-6, W.Nr. 15796, tactical number 'White 8', piloted by *Under-Officer* G. Schneider, landed on the western coast of Rybachiy and was taken prisoner. Judging by the description of the air battle, it was the victim of Junior Lieutenant D.P. Dzyuba. The second, Bf 109G-6, W.Nr. 412304, piloted by *Unteroffizier* Friedrich von Veltheim, went missing. The only loss of the S.S. Rolbin's group was a Kittyhawk flown by one of the most experienced pilots of the regiment, Captain M.N. Veryovkin, but it was an unfortunate accident after the battle. From the report of Junior Lieutenant I.P. Albul of the 78th IAP: "I saw the Kittyhawk of Veryovkin falling 10km from Vaitolahti, it turned over at a low altitude and hit the water."

In the meantime, the strike groups were returning after the attack on the convoy, so the Northern Fleet Air Force Command gave the order to strike the convoy again. Since the convoy had entered the flight range of the attack aircraft, they, together with the fighter-bombers, were to strike at the escort ships, ensuring the attack of high-altitude and low-altitude torpedo bombers against the convoy transports.

The first to attack the convoy in the repeated strike were the attack aircraft from Vaenga-2 airfield. It was the group of Captain D. Osyka's that included five Il-2s of the 46th ShAP (leader – Captain D. Osyka), six Kittyhawk fighters of the 78th IAP (leader – Major N. Osipov) and six Airacobras of the 2nd GKAP (leader – Guards Captain S.M. Loginov). At 8:30, south of Kibergnes Cape, Captain D.V. Osyka spotted the convoy. At 8:32 a dive-bombing attack followed. According to the documents of the Northern Fleet Air Force Headquarters, the attack aircraft mistakenly dropped their bombs before reaching the target. However, left without bombs, they used rocket projectiles and cannon and machine-gun fire against the escort ships. As a result of the attack, two crew members were wounded on the submarine hunter UJ-1211. When exiting the strike, the attack aircraft were counterattacked by the Bf 109s. One of the Bf 109s attempted to engage the aircraft flown by Captain V. Osyka, but was shot down by the wingman's Il-2, piloted by Lieutenant L.V. Uskrebkov. All further attacks of the Bf 109s were repulsed by Soviet fighters. From the report of Captain Kh.I. Abishev, the fighter pilot of 2nd GKAP:

> We met one Bf 109 above transports at an altitude of 1,500m. We attacked in an incoming direction at target aspect ratio of 2/4 with the subsequent transition to the fight in turns. I opened fire from a distance of 70–50m at 2/4 target aspect ratio and gave three short bursts. The Bf 109 fell to the right, in front of the enemy convoy. Above the convoy I saw two He 115s at an altitude of 200m. A group of Kittyhawks shot down one Bf 109. When Il-2s were exiting the dive bombing, one Kittyhawk was attacked by Bf 109 and shot down. The Bf 109 was shot down by another Kittyhawk.

From the combat flight log of the 6th IAD:

> At 8:21, in the area of Eckerö – Vaitolahti at an altitude of 600–800m, six Kittyhawks were engaged in an air battle with four Bf 109s. As a result of the air battle, Lieutenant Nikolayev shot down one Bf 109 near the convoy.

Based on the results of the air battle, the Northern Fleet Air Force Headquarters credied one shot down Bf 109 to Captain Kh.I. Abishev of the 2nd GKAP and Lieutenant A.F. Nikolayev of the 78th IAP each. During the air combat one Kittyhawk was shot down; the pilot, Junior Lieutenant I.I. Chekanov, was killed.

Major D.V. Osyka's group was followed by the attack of the high-altitude torpedo bombers of Guards Major A.N. Voloshin. This group consisted of six Il-4 torpedo bombers of the 9th GMTAP (leader – Guards Major A.N. Voloshin), 13 Kittyhawk fighter-bombers of the 27th IAP (leader – Senior Lieutenant A.P. Anuchin) and six Airacobras of the 255th IAP (leader – Captain I.P. Konev). On approaching the target, Airacobras of the 255th IAP were met by enemy fighters. From the report of Captain Konev: "20km before reaching the target, I saw two Bf 109s below us and attacked them. As a result of the combat, I shot down one of them". All further attempts of the Luftwaffe fighters to break through to the torpedo bombers are well described in the report of the gunner of the torpedo bomber, Guards Senior Sergeant G.S. Aseev: "Luftwaffe fighters tried to attack, but the Airacobras repulsed the attack".

At 8:36 near Kibergnes Cape, the fighter-bombers dropped bombs from a dive, and were followed by torpedo bombers which dropped six torpedoes at 8:38. Though the bombs and torpedoes passed by, one crew member was wounded by cannon and machine-gun fire on the submarine hunter UJ-1209. Judging by the pilots' reports, most of the Luftwaffe fighters of the 7. *Staffel* and the *Stab* III./JG 5 were engaged in combat with Captain D.V. Osyka's group. Some tried to attack the group of Guards Major A.N. Voloshin, but did not succeed. The Luftwaffe fighters claimed five victories, but actually managed to shoot down only one Kittyhawk. According to the combat operations report of the Commander of the Kirkenes Naval Defence, two of the 14 Bf 109s engaged in air combat over the convoy were lost, one made a forced landing, and the others were damaged and needed repair. Due to the losses in the air battles over the convoy Rp.118.Ki, the German fighters were not able to cover their ships in Kirkenes two days later.

A mixed group of attack aircraft and fighter-bombers followed the high-altitude torpedo-bomber group, which was to prepare the battle area for the strike by the low-altitude torpedo bombers. Lieutenant S.V. Vasilyev commanded the group which consisted of six Il-2s of the 46th ShAP (leader – Lieutenant S.V. Vasilyev), eight Kittyhawk fighter-bombers of the 78th IAP (leader – Senior Lieutenant V.P. Strelnikov), four Airacobras and two Yak fighters of the 20th IAP (leader – Senior Lieutenant K.V. Boychenko). At 8:36 the group spotted the convoy south of Kibergnes Cape. The Kittyhawks were the first to attack, dropping bombs from dive, but, according to reports from the pilots of the 78th IAP, were unsuccessful. At 8:40 the attack aircraft dropped bombs on the convoy's transports and escort ships. According to German documents, one of the bombs hit the steamship *Belpamela*, but it failed to explode and fell into the sea. It is very likely that this ship was damaged by the Kittyhawks because, according to the reports of the attack aircraft pilots, they struck the transports at the head of the convoy, while the *Belpamela* was at the tail of the convoy. In addition, according to the documents of the 5th Minesweepers Flotilla, the minesweeper M-252 was damaged by close explosions. The ship sustained damage to machinery in boiler room #2. The attack aircraft of Lieutenant S.V. Vasilyev, group commander, was shot down by anti-aircraft fire from German ships. Other pilots saw his aircraft land on the water near the convoy, but the crew didn't survive.

The group of Lieutenant S.V. Vasilyev was followed by the low-altitude torpedo bombers of the Guards Captain N.I. Zaitsev. The group consisted of five Bostons of the 9th GMTAP and 10 Airacobras of the 255th IAP (leader – Captain V.A. Burmatov). At 8:47 near Kibergnes, the torpedo bombers attacked the convoy, but, according to German documents, none of the torpedoes hit the target. From the report of Captain V.A. Burmatov: "I observed two Airacobras shoot down a BV 138". However, the Northern Fleet Air Force Headquarters credited Lieutenant I.I. Rossiychuk and Junior Lieutenant S.S. Trope only with a presumable victory over the Luftwaffe BV 138 seaplane. The report of Captain V.A. Burmatov also says: "On approach [to the convoy – *Author's note*] I saw a heavily smoking escort ship, which I assume had been damaged in the previous strike. On departure from the target I, with my wingman Captain Gladkov, attacked the escort ship. I observed how the port engine of the Boston was burning and it subsequently went down on the water." The ditched Boston was piloted by the Guards Captain N.I. Zaitsev, the leader of the group of low-altitude torpedo bombers. The crew went into the inflatable raft, but the rescue torpedo-boats did not find them.

Having repulsed the attacks of four groups of Soviet aircraft, the convoy commander requested the ships and vessels to report the losses and damage. According to his documents, during the attacks between 8:30 and 8:50 (Moscow time), in addition to those mentioned above, five men were wounded on the minesweeper M-251 and one on the patrol boat V-6115.

The last group to strike the convoy in the course of the second attack, as in the first, were the attack aircraft from the Pummanki airfield. This group was commanded by Lieutenant L.M. Kalmykov and consisted of three Il-2s of the 46th ShAP (leader – Lieutenant L.M. Kalmykov), three Kittyhawk fighters of the 78th IAP (leader – Senior Lieutenant A.I. Batrakov) and four Yak fighters of the 20th IAP (leader – Lieutenant I.P. Kuzhanov). The group took off from

Kittyhawks in flight.

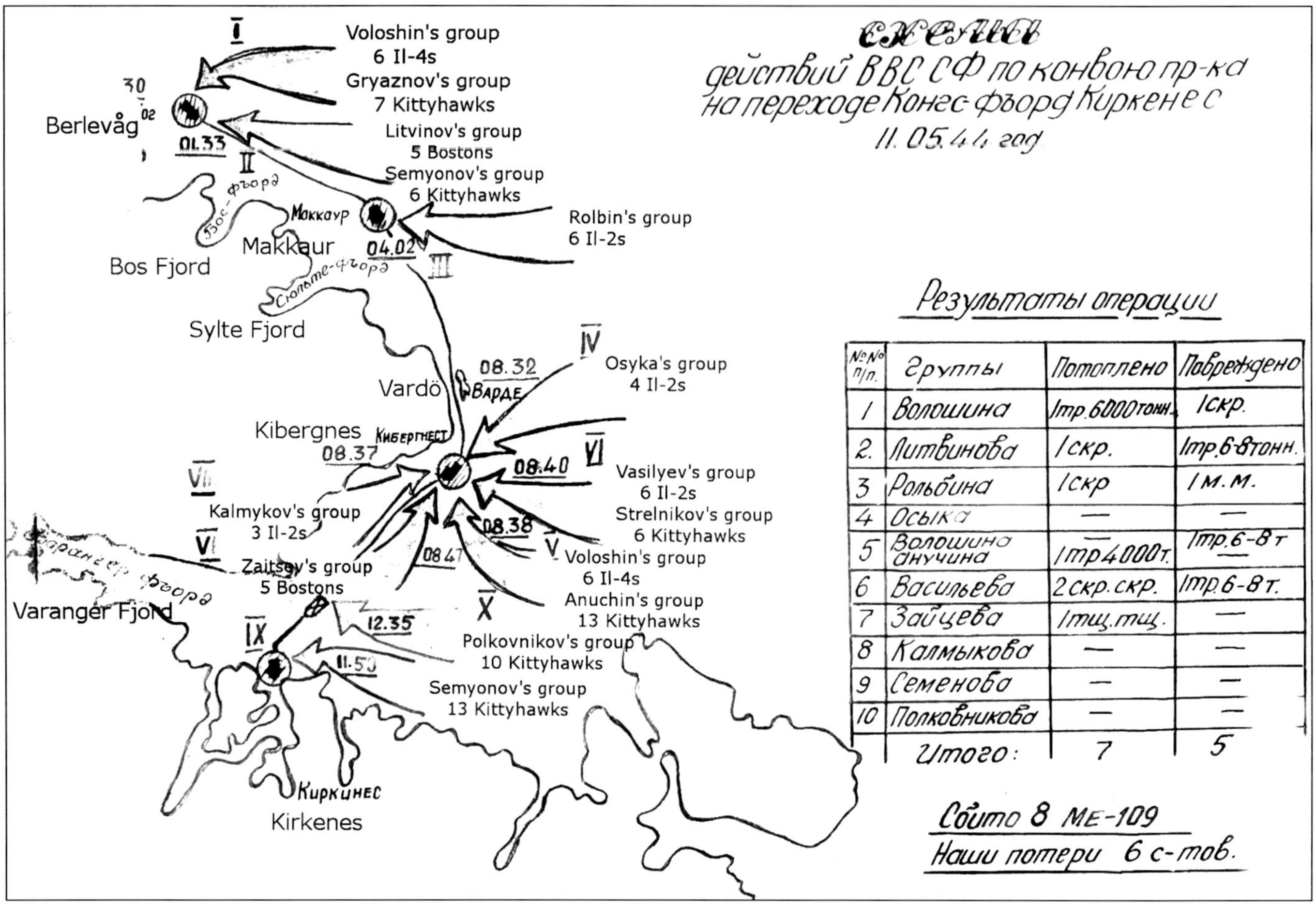

Plan of the strike by the Northern Fleet Air Force on the German convoy Rp.118.Ki (route from Kongs Fjord to Kirkenes), 11 May 1944.

Pummanki airfield at 9:03 and headed towards Svartnes. At 9:37, in the vicinity of Svartnes, the group dropped bombs on enemy ships from dive. According to German documents, there were no casualties from this attack. Two more groups of Kittyhawk fighter-bombers carried out the final strikes against the convoy that day. At 11:50, 13 Kittyhawks of the 27th IAP (leader – Senior Lieutenant L.M. Semyonov) under cover of six Airacobras of the 2nd GKAP (leader – Guards Major D.F. Marenko) bombed the ships of the convoy from dive at the entrance to the Böck-fjord, but according to pilots' reports, there were no hits.

Half an hour later, at 12:35, a second group of 10 Kittyhawk fighter-bombers of the 78th IAP (leader – Major A.V. Polkovnikov) and six Airacobras of the 2nd GKAP (leader – Guards Captain S.M. Loginov) struck the patrol ship which was following the convoy near Eckerö, judging by the pilots' reports. The Kittyhawk pilots reported that they observed explosions near the ship, but according to the logbook of the German Patrol Boats Flotilla, the 37mm cannon muzzle was burst and one crew member was wounded on the motor minesweeper R-173.

Completing the story about the combat against convoy Rp.118. Ki, it should be noted that when repulsing the attacks of Soviet aircraft, the III./JG 5 had no serviceable fighters left and in two days this resulted in further losses of the German fleet.

Results of the operation

Group leader	Sank ship	Damaged ship
1 Voloshin	1 transport, 6,000grt	1 patrol ship
2 Litvinov	1 patrol ship	1 transport 6-8,000grt
3 Rolbin	1 patrol ship	1 destoyer
4 Osyka	-	-
5 Voloschin	-	1 transport, 4,000grt
5 Anuchin	1 transport, 6,000-8,000grt	-
6 Vasilyev	2 patrol ships	1 transport 6,000-8,00grt
7 Zaitsev	1 minesweeper	-
8 Kalmykov	-	-
9 Semyonov	-	-
10 Polkovnikov	-	-
Total	7	5
Shot down eight Bf 109s		
Our losses – six aircraft		

Pilot of the 118th RAP, Junior Lieutenant A.V. Bystrov.

13 May

The passage of the large convoy Rp.118.Ki to Kirkenes caused a surge of reconnaissance activity by the Northern Fleet Air Force. Initially the plan was to strike at the Kirkenes roadstead on 12 May, but the weather wasn't favourable.

On the morning of 13 May 1944, a Kittyhawk reconnaissance aircraft of the 118th RAP piloted by Junior Lieutenant S.I. Pankrashin, flew on a reconnaissance mission of the enemy ships in Varanger Fjord. At 3:30 it was over Kirkenes, and spotted nine transports and up to a dozen escort ships.

At 9:45 a Spitfire reconnaissance aircraft of the 118th RAP piloted by Junior Lieutenant I.A. Bugakov appeared over Kirkenes. The photo equipment of the British aircraft made it possible to take good-quality pictures of the ships in the Kirkenes area. After analysing the photos, intelligence of the fleet counted 16 transports and 31 warships.

The main areas where the ships were concentrated were:

a) South of Renö Island – three transports and four warships. The command named this area as Target No. 1.
b) Jakobsnes roadstead – six transports, two destroyers, four motorboats. The command designated this area as Target No. 2.
c) Lang Fjord – six transports and three warships were stationed there. The command designated the area as Target No. 3.

At 18:28 the Northern Fleet Air Force Headquarters issued a preliminary order to prepare to attack the transports in Kirkenes.

At 19:30 the commander of the Northern Fleet Air Force Major General A.Kh. Andreev summoned the division commanders to his command post where he briefed them on the task of the operation. Taking into account the strong air defence of Kirkenes, it was decided to conduct a massive combined strike by the fleet aircraft. The plan was to use four attack groups, which were to strike ships in the Kirkenes area simultaneously from different altitudes and directions.

The first group, consisting of high-altitude Il-4 torpedo bombers of the 9th GMTAP, in cooperation with Kittyhawk fighter-bombers of the 27th IAP and under the cover of Airacobras of the 255th IAP, were to attack the Target No. 1 (transports to the south of the Renö Island).

The second group, consisting of Il-2s of the 46th ShAP, in cooperation with fighter-bombers of the 78th IAP and under cover of fighters of the 20th IAP, was to attack Target No. 2 (transports at Jakobsnes roadstead).

The third group was from the Pummanki Task Group. It was to include the Il-2s of the 46th ShAP attacking the Target No. 3 (transports at Lang Fjord) from a dive under cover of fighters of the 20th and 78th IAPs.

The fourth group consisted of Il-2s of the 46th ShAP striking by a skip-bombing method, in cooperation with fighter-bombers of the 78th IAP and under cover of fighters of the 255th IAP, and was to attack the Target No.2 as well (transports at Jakobsnes roadstead).

Operating in the first, second, and fourth groups, the Kittyhawks were to bomb from diving one to two minutes before the strike by torpedo-bombers and attack aircraft, after which they were to provide fighter cover for them. All fighter-bomber Kittyhawks carried two FAB-100s each, and some carried camera equipment instead of bombs, in order to monitor the results of the mission.

The time of attack for all aircraft was set at 23:30. As the commander of the Pummanki Task Group was unable to reach the command post in time due to lack of passable roads, the task for the mission for the third group was given by telephone.

In order to block the enemy airfields of Luostari and Salmijärvi, the command of the 7th Air Army of the Red Army Air Force was requested to send fighter aircraft to those airfields 15 minutes before Kirkenes attack.

Having received the orders from the Northern Fleet Air Force Headquarters, the units began to prepare the aircraft for take-off. Soon the aircraft took off and headed for their targets.

The operation was started at 23:15–23:35 when 32 Airacobras of the 1st Guards SAD of the 7th Air Army carried air patrol in the area of Luostari and Salmijärvi airfields. While they were blocking the German airfields, the strike groups of the Northern Fleet Air Force approached the targets and attacked them.

The first group attacked at 23:31. It consisted of five Il-4 torpedo bombers of the 9th GMTAP (leader – Major A.N. Voloshin) armed with high-altitude torpedoes, 13 Kittyhawk fighter-bombers of the 27th IAP (leader – Major A.Y. Dizhevskiy) and eight Airacobras of the 255th IAP (leader – Major A.E. Tulskiy). The torpedo bombers dropped torpedoes from an altitude of 2,900m on the transports south of Renö Island, but, according to the crews' reports, they missed the targets. At the same time, three Kittyhawks dropped bombs from an altitude of 1,000m on the same targets, with the same result. Nine other Kittyhawks, having mixed up their targets, bombed three transports at Jakobsnes roadstead (actually, it was Target No. 2). As a result, the crews observed two FAB-100s hitting a transport with a displacement of 6,000–7,000 tonnes, according to the pilots' estimates. The transport, according to the pilots' observations, was badly damaged. Unfortunately, the Kittyhawk which carried out photo footage was not able to capture the moment when the target was hit.

The second group attacked almost simultaneously with the first. The group consisted of six Il-2s of the 46th ShAP (leader – Senior Lieutenant V.I. Belashev), eight Kittyhawk fighter-bombers of the 78th IAP (leader – Senior Lieutenant A.I. Batrakov), six Airacobras and two Yak fighters of the 20th IAP (leader – Captain E.V. Petrenko). At 22:36, the group took off from Vaenga-2 and gathered over the airfield. It turned out that one attack aircraft had a technical failure, which made the pilot go for an emergency landing. The other aircraft made their way towards the target. When approaching the target, five to seven kilometres eastward from Jakobsnes Cape, the pilot of the Kittyhawk of 78th IAP, Junior Lieutenant Vasilyev spotted an enemy Bf 110. Approaching from behind and from above, Vasilyev attacked it from the target aspect ratio of 1/4 and from a distance of 200–80m. He fired three machine-gun bursts, but did not observe the enemy aircraft any further. According to the observations of the Il-2 and Kittyhawk crews, the Bf 110 crashed five to six kilometres east of Jakobsnes Cape in the hills and burned out. As a result of the air combat, the Northern Fleet Air Force Headquarters credited one shot down Bf 110 to the combat account of Junior Lieutenant N.V. Vasilyev.

At 23:30, seven Kittyhawks gained an altitude of 2,000m, approached their target from the north-east, set on the combat course in pairs and performed a dive-bombing attack on the transports and the escort ships near Jakobsnes Cape. Senior Lieutenant A.I. Batrakov and his wingman Junior Lieutenant N.P. Proyavko attacked the transport vessel with a displacement of 3,000–4,000 tonnes, the crews observed one direct hit at the bow of the transport, two bombs exploded near the sides. The other crews also dropped bombs on the transports and ships, with no results observed. Coming out of the dive, they fired machine guns at the anti-aircraft artillery positions on Renö Island, which were firing at them.

Four minutes later, at 23:34, five Il-2s made dive-bombing attack from an altitude of 400m on the same four transports in the area of Jakobsnes. The crews observed the bombs hitting the transport of 6,000–7,000 tonnes displacement and the fire on it. From the report of Senior Lieutenant V.I. Belashev: "I observed two large columns of smoke after exiting from the target". From the combat flight log of the 6th IAD:

> On the return route in Jar Fjord from an altitude of 400m, we fired machine-guns at a deport, transport on unloading and small-calibre anti-aircraft artillery battery. As a result of the attack, the small-calibre anti-aircraft artillery was suppressed and an explosion was observed at the depot.

According to German documents, three Soviet fighters in the Taarnet area fired at a motorboat, seriously wounding its passengers – an officer and a private. There is a version that it was the Airacobras of the 20th IAP, but it could also have been other aircraft, such as the Kittyhawks of A.I. Batrakov's group.

The third group attacked ships and vessels in the Lang Fjord. The group consisted of five Il-2s of the 46th ShAP (leader – Senior Lieutenant S.S. Rolbin), eight Kittyhawks of the 78th IAP (leader – Major A.V. Polkovnikov) and four Yak fighters of the 20th IAP (leader – Lieutenant L.P. Lapin). At 22:45 the group took off from Pummanki, gathered above the airfield and flew along the route Bugö Island – Skogerre Island – Lang Fjord.

At 23:28, diving from an altitude of 400m, three Il-2s attacked a transport with displacement of 3,000–4,000 tonnes, two more Il-2s attacked a patrol ship. Three people were wounded on the floating base *Südmeer* by the cannon and machine gun-fire of the attackers. Anti-aircraft fire from enemy ships shot down one attack aircraft, its crew died.

According to German documents, Soviet aircraft shot at a Do 24 floatplane at the Kirkenes roadstead. Most likely it was the prey of the pilots of the third group. However, no mentioning of this attack has yet been found in Soviet documents.

The fourth group included the skip-bombing aircraft. The pilots of the 46th ShAP had been practicing skip-bombing technique since April, and they were the first in the history of the Northern Fleet to perform the skip-bombing attack against German transports. The group consisted of four Il-2s of the 46th ShAP (leader – Major G.V. Pavlov), seven Kittyhawk fighter-bombers of the 78th IAP (leader – Senior Lieutenant V.P. Strelnikov) and eight Airacobras of the 255th IAP (leader – Captain I.P. Konev). At 22:55 the group took off from the Vaenga-2 airfield and followed the route Vaenga-2 – Tsyp-Navolok – Sredniy Peninsula – further to Jakobsnes.

At 23:36, four aircraft attacked the transports, which were staying at the Jakobsnes roadstead, using the skip-bombing method. From an altitude of 25–30m and a distance of 150m to the target, they dropped eight FAB-250s. The crews witnessed the explosion of a transport with displacement of 8,000 tonnes and the loss of a support vessel of 600 tonnes displacement. At 23:37, seven Kittyhawks dropped bombs on the ships at Jakobsnes roadstead in a dive from an altitude of 1,000m. From the combat flight log of the 6th IAD:

> A direct hit by one FAB-100 damaged the Jakobsnes pier. The enemy motorboat didn't suffer any damage from our machine-gun fire. At 23:41 near Kobbholm-fiord, the aircraft engaged in an air battle at ground level with six Bf 109s. As a result of the combat, Lieutenant Nikolayev shot down one Bf 109. The enemy aircraft crashed five kilometres north-west of Kobbholm Fjord. The pilots, Junior Lieutenants Venikov and Logvinov, dropped bombs on the self-propelled barge in the area of Renö Island and fired machine guns at it. As a result of the strike, the enemy self-propelled barge was sunk.

The Northern Fleet Air Force Headquarters credited one shot down Bf 109 to Lieutenant A.F. Nikolayev.

According to available German documents, in the course of the attack two large transports were damaged. The refrigerator steamship *Patagonia* (5,898grt) was hit by one bomb, but it exploded only after it went through the port side and hit the water. A leak developed and the tug *Staerkodder* came to the rescue. It is now established that this steamship was repaired fairly quickly, but remained in Kirkenes until October 1944 acting as a floating warehouse for perishable goods (refrigerator). So far, there are no available German records to establish which of the pilots hit it.

The steamship *Pernambuco* (4,121grt), anchored at Jakobsnes, was attacked by four aircraft which dropped bombs and fired at it from their cannon and machine guns, according to the report of the onboard anti-aircraft gunners. The attacking aircraft achieved one bomb hit between the ship holds 4 and 5. In addition to one direct hit, many bombs dropped by the attacking aircraft exploded 50m from the steamship. One bomb hit caused a fire on the ship, threatening to explode the ammunition. The vessel ran aground and the crew intentionally flooded some of the compartments to extinguish the fire. The ship was saved, but the fire destroyed 298 tonnes of straw and 1,923 tonnes of oats. After the fire was extinguished, the ship was brought afloat and repaired. It left Kirkenes with convoy Ki.121. Rp. on 10 June 1944.

German transport ships after the attack on Kirkenes by aircraft of the Northern Fleet Air Force, 13 May 1944.

Taking into account the minor damage (clearly from an FAB-100) and the description of the attack, it is most likely that the damage was sustained during an attack by a group of attack aircraft of the 46th IAP led by Senior Lieutenant V.I. Belashev. It makes no sense to credit this damage to the Kittyhawks of the 78th IAP, as some authors have done, because the description of the strike was clearly more consistent with the one by attack aircraft.

The Luftwaffe fighters had not yet recovered from the fighting over the convoy on 11 May, and were apparently kept busy by the fighters of the 7th Air Army. The Germans proudly reported one shot down Airacobra with no losses of their own.

14 May

A Kittyhawk reconnaissance aircraft of the 118th RAP, which flew out to the Kirkenes area, reported at 1:08 that the German ships were still in the areas where they had been attacked the previous evening by strike groups of the Northern Fleet Air Force aircraft. Having received the report, the Air Force Headquarters ordered the 5th MTAD, the 6th and 14th SADs to prepare for a second strike. In fact, after numerous changes, the task of striking the enemy ships was divided as follows: the first group, consisting of Kittyhawk fighter-bombers of the 78th IAP under the cover of Airacobras of the 255th IAP, to attack the enemy transport at Jar Fjord by the skip-bombing method. Initially the task of the group was to attack Target No. 1 (transports south of Renö Island), but the target was changed just before the flight, and, as it turned out later, this order would prove to be successful. The second group, consisting of Il-4 torpedo bombers, in cooperation with Kittyhawk fighter-bombers of the 27th IAP covered by the fighters of the 255th IAP, attacked Target No. 1 (transports south of Renö Island). One of the main changes was that the torpedo bombers carried bombs instead of high-altitude torpedoes: two FAB-250s and six FAB-100s per aircraft. The torpedo-bomber crews were ordered to drop FAB-250s on transports and FAB-100s on the port of Kirkenes. The bomb load on the Kittyhawks of the 27th IAP also changed – they were ordered to have one FAB-250 in addition to the two FAB-100s on each aircraft. The Kittyhawks were to drop their bombs following the lead Il-4 torpedo bomber. The third group, consisting of Il-2s of the 46th ShAP, together with Kittyhawk fighter-bombers of the 78th IAP under the cover of the fighters of the 20th IAP, attacked Target No. 2 (transports at Jakobsnes roadstead). The fourth group was to take off from Pummanki airfield. It consisted of the Il-2s of the 46th ShAP, which were to attack the Target No.3 (transports in the Lang Fjord) from a dive under cover of the fighters of the 20th and 78th IAPs.

According to the original plan, the time of attack for all groups was set at 4:30. However, unit commanders reported that they did not have enough time to prepare aircraft, and as a result the strike time for all groups was changed to 5:00. Vadsø was set as the reserve target for all the groups.

The first group achieved the greatest success. The group consisted of eight Kittyhawks fighter-bombers of the 78th IAP (lead Captain F.S. Plotko) under the cover of four Airacobras of the 255th IAP (lead Captain I.P. Konev). After take-off, the 255th IAP Airacobras mistakenly joined another group of attack aircraft, but the fighter-bombers were not deterred by this fact.

At 4:50, three Kittyhawk fighter-bombers piloted by Captain F.S. Plotko, Lieutenant I.L. Antonov and Junior Lieutenant A.S. Kovalenko attacked the German transport of 3,000 tonnes displacement in the Jar Fjord using a skip-bombing method. Several bombs hit the steamship *Johann Faulbaums* (2,944grt) and seriously damaged it.[1] Two of the ship crew members were seriously wounded and one lightly wounded as a result of the bombing and machine-gun fire. The Germans sent two artillery MFPs to help the transport, but they arrived too late to reload the cargo: at 7:05 the ship sank. For the first time the Northern Fleet succeeded in sinking a German transport using the skip-bombing method. This victory wasn't the last…

The pilots of three other Kittyhawks dropped bombs on the pier. After dropping the bombs, the aircraft fired machine guns at the motorboat and the harbour depot, however, to no avail, according to the pilots' observations. However, the sinking of the steamer was paid for by a high price: one Kittyhawk was shot down. From the accident report of the loss of the aircraft: "When it appeared over the target, it was subjected to intensive anti-aircraft artillery fire. There were no encounters with fighter aircraft. On departing from the target, it was shot down by a direct hit from anti-aircraft artillery." The pilot, Junior Lieutenant I.N. Sapronov, was killed. According to German documents, he was shot down by fire of the *2 Kompanie Festungs-battailon 664*.

The second group of attack aircraft also soon reached Target No. 1 (transports south of Renö Island). The group consisted of five Il-4 bombers of the 9th GMTAP (leader – Guards Major A.N. Voloshin), 13 Kittyhawk fighter-bombers of the 27th IAP (leader – Senior Lieutenant L.M. Semyonov) under the cover of eight Airacobras of the 255th IAP (leader – Captain V.A. Burmatov). The group began to approach the target, and it became clear that the Kittyhawks, which were supposed to drop bombs following the leading Il-4, were unable to maintain low speed equal to that of the Il-4 on its course because of the increased bomb load (Kittyhawk had problems with controllability at low speeds when carrying bombs). At 5:00 the Kittyhawks advanced and dropped bombs from a horizontal flight from an altitude of 2,500m on transports south of Renö Island. According to German reports, the transports were not hit. After them, at 5:03, two transports and a patrol ship to the south of Renö Island were bombed by Il-4s from a horizontal flight from an altitude of 2,700m. According to the reports of the crews, all the bombs missed their targets.

The third group consisted of six Il-2s of the 46th ShAP (leader – Captain S.A. Gulyaev), six Kittyhawk fighter-bombers of the 78th IAP (leader – Lieutenant A.F. Nikolayev), and six Airacobras and two Yaks of the 20th IAP (leader – Senior Lieutenant A.K. Tarasov). The group took off at 4:19 from Vaenga-2 airfield. At 4:55, the Kittyhawks dive-bombed two transports at Jakobsnes from an altitude of 1,100m. According to the pilots' reports, there were no hits. At 5:07 the attack

1 Historical note: The steamship *Johann Faulbaums* was commissioned as the cargo steamer *Vittoria*, ship number 587, at the Richardson, Duck & Company, Thornaby shipyard in July 1907. Capacity 2,817grt. Length 100m, width 14m. The first owner was Scholefield Steam Shipping Co. Ltd (H. Scholefield & Son), Newcastle. In 1916 the vessel was sold to Century Steam Shipping Co. Ltd (Harris & Dixon), London, leased by the Admiralty in 1917 and served as a decoy ship (Q-Ship) under the code names *Pargust, Friswell, Pangloss* and *Snail*. Under the first name it sank the German submarine UC 27 on 7 June 1917. From 1919 the vessel was taken over by the S.S. Vittoria Ltd (Cadman, Gardner & Co.), Liverpool. In 1927 it was sold to Greece and named *Dimitrios G. Thermiotis*, owned by A. Tatakis & A. Kyrtatas, Andros. In 1929 resold to Latvia and named *Janis Faulbaums*, owner – M. Faulbaum & W. Hummel, Riga. From 1937 the company had a new name – Max Faulbaum Steamship Lines (James Siering & Co.). In 1940, the owner with his steamships preferred to join to the Germans and changed all ship names to German. The steamship became *Johann Faulbaum* and its home port was Stettin. It arrived in Kirkenes with convoy Rp.116.Ki on 29 April 1944.

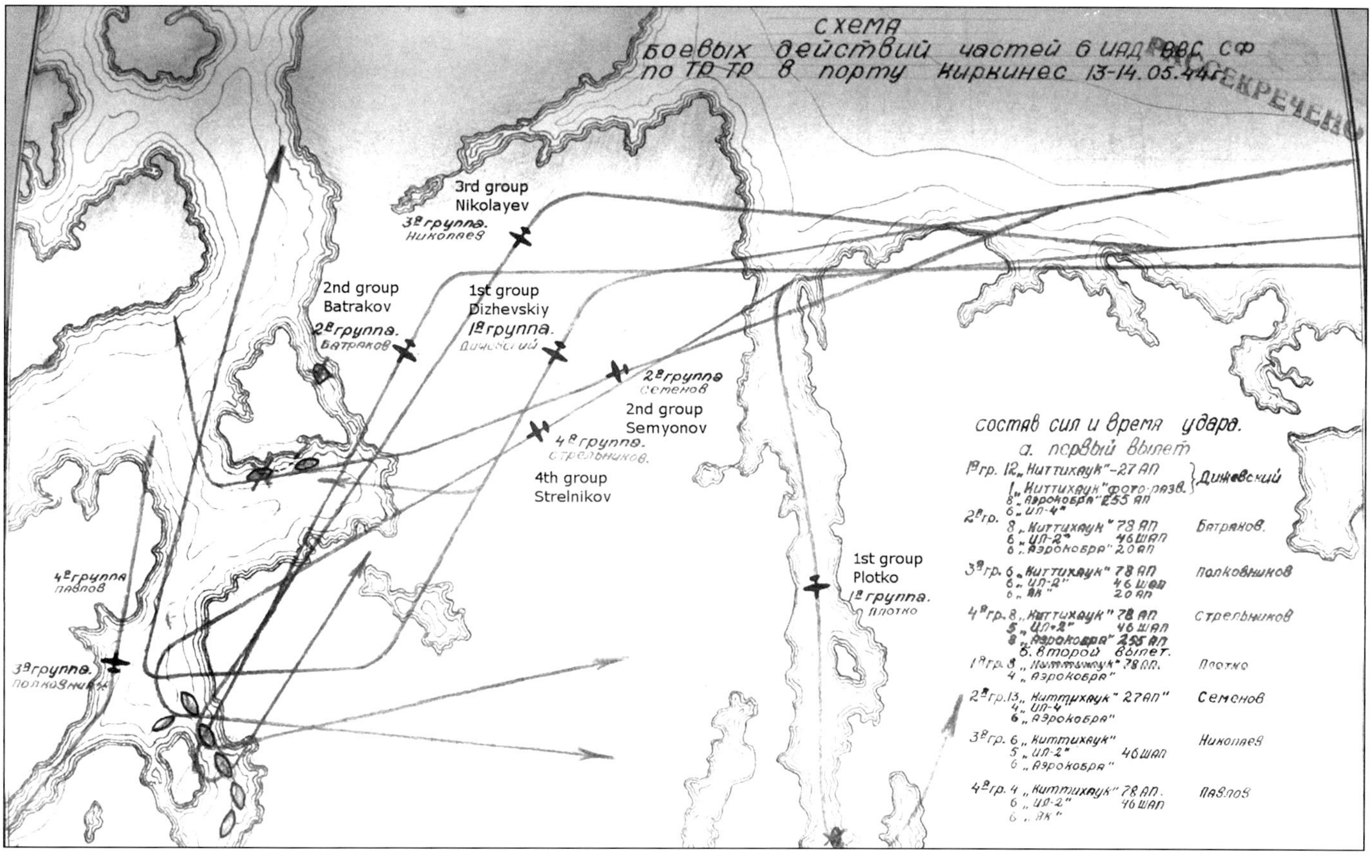

Plan of attacks of the 27th and 78th IAPs against the German transport ships in Kirkenes on 13–14 May 1944.
Composition of forces: **a – the first sortie**; – 12 Kittyhawks, 1 photo recce Kittyhawk, 27th IAP, Leader – Dizhevskiy; 8 Airacobras, 255 IAP, 6 Il-4s; – 8 Kittyhawks, 78th IAP, Leader – Batrakov; 6 Il-2s, 46th ShAP; 6 Airacobras, 20th IAP; – 6 Kittyhawks, 78th IAP, Leader – Polkovnikov; 6 Il-2s, 46th ShAP; 6 Yaks, 20th IAP; 4th group – 8 Kittyhawks, 78th IAP, Leader – Strelnikov; 5 Il-2s, 46th ShAP; 8 Airacobras, 255th IAP. **b – the second sortie**; – 8 Kittyhawks, 78th IAP, Leader – Plotko; 4 Airacobras, – 13 Kittyhawks, 27th IAP, Leader – Semyonov, 4 Il-4s; 6 Airacobras; – 6 Kittyhawks, Leader – Nikolayev; 5 Il-2s, 46th ShAP; 6 Airacobras; – 4 Kittyhawks, 78th IAP, Leader – Pavlov; 6 Il-2s, 46th ShAP; 6 Yak.

aircraft dive-bombed the same two transports near Jakobsnes Cape. Despite the victorious report, German documents claimed that their ships were unharmed.

Soviet pilots spotted one German transport, which, after sustaining damage during the evening attack, was stuck on the shoal. It was the transport *Pernambuco* (4,121grt).

The fourth group attacked the ships in Lang Fjord. The group consisted of three Il-2s (leader – Lieutenant L.M. Kalmykov), four Kittyhawk fighters of the 78th IAP (leader – Lieutenant A.S. Pavlov), and four Yaks of the 20th IAP (leader – Lieutenant I.P. Kuzhanov). The group took off from Pummanki at 4:30, gathered above the airfield and set off on a course for the target. At 5:01, from an altitude of 1,200m, the attack aircraft dropped bombs on transports in the Lang Fjord. Germans recorded an attack on the floating base *Südmeer* near Storbukt (Neidenfjord) by Il-2 and SB aircraft. No German losses or damage were recorded.

In the result of the two-day attack, the Northern Fleet Air Force achieved a significant success in the fight against enemy ships – one transport ship was sink and two transports were seriously damaged at the cost of only two aircraft. This was also the beginning of the successful use of the skip-bombing method in the Northern Fleet.

Captain F.S. Plotko, leader of Kittyhawks group of the 78th IAP during the strike on Kirkenes on 14 May 1944.

15 May

On this day the 27th IAP lost one of its most experienced pilots. At 12:30 the Kittyhawks of the 27th IAP were conducting skip-bombing exercises at the Gryaznaya Bay naval range. Senior Lieutenant L.M. Semyonov, being an experienced pilot, made a tragic mistake. From the accident report on the loss of the aircraft: "While practicing skip bombing, Semyonov, leading four aircraft at a low altitude of one to two metres on a straight course, tried to make a turn to the right and pushed the aircraft to the water with a right tilt. Performing a turn at a critically low altitude, the aircraft hit the water with the wing. The wing panel warped causing the aircraft to bounce, it turned over, fell into the water at 12:25 and sank." Senior Lieutenant L.M. Semyonov, a pilot, who had previously led the group into battle not once, died.

16–17 May

On 16 May 1944 there was another battle of the Northern Fleet Air Force against a German convoy. This seemingly ordinary event of the war turned out to be one of the most confusing battles in the North. On that day, at 17:40, a reconnaissance Kittyhawk of the 118th RAP transmitted a radio message: 'Makkaur Cape, a convoy'. The convoy observed was the Rp.119.Ki which included the gunboat K-1, patrol boats V-6110, V-6108, UJ-1209, UJ-1210, UJ-1211 and minesweeper M-35; it set out from Reppa Fjord heading to Kirkenes. At the time of departure from Reppa Fjord it also included the steamer *Solviken* (3,502grt), but by the beginning of the events described the steamer had left for Honningsvåg and the convoy essentially became a warship unit. After discovering the enemy, the Northern Fleet Air Force Headquarters began to devise an air strike operation. As a result, the following orders were given:

a) The command of the 5th MTAD – to launch a torpedo attack on the convoy by low-altitude Boston torpedo bombers. The first strike at Vadsø, the second at the area of Kibergnes – Eckerö.
b) Command of the 14th SAD and 6th IAD – to conduct a bomb strike on the enemy convoy in Varanger Fjord by two groups of aircraft.

According to the plan, the Il-2s of the 46th ShAP and Kittyhawk fighter-bombers of the 78th IAP were to attack the convoy jointly. The first group of attack aircraft and Kittyhawk fighter-bombers were to strike in the following order: the attack aircraft to carry out the dive bombing first, followed by the Kittyhawk fighter-bombers using the skip-bombing method. On the second approach, the Il-2s were to attack the enemy ships in order to secure the exit of Kittyhawks from the attack. The second group of fighter-bombers and attack aircraft, covered by Airacobras of the 255th IAP, were to attack the convoy using dive-bombing and skip-bombing methods. After landing, both groups were to prepare to strike again. The Pummanki task force was to conduct a dive-bombing attack on the spotted convoy. Time of the strike – upon readiness; location – to be decided by the task force commander. After landing to be ready for the next mission.

At 19:00 a Kittyhawk reconnaissance aircraft flown by Junior Lieutenant S.I. Pankrashin of the 118th RAP took off to track the convoy. Forty-five minutes later he observed a group of torpedo bombers attacking the convoy and reported: "Our aircraft are approaching the target, sustaining a terrible anti-aircraft fire, water columns are being put in the way of our torpedo bombers."

Four Boston torpedo bombers of the 9th GMTAP (leader – Guards Captain P.P. Gusev) under the cover of 10 Airacobras of the 255th IAP (leader – Captain P.A. Rassadkin) and eight Kittyhawks of the 27th IAP (leader – Senior Lieutenant A.P. Anuchin) attacked the enemy at Pers Fjord. From combat report No. 138 of the Northern Fleet Air Force Headquarters:

> At 19:45, altitude 30m, distance of 800–3,000m, Guards Junior Lieutenant Rybchinskiy and Guards Junior Lieutenant Sushitskiy unsuccessfully attacked the enemy convoy. Two torpedoes 45-36-AN were dropped. Guards Captain Gusev did not drop two torpedoes, and Guards Junior Lieutenant Nikolayev did not drop one torpedo because of the fault of the crews.

The German reports do not describe the results of the attack as successful either. From the report of K-1 commander *Kplt.d.R.* Arretz: "18:43. Fire was opened at 12km. Four Boston-type torpedo bombers attacked the convoy in open formation. Because of the powerful anti-aircraft fire, the exact moment of the torpedo drop was not observed. At 2,5km the enemy turned to the north and south. One torpedo, approaching on the surface, was easily evaded." Another torpedo was evaded by UJ-1210. From the report of its commander, *Oberleutnant z.S.d.R.* Friedrich Ulrich: "We saw one torpedo track and dodged it by turning the rudder abruptly to the left. The torpedo passed at a distance of about 150m on the port side."

On leaving the target, a pair of Kittyhawks of the 27th IAP were engaged in an air battle with two Bf 109s, but neither side claimed any victories. One of the Bostons, piloted by Guards Captain P.P. Gusev, was hit by anti-aircraft fire during the attack and landed in the vicinity of Tsyp-Navolok. From the accident report about the loss of the Boston:

> The aircraft flown by Gusev, when attacking the convoy, received four direct hits by shells. In spite of this, the aircraft remained under control and returned to home airfield. While flying in the Tsyp-Navolok area, the pilot noticed a failure of the trimmers and ordered the gunner to inspect the cables. The gunner, having found the break, tried to repair it by tying it up and put the aircraft into pitching-up position. The aircraft did not steer well and the pilot landed on the water.

The pilot of the reconnaissance aircraft, S.I. Pankrashin, having spotted a life raft with the crew of the Boston, radioed a request to send a rescue boat, and then flew eight tracks directing the boat towards the life raft, thanks to which the torpedo bomber crew was saved.

Around this time, a Spitfire reconnaissance aircraft (British registration number BP917) of the 118th RAP, which was sent to record the results of the attack on the convoy, went missing in the battle area. Most likely, it was shot down by a Bf 109 of the 9./JG 5. The pilot, Captain V.A. Aleksandrov, was missed in action.

The next to attack the enemy ships were four Il-2s of the 46th ShAP (leader – Lieutenant L.M. Kalmykov) under cover of four Kittyhawks of the 78th IAP (leader – Major A.V. Polkovnikov) and four Yaks of the 20th IAP (leader – Lieutenant I.P. Kuzhanov). Having taken off from Pummanki airfield at 20:06, this group set course for Vardö. However, one of the attack aircraft had to return due to the engine problems. At 20:32 the attack aircraft performed a dive bombing from 300m altitude and then fired rocket projectiles and machine guns at the enemy ships. According to the Northern Fleet Air Force Headquarters, L.M. Kalmykov's group did not cause any damage to the enemy. However, this was not entirely true.

While the bombs did not hit the German ships, the 37mm cannon fire of the attack aircraft was quite effective. From the report of the commander of K-1:

> At 19:28, fire was opened. Three enemy aircraft attacked from diving with bombs and cannon/machine-gun fire the group headed by V-6110, K-1 and UJ-1210. The bombs fell 20–30m to the port side in front and on the traverse of the K-1. Many hits by cannon and machine-gun fire damaged the bridge of the K-1 and the ammunition winch of the forward 3.7cm cannon. One sailor was lightly wounded and the other was heavily wounded by the enemy fire. The enemy conducted the attack very bravely.

The mechanical engineer of K-1 *Stbs. Ob. Masch.* Held described damage from the attack in detail:

> The steering gear ventilation shaft and main calibre control equipment were damaged by cannon/ machine-gun fire, the ammunition winch for 3.7cm cannon was put out of action. Due to the failure of the winch, two more men had to be assigned to carry the ammunition and replace the disabled gunners. The shell splinters hit the cellars of the 12cm and 3.7cm cannon.

The Soviet attack aircraft also hit UJ-1210. From the report of its commander:

> 19:28. Three Il-2s made a dive attack on the K-1 and UJ-1210. The aircraft fired at the coastal batteries and then on the ships. Three aircraft were approaching very low (at about 80m altitude), firing cannons and machine guns. They dropped three bombs. One exploded on the starboard side about 50m away and two on the port side about 150m away from the ship. No damage sustained.

The commander of the UJ-1210 was clearly overoptimistic. The ship's engineer-mechanic E. Fieseler was more realistic, as his report says:

> At 19:20, another attack followed in which the washing room, the deck between it and the canteen for petty officers were hit by cannon fire. In addition, the intercom pipe from the bridge to the acoustic was punctured. The port-side expansion tank I of the fuel bunker had one hole of about 20cm in diameter, presumably caused by a 3.7cm calibre shell.

Luftwaffe fighters attempted to pursue the departing Soviet aircraft. From the report of commander of the K-1: "Shortly after the attack, our fighters rushed in pursuit". However, the Luftwaffe pilots were not too eager to fight. From the documents of the 78th IAP:

> The Il-2s took up the attack formation, the Kittyhawks moved north-east of the target; at this moment four to six Bf 109s appeared, hiding in pairs in the clouds from the Vardö side. One pair began to approach from tail to the leading Kittyhawk. Lieutenant Mitrofanov noticed the approach, attacked the wingman Bf 109 from a range of 130–50m, fired two bursts at 3/4–0/4 target aspect ratio; the enemy aircraft plunged into the sea five to eight kilometres from Vardö. The leading Bf 109 made an unsuccessful attack and went into the clouds. From that moment on, the crews did not observe any enemy aircraft.

From the German side, the Bf 109 fighters of 9./JG 5 took part in the air battle, their pilots claimed seven victories, but the Soviet aircraft sustained no losses. Only one victory was credited by the Northern Fleet Air Force Headquarters: Lieutenant V.G. Mitrofanov of the 78th IAP shot down one Bf 109. Perhaps in the course of the battle the Soviet aircraft managed to damage the Bf 109G-2, W. Nr. 13692, tactical number 'Black 4' which nosed over when landing at the Svartnes airfield and its pilot, *Obfw.* Josef Bößenecker was wounded. However, the information about the time of the loss of this aircraft is somewhat contradictory.

At 21:01, the radio message came from the reconnaissance aircraft: "Enemy convoy approached Kibergnes. The composition of the convoy remains the same". At 21:47, the group of six Il-2s of the 46th ShAP (leader – Senior Lieutenant V.I. Belashev, he was also the group commander), six Kittyhawk fighter-bombers of the 78th IAP (leader – Senior Lieutenant A.I. Batrakov) and six Airacobras of the 20th IAP (leader – Captain E.V. Petrenko) took off from the Vaenga-2 airfield to attack. The route of the group: Vaenga-2 – Tsyp-Navolok – Pummanki – convoy. On the way to the target, one Il-2 and one Kittyhawk had to turn back due to equipment failures, with the Kittyhawk landing on the water and its pilot, Junior Lieutenant L.N. Priz, being rescued by motorboats. From the accident report on the loss of Kittyhawk aircraft: "En route to the target, with the mission of destroying the enemy transports sailing as a part of a caravan by the method of skip bombing, before reaching the target in area to the north of Set-Navolok Cape, the pilot made an emergency landing in the sea due to the engine failure. The pilot was rescued by the boats, the aircraft sank."

The second group of strike aircraft took off from Vaenga-2 at 21:55. It consisted of four Il-2s of the 46th ShAP (leader – Lieutenant V.M. Skopintsev), eight Kittyhawk fighters of the 78th IAP (leader – Senior Lieutenant P.I. Sakharov), four of them carrying bombs, and six Airacobras of the 255th IAP (leader – Lieutenant P.D. Bogdanov). On the way to the convoy, one Kittyhawk had engine failure and was forced to return to home airfield. Having discovered the convoy, the Kittyhawks moved forward to attack it. The Kittyhawk fighter-bombers of P.I. Sakharov's group attacked from a dive from the sea side, while those of A.I. Batrakov's groups attacked from the shore side using the skip-bombing method. Most likely, P.I. Sakharov's group was the first to attack. Time of its strike varies in different documents from 22:35 to 22:39. Four fighter-bombers split into pairs and dropped bombs on UJ-1209 and UJ-1212. None of the German ships were damaged in this attack. From the report of *Ober-Lieutenant* Flunkert, commander of UJ-1209:

> 21:36. Air alert. Our true course 235 degrees. Formation: anti-aircraft defence order. Enemy aircraft – eight Il-2s and 16 fighters on true course 80 degrees, course 350 degrees, four aircraft left the group and turned east. The rest flew over the convoy and at 21:40 attacked with bombs and cannon/machine-gun fire. Return fire was opened. Of the four aircraft that turned eastward, two Il-2s attacked from a dive the UJ-1209, from true course 65 degrees, with cannon/machine-gun fire and bombs (two by each). By manoeuvring at full throttle and steering steeply to port (course east), bombs dropped to starboard (10–40 m away).

Luftwaffe fighters attacked the Kittyhawks on their exit from the attack. From the report of Junior Lieutenant A.S. Volkov, Kittyhawk pilot of 78th IAP: "The leader Sakharov, after seeing eight Bf 109s, turned for the head-on attack, so then four of them went down towards the Kittyhawk group below. The remaining four Bf 109s, after engaging into air combat with us, tried to approach us from the tail, but after two turns the four-formation of the Bf 109s scattered. One of them tried to attack the leading aircraft on the turn, having previously skipped me, firing on me. I, repulsing the attack of the Bf 109s, fired two bursts at the leader from 50–70 m distance at 1/4–2/4 target aspect ratio. The Bf 109 made a turn with a small climb and then came out of the battle towards the convoy, where it landed in the water." The Northern Fleet Air Force Headquarters credited the victory over the Bf 109 to Junior Lieutenant Volkov.

While the Germans repulsed the attack of the Kittyhawk dive bombers, they missed the approaching Senior Lieutenant A.I. Batrakov's skip-bombing Kittyhawks which came in from the shore side. Five Kittyhawk fighter-bombers of the 78th IAP (leader – Senior Lieutenant A.I. Batrakov) attacked the patrol ship and the first transport which were in the head of the convoy, but which in reality were UJ-1210 and K-1. As reported by the pilots, two Kittyhawks, piloted by Junior Lieutenants N.P. Proyavko and N.V. Vasilyev attacked the 'minesweeper in the head of the convoy'. Initially, the pilots reported four direct hits of FAB-100s into the ship, later they stated about two hits and two close-range explosions. The latter was fully consistent with reality. The machine-gun fire of the Kittyhawks took out the stern 37mm automatic cannon. From a report by a member of the UJ-1210 crew, *Ob.strm.* Herbert Strauchmann: "As the rear gunnery commander, I ordered that fire should be transferred to the three aircraft approaching from the starboard side. At this moment *Ob.btsmt.* Fiebeg (commander of the 3.7cm cannon) was killed by machine-gun fire."

From the report of the Commander of UJ-1210, *Oberleutnant z. S. d. R.* Friedrich Ulrich:

> 21:36. Formation: anti-aircraft defence order, course 235 degrees. Air alert! Eight Il-2s and about 15 other aircraft were flying with true course 80 degrees, course 350 degrees. The Il-2s split into two groups, one of which flew to the convoy, while the second remained on course. The first group came under fire from all guns. Immediately after them three Il-2s approached from starboard at true course 230 degrees. Change of targets to starboard. The aircraft approached the ship and opened cannon and machine-gun fire. The first aircraft dropped two bombs which hit the ship in the area of the aft 37mm cannon. The second and third aircraft each dropped a bomb, one of which fell into the water on the starboard side in the centre of the ship, and the second fell in front of the bow five metres away. Two men were thrown overboard by the explosions. Of the two bombs that hit the ship, the first, which exploded on the deck, disabled the entire aft armament of the ship, while the second hit the wheelhouse and damaged the steering gear. The rudder was jammed in the 'right 15' position. The bomb which exploded near the starboard side damaged the hull in the boiler room area.

The damage to the UJ-1210 was also recorded by other ships of the convoy. From the report of the UJ-1212 commander: "21:42… UJ-1210 was hit by a bomb in the aft area, let out steam and stopped moving'". From the report of the V-6108: "At 21:42, UJ-1210 was hit by a bomb". The crew of UJ-1210 tried to fight for keeping the vessel afloat but the damage to the ship was very severe. In official documents, the sunken ship was converted from a 'minesweeper' to a 'patrol ship' and as such was recorded on the combat record of the Junior Lieutenants N.P. Proyavko and N.V. Vasilyev. It remains unknown why the Germans spotted three attackers instead of two.

Junior Lieutenant N.V. Vasilyev, after striking UJ-1210, attacked a Luftwaffe flying boat and, according to his report, shot it down, but the victory was not credited by the Northern Fleet Air Force Headquarters. This victory is not present both in the Operational Summary No.138 of the Northern Fleet Air Force Headquarters and in the official list of aircraft shot down by the 6th IAD.

Three Kittyhawks piloted by Senior Lieutenant A.I. Batrakov, Lieutenant I.L. Antonov, and Junior Lieutenant A.S. Kovalenko attacked the gunboat K-1, but did not succeed. Unfortunately, one Kittyhawk was shot down on leaving the attack. From the report of the commander of the UJ-1209:

> 21:42. One Il-2, at a distance of 300m from the stern, approached towards UJ-1209 from the starboard side. After direct hits in the engine by 3.7cm and 2cm shells, the aircraft flipped over the port wing. At the same time, a *Vierling* [20mm quadruple cannon] hit the right wing of the aircraft causing it to break off. The aircraft fell down at the true course of 310 degrees. Observed from K-1, M-35, UJ-1212 and 1209.

Later in the report, commander of the UJ-1209 indicated that the shot down aircraft was also fired upon from gunboat K-1 after flying over his ship. However, the Soviet documents give a different picture of what happened. From the accident report on the loss of the Kittyhawk: "In the vicinity of the target the aircraft withstood intensive anti-aircraft artillery fire. Above the target it was hit by anti-aircraft fire. On the return route, as a result of engine failure, it crashed into the sea 20–30km south-east of the target. Burning, it made a landing on water."

Two days before his death, the Kittyhawk pilot, Lieutenant I.L. Antonov, took part in the sinking of the transport *Johann Faulbaums* (2,944grt) in the Jar Fjord. For him it was the 22nd combat flight and the third attack. A Kittyhawk flown by Senior Lieutenant A.I. Batrakov was also damaged by anti-aircraft fire, but the experienced pilot managed to bring his aircraft home.

Two groups of Kittyhawk fighter-bombers were followed by the attack aircraft of the group led by Senior Lieutenant V.I. Belashev. According to archival documents, five of his Il-2s attacked the German ships in the tail of the convoy at 22:43. However, according to the pilots' reports, Senior Lieutenant V.I. Belashev, Lieutenant M.M. Tamarov and Junior Lieutenant S.I. Pantyukhov indicated the time of the attack at 22:43, while Junior Lieutenants P.V. Serdyuk and S.N. Daurov attacked at 22:47. According to the plan of attack from the report of Senior Lieutenant V.I. Belashev, he attacked the central part of the convoy. If we compare his plan from the report with the plan of the convoy formation from the combat report of the 12th Submarine Hunters Flotilla, it turns out the following – he dropped bombs on minesweeper M-35, then opened cannon and machine-gun fire on gunboat K-1 and the submarine hunter UJ-1209. The bombs dropped by the Il-2 of Senior Lieutenant V.I. Belashev caused light damage to the minesweeper M-35. From the report of the K-1 commander: "21:42 … M-35 reported a water leakage in compartment I (steering gear)." The nature of the damage is described in the combat log of the 5th Minesweepers Flotilla: "Due to strong explosions [caused by bombs – author's note] water penetrated through the rudder axle gland. The water level was contained by pumping it out with an auxiliary pump when it had almost reached the rudder gland. The gland was tightened and thus the threat [of flooding – author's note] was eliminated".

The report of the commander of submarine hunter UJ-1209 records: "21:43 … At the same time one Il-2, approaching us from the stern, was fired upon by many ships. It was shot down by M-35 and fell at the true course of about 100 degrees, at a distance of 900m". However, despite the victorious report from the German ships, V.I. Belashev's Il-2 was not even seriously damaged.

A pair of attack aircraft, piloted by Lieutenant M.M. Tamarov and Junior Lieutenant S.I. Pantyukhov, attacked the convoy at 22:43. If we compare the plans from their reports with the plan from the combat operations report of the convoy of the 12th Submarine Hunters Flotilla, the following can be surmised – both pilots attacked V-6108, and then Lieutenant M.M. Tamarov attacked V-6110 and proceeded to attack gunboat K-1. Junior Lieutenant S.I. Pantyukhov, after attacking V-6108, attacked K-1. Both pilots indicate in their reports that they saw a "heading transport on fire" which, to all appearances, was the critically damaged UJ-1210, but they write nothing about the attacks on it. It should be noted that the plan of attack of the 46th ShAP Il-2s on 16 May 1944, which is used by some historians, shows two patrol ships on the starboard side of the convoy, while the scheme in the report of the 12th Submarine Hunters Flotilla – three (the leading UJ-1210, followed by V-6110 and last V-6108). Two patrol ships V-6110 and V-6108 were hit by the attack aircraft, as UJ-1210, after being hit by the Kittyhawks, became the "heading transport on fire".

In chronological order, the next to attack were the skip bombers of Senior Lieutenant V.M. Skopintsev. According to the reports of the skip-bomber pilots, they began the attack at 22:45, but according to the documents of the German ships, everything happened two minutes earlier. From the operations log of the 12th Submarine Hunters Flotilla: "21:43. Approach of six Il-2s from the west". The same is said in the report of the commander of UJ-1209: "21:43. Approach of six Il-2s from the west (Varanger Fjord)". According to the reports of the skip-bomber pilots, the group split into two pairs and attacked the German ships. The first pair (pilots Senior Lieutenant V.M. Skopintsev and Lieutenant G.V. Starchikov) attacked the K-1, but the gunboat was not damaged by their strike. However, both attacking aircraft sustained serious damage from anti-aircraft fire, but managed to land safely at the Pummanki airfield on the Sredniy Peninsula. The second pair of skip bombers (flown by Lieutenants A.P. Bondarenko and I.V. Maksimenko) attacked minesweeper M-35. Comparison of the diagrams from the pilots' reports with the convoy formation diagrams from the documents of the 12th Submarine Hunters Flotilla shows that both attack aircraft bypassed V-6108 from the bow and attacked minesweeper M-35, taking it for a transport. It should be noted that this is by no means the only case where the pilots mistakenly identified ships due to poor visibility. However, the attack was effective. From the report of I.V. Maksimenko: "As a result of the strike, I saw an explosion in the transport". The bombs of the Il 2s did not hit the target, but the fire of cannon and machine guns was accurate. From the operations log of the 5th Minesweepers Flotilla: "The cannon and machine-gun fire damaged the water separator in the pipe and the howler with the siren, which caused a large outflow of steam. The steam flow there was shut off by a valve and the breach was repaired in port" Thus, the pilot mistook the release of steam for an explosion on the ship. Apart from the problems with the steam pipe, the ready ammunition boxes of the bow 105mm gun were damaged.

Meanwhile, the Airacobras of the 255th IAP spotted a pair of hydroplanes and attacked them, but on their way out of the attack they themselves were attacked by Luftwaffe fighters and lost one aircraft. From the accident report on the loss of the Airacobra fighter: "Two Blohm und Voss BV 138 aircraft were seen in the target area and attacked. On exiting the attack, Rossiychuk was attacked by an enemy fighter and shot down. On the way out of the attack using a zoom climb maneuver, a Bf 109 came from behind and below and shot down Rossiychuk's aircraft from short range. The enemy aircraft was immediately shot down by Lieutenant Bogdanov". The pilot of Airacobra, Lieutenant I.I. Rossiychuk, died. Following the results of the air battle, the Headquarters of the Northern Fleet Air Force credited the following victories to the pilots of the 255th IAP: Senior Lieutenant P.D. Bogdanov added one Bf 109 to his score, and Lieutenant P.I. Kalekin one BV 138. The victories of both pilots, including Lieutenant P.I. Kalekin, are also recorded in the Operational Summary No. 138 of the Northern Fleet Air Force Headquarters. The victim of P.I. Kalekin's attacked was flying boat BV 138 C-1, W.Nr. 2300113, of 3.(F)/130 which performed the function of anti-submarine patrol; the entire crew survived. The end of the attack of the second group is described in the report of the Commander of UJ-1212: "21:47 … Another six Il-2s attacked from the west, flying at the course of 150 degrees".

At 22:47, judging from the pilots' reports, two attack aircraft of the 46th ShAP from the group of Senior Lieutenant V.I. Belashev were the last to attack. The aircraft were piloted by Junior Lieutenants P.V. Serdyuk and Sh.N. Daurov. Some documents indicate that the task of the pilots was to monitor the results of the strike. Both pilots attacked V-6108 and managed to achieve one hit on the patrol boat. From the report of Junior Lieutenant P.V. Serdyuk: "I attacked the patrol boat on the right. The gunner [Anikin – author's note] observed two direct hits to the right patrol boat by two FAB-100s, two of the other bombs missed the target, the boat was burning on the surface. On the way out of the attack I saw smoke and fire from the leading transport. No enemy fighters were observed." From the report of the commander [since the commander of the patrol ship V-6108 was killed in action, this report was made by the first officer of the watch, the navigator. No name was found in the document – author's note] of the patrol ship V-6108:

> 21:44. One Il-2 started a low-level attack from 350 degrees direction at V 6108. We started firing [at the aircraft – author's note] from a range of six kilometres from all weapons. The *Vierling* achieved numerous hits. The ship received hits from cannon and machine-gun fire.
>
> 21:45. The commander was severely wounded by cannon and machine-gun fire, one crew member was killed. The aircraft dropped two bombs. The ship was hit by one bomb in the stern. The second bomb exploded near the port side. The aircraft flew over the ship at an altitude of about 40m and plunged into the water in the direction of 115 degrees, at a distance of 700m.
>
> 21:46. Bomb explosion at the stern. A 3.7cm anti-aircraft gun with five sailors was thrown overboard. None of the sailors who were thrown overboard were seen again.
>
> The ship's crew has two seriously injured and many lightly wounded. The steering is damaged. The ship is restricted in manoeuvring. Ammunition consumption when firing on this aircraft was: six rounds of 8.8cm, 20 rounds 3.7cm and 160 rounds 2cm. The engine is not damaged as is the rest of the armament.

This attack against V-6108 was the last for the aircraft flown by Junior Lieutenant Sh.N. Daurov and his air gunner, Junior Sergeant A.L.

Lukin. From the report of Junior Lieutenant P.V. Serdyuk: "Wingman Daurov went into attack firing from cannons and machine guns, he was not seen further: according to the gunners' evidence, his aircraft fell into the sea".

From the report of the commander of submarine hunter UJ-1209: "21:45. Another fall [of aircraft – author's note] was observed at about true course of 100 degrees, at a distance of about 1,200m. Presumably shot down by V-6108". Unfortunately, unlike the report on the death of Il-2 of Senior Lieutenant V.I. Belashev, this one turned out to be correct. From the accident report on the loss of the Il-2: "On the distant approaches to the target, enemy ships opened heavy anti-aircraft fire. The crews resorted to a counter-attack manoeuvre and began to break through to attack the ships. On leaving the dive, the aircraft was hit by anti-aircraft fire. Having made a half roll, the aircraft hit the water. The crew was killed." Some discrepancy of the bombing time of V-6108 in German and Soviet documents is possible because of the fact that in the war neither of the sides would synchronize their watches.

It should also be noted that the bomb that hit V-6108 was clearly not a FAB-250. Abstract from ;Source book No 14 on the experience of combat operations of the Naval Air Force':

> Against transports with a displacement of more than 3,000 tonnes, it is most expedient to use the FAB-250TsK bombs (by aircraft not able to carry bombs over 250kg), with fuses set to delay by five to seven seconds. This bomb, dropped even from low altitudes of about 100–200m, would penetrate two iron decks and detonate at the bottom of the transport. The FAB-100 bomb with the same delayed-action fuse breaks through one deck and explodes in the space between decks.

It should be noted that the conclusion on the effectiveness of the bombs was based on a wide range of factual material – Soviet commissions on determining the effectiveness examined a large number (up to two hundred) of destroyed German ships and vessels in the Pillau – Hela Peninsula area. And, as a rule, the picture was the same. A single FAB-250 hit on ships of up to 4,000 tonnes displacement was fatal to them. Hence it is clear that a FAB-250 hit would have resulted in the destruction of V-6108. Unfortunately, it was hit by an FAB-100. Meanwhile, the crew of the submarine hunter UJ-1210 tried to save their ship. From the report of its commander:

> There was steam coming from the engine room. The chief mechanic reported that it was no longer safe to go in due to the threat of hot steam. In addition, there were reports of leaks in the engine room and boiler room. Thus, I gave orders to close the main shutoff valve and open the safety valve. The engine was now stopped. The ship in the meantime had made a full circle to starboard, but we had managed to rescue both sailors who had fallen overboard with the help of a rope and inflatable raft. The flagship of convoy K-1 was given a signal by searchlight: "Urgent help needed". UJ-1212 and 1209 approached in response, but were delayed due to another air raid.

From the report of the commander of submarine hunter UJ-1209: "21:52. The convoy lay back on course (accident at UJ-1210). Approached by 10 Il-2s from 50 degrees direction". This was another group of attack aircraft striking the German convoy. The aircraft, which returned to Pummanki airfield after the first attack, had been refuelled and re-armed for a second raid on the enemy. The group consisted of four Il-2s of the 46th ShAP (leader – Lieutenant L.M. Kalmykov), four Kittyhawk fighters of the 78th IAP (leader – Major A.V. Polkovnikov) and six Yak fighters of the 20th IAP (leader – Lieutenant L.P. Lapin). Having taken off at 22:38, they struck the target twelve minutes later, with the Il-2s dispersed and attacked the German ships individually. This time, the Northern Fleet Air Force Headquarters credited the group of Lieutenant L.M. Kalmykov with a damaged patrol ship and the patrol boat, which was quite true. From the report of K-1 commander:

> At 21:53, a new approach by 10 Il-2s from a true course of 50 degrees. Anti-aircraft fire was opened from eight kilometres. The aircraft dropped bombs and attacked ships with cannon and machine-gun fire. Many close bomb explosions behind the stern of K-1 and UJ-1212. Damage report: on UJ-1212, the radio room is damaged, shells exploded in the first shot locker of the 2cm aft gun. On M-35, ready ammunition boxes of the 10.5cm cannon were damaged by cannon/machine-gun fire.

The worst damage was sustained by the submarine hunter UJ-1212. From the report of its commander, *Oberleutnant zur See d. R.* Jungkurth:

> 21:52. Ten Il-2s attacked from a true course of 50 degrees, then flew over the convoy, firing from on-board weapons. One aircraft dived on UJ-1212, frantically firing cannons and machine guns, dropped three fragmentation bombs near the ship and flew over UJ-1212 at about 60m altitude. Cannon and machine-gun fire and bomb splinters caused numerous holes in the UJ-1212 superstructure and deck. Shells and bullets hitting the radio room caused the radio station to break down and the ready ammunition boxes of the 2cm aft firings to explode. Of the crew, one sailor was seriously and one lightly wounded.

In addition to K-1 and UJ-1212, the attack aircraft also struck M-35 and the already damaged UJ-1210. The above report of the K-1 commander indicates that the ready ammunition boxes of the 105mm cannon of the minesweeper were again damaged by cannon and machine-gun fire. The agonising UJ-1210 sustained no further damage.

From the report of the commander of UJ-1212: "21:57. Heavy fire from all weapons caused one of the Il-2s to fall down while flying away in the 340 degrees direction at a distance of about 800m, through the left wing into the water". The statement on the downed aircraft made after the battle by the commander of UJ-1212 recorded:

> When the enemy was approaching, fire of the stern *Vierling* was well targeted. While the Il-2 was flying over the ship, it was hit by our bow 2cm cannon. I observed hits to the fuselage and wings. The aircraft then overturned through the port wing and plunged into the water at a distance of about 600–700m. The Il-2 downed by UJ-1212 was observed by K-1, UJ-1209 crews and Commander of UJ-1210.

It would seem that the aircraft was lost, the more so as one Il-2 from the L.M. Kalmykov's group did not return to the home airfield. However, the attack aircraft piloted by Junior Lieutenant Vasin ditched 20km away from the German convoy.

Returning to the report of the commander of UJ-1212: "21:57. The remaining aircraft flew away at about 160 degrees direction, being pursued by several Luftwaffe fighters". However, the German pursuit of Soviet aircraft was clearly inefficient. From the documents of the 78th IAP:

> Approaching the target, the crews noticed a group of six to eight Bf 109s aircraft approaching Il-2s and Kittyhawks from the north-west (our aircraft were in the north-eastern part of the target); the signal 'Attack' was given by the leading aircraft. Junior Lieutenant Albul spotted a Bf 109 approaching from tail the leading Major Polkovnikov, fired a barrage burst, so the enemy aircraft turned right and ended up in front of Major Polkovnikov's aircraft. Major Polkovnikov fired two bursts of machine-gun fire from a distance of 150–80 m and at 3/4 target aspect ratio. The enemy aircraft rolled to the right and fell onto the ground at Svartnes Cape. A second Bf 109 started attacking the leading Il-2 from below and behind. Junior Lieutenant Albul turned his aircraft and attacked the Bf 109 from behind and below at 2/4 target aspect ratio, fired two to three bursts from 150–100m distance, the enemy aircraft made a left turn and fell into the sea in the north-eastern part of Eckerö Cape. The remaining enemy aircraft were engaged in combat with the Yak-9s. When moving away from the target, two Bf 109s pursued the group and tried to attack the Il-2 aircraft. Junior Lieutenant Dzyuba attacked the wingman Bf 109 from above and behind, fired two bursts from 70–160m distance at 1/4 target aspect ratio, the enemy aircraft fell into the sea. The second Bf 109 made a right turn at low level and flew back to home territory.

As a result of the air battle, the Northern Fleet Air Force Headquarters credited one shot down Bf 109 to Major A.V. Polkovnikov and Junior Lieutenant I.P. Albul each.

The Kittyhawk pilots observed an Il-2 aircraft shot down by anti-aircraft artillery fire in the target area, which ditched into the water, and the crew escaped on a life raft. From the accident report on the loss of the Il-2: "While attacking the enemy, the aircraft sustained heavy anti-aircraft artillery fire at an altitude of 800–900m, a smoke screen was put up by the enemy, so the leading aircraft, followed by the whole group, broke through the smoke screen and attacked the transports. The aircraft was hit above the target by anti-aircraft artillery fire, managed to continue flying 10–15km from the target, landed on the water and sank." Pilot N.I. Vasin succeeded in ditching the aircraft on water, but the torpedo boats sent to rescue the crew found only a life raft with bullet and splinter holes... It is quite likely that the Luftwaffe fighters, having failed in the air battle, killed the crew (pilot Junior Lieutenant N.I. Vasin and gunner Junior Sergeant I.F. Skupinskiy) who were escaping on the life raft.

From the report of the commander of UJ-1212: "22:15. The air-raid alert was over".

After the departure of the last Soviet aircraft the Germans began to take measures to help their damaged ships. Patrol ship V-6108 was relatively lucky. From the report of V-6108:

> 22:10. V 6110 approached to transfer medics and bandaging material.
> 22:43. The ship, by permission of the convoy commander, proceeded to Kirkenes to transfer the seriously wounded crew members. The ship's commander and one seriously wounded man died on the way to Kirkenes.
> 17 May. 0:57. We docked in Kirkenes, and unloaded the wounded.
> Losses of the crew: eight dead, one seriously wounded, four lightly wounded.

Already on 17 May, the V-6108 was docked for repairs at the floating workshop *Südmeer* in Kirkenes, for regaining its ability for the further crossing after being hit by a bomb. Most likely repairs were being made to the damaged steering gear. Once the work was completed, the ship was declared combat-ready and on 10 June V-6108 set out westward with another convoy. On 12 June it reached Hammerfest and from there continued its journey with the patrol ship NKI-11. On 13 June both ships arrived in Tromsø, from where they continued southwards, arriving in Horten on 28 June. There, the ammunition, barrages and artillery were removed, after which the shipyard in Sande Fjord started repairing the damaged engine and hull of the V-6108. This lasted at least until January 1945, but by April the repairs had been completed, as the ship, according to German documents, was escorting convoys in Southern Norway.

In the meantime, the crew of UJ-1210 began to realise that they could not save their ship. From the report of *Strm.Mt.* (Chief Helmsman) Egon Bächle, member of the crew of UJ-1210: "As the signallers were wounded or killed, the Commander ordered me to send a semaphore message to K-1 and UJ-1209: 'I urgently require assistance'." From the report of the commander of UJ-1209: "21:57... UJ-1210 reported in Morse code: 'I urgently need assistance'." Report from UJ-1210: "UJ-1209 was able to receive one of the sailors who had fallen overboard. UJ-1212 cast off a tow line. After UJ-1209 picked up the man, it approached from the port side". From the report of UJ-1209 commander: "After UJ-1209 rescued one sailor who had fallen overboard from UJ-1210, it approached from the port side of UJ-1210. We took on board the seriously wounded [from UJ-1210 – author's note]."

From the report of the commander of UJ-1210: "The doctor, meanwhile, arrived by boat from K-1. As with the rudder position 'right 15' towing with one line was difficult, I ordered to cast off the hawsers. UJ-1212 came close to the starboard side. Now they [UJ-1209 and UJ-1212 – author's note] tried to support the ship, however failing as the ship was taking on too much water. Both ships were now towing UJ 1210 to the shore".

From a report of *Strm.Mt.* Egon Bächle, member of the crew of UJ-1210:

> They [UJ-1209 and UJ-1212 – author's note] tried to support the ship, but did not succeed. By order of the commander, all classified materials were transferred to UJ-1212, which I did myself. When the classified materials and the wounded were handed over, most of the crew moved to UJ-1209 and UJ-1212, but I remained on board and went back to the bridge to see the commander. After both ships had to move away, our ship pushed up against the shore. I passed the following semaphore message to UJ-1212 on the commander's order: 'Please push the stern towards the shore'.

From the report of the commander of UJ-1210:

> The wounded and the classified materials were transferred. In the meantime, the ship had settled so much that water was overflowing over the lower deck. Approximately 800m from the shore, the UJ-1209 put off and the sinking ship was now dragged further to land by UJ-1212 alone. On the southern edge of the Eckerö Cape at 70.00,5,1'-30.15,9' it ran aground with its bow, shortly after UJ-1212 had withdrawn with

> most of its crew. The ship's sternpost was lifted off onshore but slipped off again due to the steepness of the bottom. UJ-1212 was now pushing its stern ashore with its sternpost. During this manoeuvre the ship's aft settled more and went to starboard. 22:45. The ship rolled over. It settled even more, so that only part of the tank and part of the bridge were sticking out of the water. I, with the rest of the crew on the ship, moved to the bow and gave the order to jump out. When all men were taken by boats from K-1 and UJ-1212, I was the last to leave the ship and go over to the boat from K-1.

From the report of the mechanical engineer of UJ-1210: "The ship was lying starboard and with its aft sinking when I executed the commander's order to go forward and was received by the UJ-1212 boat from the port side." From a report by *Strm.Mt.* Egon Bächle, a member of the crew of UJ-1210: "In the meantime the ship was settling on the stern and turned over to starboard. The rest of the crew on board, on the orders of the commander, moved to the bow and abandoned it on the port side. I was picked up by a K-1 boat". Thus was the end of the submarine hunter UJ-1210. From the report of the commander of UJ-1209: "22:45. UJ-1210 turned over to starboard". From the report of UJ-1210 commander: "23:54. K-1 transmitted the following radiogram 2345/48: UJ-1210 capsized at the spot 70.05,1-30.15,9. The crew has been rescued. Losses will be reported later. Asking for urgent assistance and mooring location for UJ-1212 and K-1. Casualties: three men completely torn to pieces when hit by a bomb to the stern. Two men wounded so badly that they died half an hour later. Injured: nine crew members, including four seriously and five lightly. One man (assigned for UJ-1211) lightly wounded."[2]

While the Germans were rendering assistance to their sailors, the Northern Fleet Air Force Headquarters tried to rescue the crews of the aircraft that had ditched in the area of the aircraft convoy. For this purpose, torpedo boats left the Sredniy Peninsula for search of the crews. Two Kittyhawks, piloted by Lieutenant Kravchenko and Junior Lieutenant D.P. Dzyuba, flew from the Pummanki airfield to provide air cover for them. What happened next is recorded in the document 'Description of Air Combat of the 78th IAP': "At the moment of approaching the torpedo boats, the crews spotted five or six FW 190s coming in at a low altitude to the torpedo boats from the direction of Petsamo. Lieutenant Kravchenko at 100-200m range at 1/4 target aspect ratio made two attacks on one FW 190, the enemy aircraft went down in the sea. Junior Lieutenant Dzyuba repulsed the attacks of the FW 190s, which unsuccessfully dropped bombs from a low-level and returned to their own territory". Following the results of the air battle, the Headquarters of the Northern Fleet Air Force credited one downed FW 190 to Lieutenant Kravchenko. German records indicate that at 1:00 [Berlin time – author's note] four FW 190s of 4./SG5 attacked two torpedo boats to the west of Rybachiy Peninsula and, according to the Luftwaffe pilots, achieved three close-range explosions of bombs near them. In reality the boats sustained no damage. There is no information about losses of FW 190 aircraft.

The outcome of the battle for the Germans was disappointing. The Northern Fleet pilots sank submarine hunter UJ-1210 and damaged patrol ship V-6108. Gunboat K-1, minesweeper M-35 and submarine hunter UJ-1212 sustained light damage from close-range explosions and machine-gun fire. Based on the German reports, it is possible to calculate the enemy's losses in personnel. On V-6108 and UJ-1210 eight and five were killed and five and 10 crewmen were wounded respectively. On UJ-1212 and K-1 two men each were wounded. In total on the German ships, 13 sailors were killed and 19 were wounded. The report of the K-1 commander lists the casualties of the Germans as 20 men (7 severely and 13 lightly wounded).

During the strike on the convoy by Il-2s and Kittyhawk fighter-bombers from 22:30 to 22:55, Luftwaffe fighters of the *Stab* III/JG 5 and 7. and 8. *Staffeln* of the JG 5 claimed 14 victories without losses on their part. However, according to the records of JG 5, four Luftwaffe aircraft were damaged but were able to return to their home airfield. Information on the level of these damage was not found in the documents. However, according to the reports made by soldiers of the 2. *Gebirgs-Division*, who observed Soviet aircraft striking the ships, two Luftwaffe fighters made forced landings, and the soldiers assisted their pilots. Of great interest is the conclusion of the Commander of the 12th Submarine Hunters Flotilla:

> The convoy proceeded in anti-aircraft defence order, following the 'T-yellow' order when passing Busse Sund, then anti-aircraft defence order again, this formation was most suitable for use of the ships' weapons.
>
> The bombs which caused sinking of the UJ-1210 were dropped by aircraft approaching from the stern, from the direction which was the weakest in terms of air defence because the UJ-1210 and UJ-1211 were equipped with only single 2cm Hotchkiss in addition to the 3.7cm cannon on starboard and port sides. The question must be raised about the installation of a *Vierling* or two 2cm paired automatic cannon at the stern of the submarine hunters, as firepower from the stern is too low. The rescue attempts made by the ship's command, as well as by the UJ-1209 and UJ-1212, could not prevent the loss of the ship because UJ-1210 took too much water into the engine and boiler rooms after being hit by a bomb. Efficient assistance from friendly ships reduced the loss of personnel and saved all of the classified materials. The case showed that with the current air superiority of the enemy in the area only the units well-armed with anti-aircraft artillery can hold their own. Therefore, now it is required to form four to five ships in close anti-submarine groups for carrying out patrol missions and anti-submarine tasks.

Very soon the pilots of the Northern Fleet would confirm the correctness of the words of the commander of the 12th Submarine Hunters Flotilla.

2 Historical note – UJ-1210 was one of six whaleships built for the Kriegsmarine at the Akers Mek. Verkst. shipyard in Oslo. Built in 1943 (No. 498), gross tonnage up to 1,060 tonnes, tonnage 538grt. From April 1943 it was registered in Hammerfest Harbour Defence Flotilla as a patrol ship NH-03; on 1 May 1944 it was reclassified to submarine hunter and received the letter-digit designation UJ-1210.

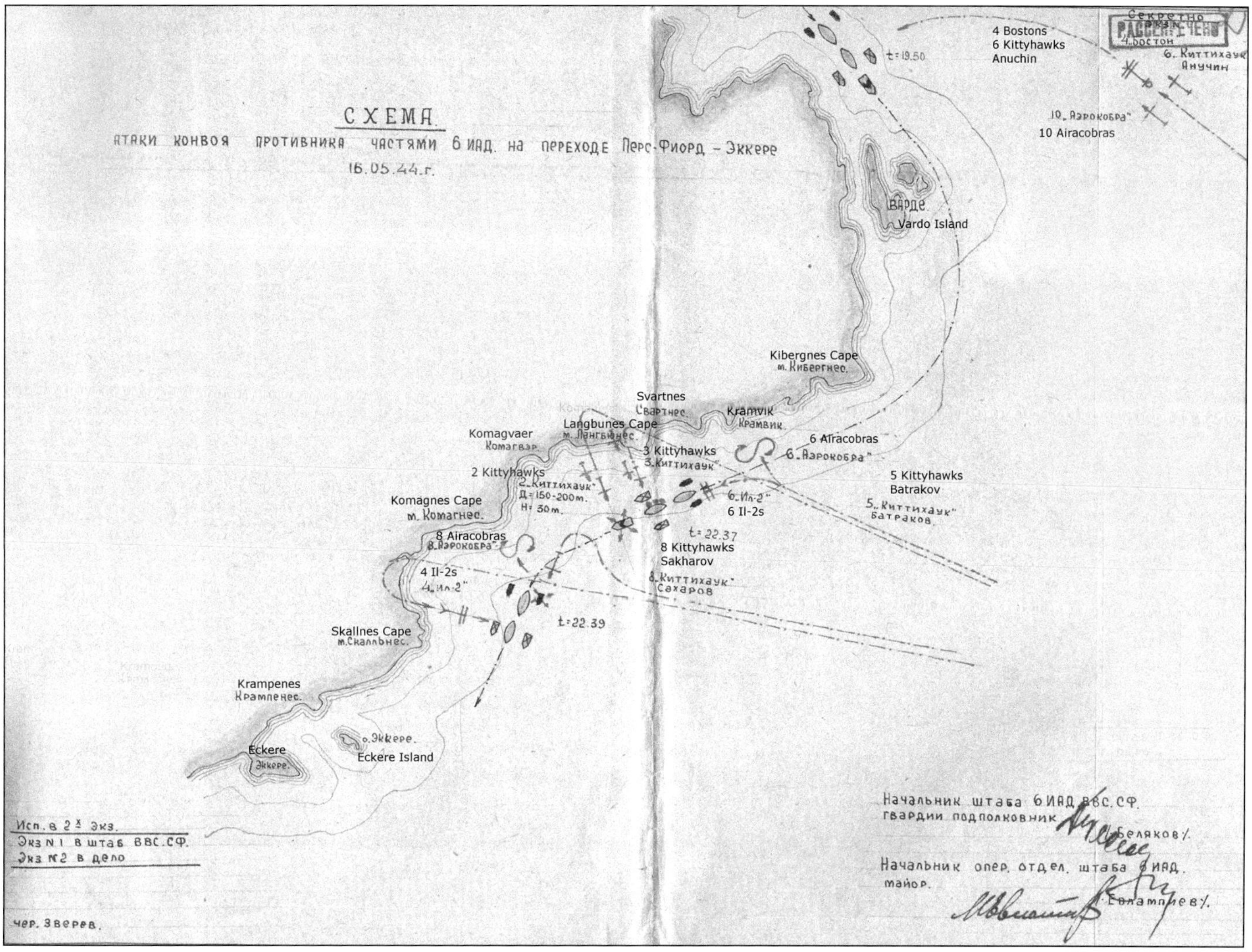

Plan of the Kittyhawks' attack on the Rp.119.Ki convoy on 16 May 1944.

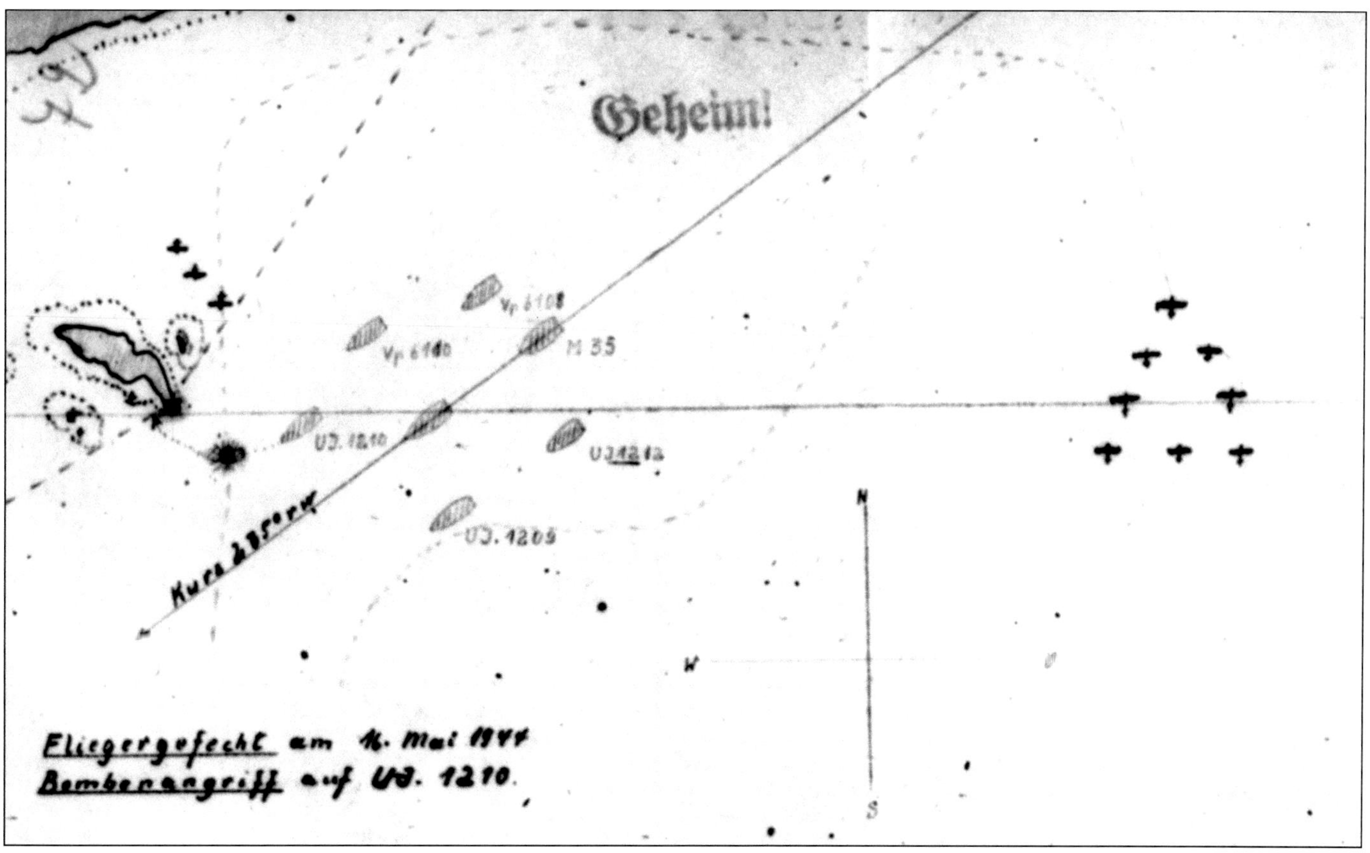

Plan of the Soviet aircraft attack on the UJ-1210 submarine hunter on 16 May 1944.

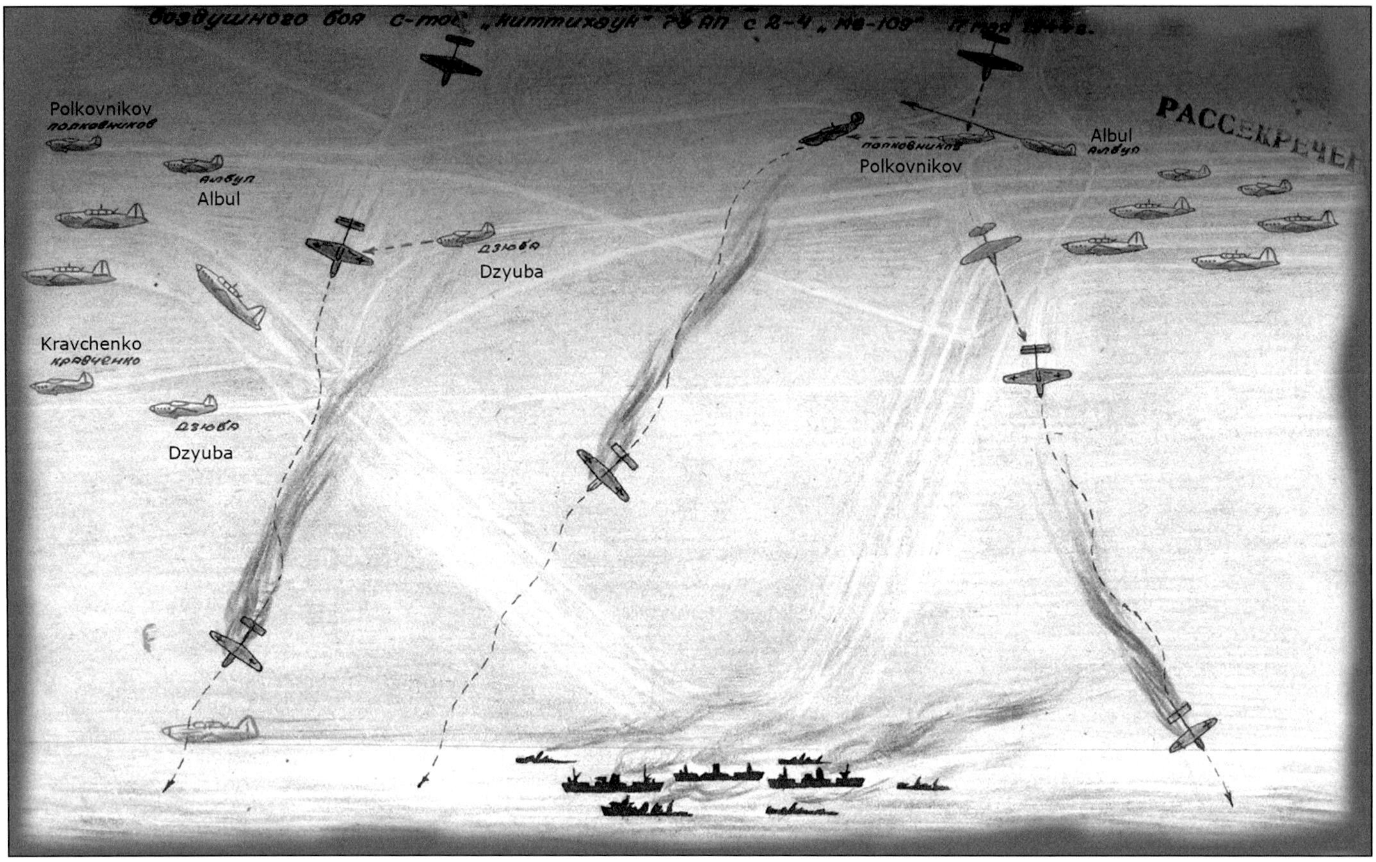

Plan of the air combat of the Kittyhawks of the 78th IAP over the Rp.119.Ki convoy on 16 May 1944.

Submarine hunter of the 12th Submarine Hunters Flotilla.

25 May

The day began with an accident and a crash in the 78th IAP. Both occurred during training exercises. The first crash occurred at 15:40. From the accident report on the loss of the Kittyhawk aircraft: "In the vicinity of the Gryaznaya Bay firing range the aircraft was practicing skip bombing. While dropping bombs, it blew up on its bombs due to the faulty installation of the bomb fuse". The pilot of the aircraft, Junior Lieutenant V.A. Khilobodchenko, died. Loss of the aircraft and death of the pilot was caused by a mistake made by technicians while preparing the aircraft. In the second case there was an accident. The accident report states that the incident happened at 18:45: "The pilot was practicing techniques of flying and air combat. Due to carelessness, the fuel from the fuselage tank was emptied and the engine stopped. The error: fuel tanks were not switched. The aircraft made a forced landing 1.5km away from the airfield". The pilot, Junior Lieutenant V.V. Venikov, was not injured. The aircraft was transferred to the repair workshop.

Left: Senior Lieutenant A.I. Batrakov, the leader of the Kittyhawks group of the 78th IAP during air combat on 16 May 1944.

Above: Pilot of the 78th IAP, Lieutenant N.P. Proyavko.

Meanwhile the war continued and at 18:45 the Northern Fleet Air Force command post received a report from a Boston reconnaissance aircraft of the 118th RAP piloted by Junior Lieutenant M.Y. Sologubov: "Cape Nordkyn, convoy at 80 degrees course, speed eight knots, clear weather in the target area". This was Convoy Rp.120.Ki which had left Lo Fjord for Kirkenes on 25 May. At the time of the attack the convoy consisted of gunboat K-1, floating base of the motor minesweepers *Bali*, patrol ships V-6101, V-6107, V-6110, V-6111, V-6115, NK-08, submarine hunters UJ-1209, UJ-1211, UJ-1212, UJ-1219, minesweepers M-35, M-154, M-202, M-251, M-252, motor minesweepers R-154, R-159, R-173, R-223, steamers *Kerkplein* (5,085grt), *Baltenland* (3,038grt), *Pompeji* (2,916grt), *Herta Engeline Fritzen* (3,672grt), *Horst* (500grt), *Solviken* (3,502grt), *Aktiv* (507grt), tankers *Marsteinen* (806grt), and *Gerdmor* (761grt).

According to the plan of attack developed at the Northern Fleet Air Force Headquarters, the strikes were to be carried out in Kongs Fjord. The first to attack were high-altitude torpedo bombers with the aim of disrupting the convoy formation. After them the fighter-bombers of the 78th IAP were to attack the escort ships in two groups, one by dive bombing and the other by skip bombing. Further, in order to suppress the convoy air defences, the attack aircraft from the Pummanki airfield were to strike the convoy, but this part of the plan was abandoned because the aircraft would not have had enough flying range to reach the convoy. After suppressing the convoy air defences, the low altitude torpedo bombers were to attack. The command of the Northern Fleet, in addition to its own forces, requested assistance from the 7th Air Army. The army fighters were to block the Luostari and Salmijärvi airfields.

The attack on the convoy was launched by army Airacobras, which appeared over the German airfields as planned. The Airacobra pilots fought several air battles and scored one downed Luftwaffe fighter. The Germans acknowledged the loss of two FW 190s, but according to the German version they collided on take-off. The most unpleasant thing is that the Luftwaffe fighters, which had gone to intercept the Soviet aircraft attacking the convoy, took off from an unblocked airfield.

The first in the strike, as planned, were the high-altitude torpedo bombers. The group consisted of six Il-4s of the 9th GMTAP (leader – Captain K.F. Shkaruba) under the cover of six Airacobras of the 255th IAP (leader – Captain I.P. Konev). At 22:32, they attacked the convoy from the bow and dropped torpedoes into the centre and end of the convoy. The operations log of the 5th Minesweepers Flotilla recorded the dropping of parachute torpedoes and their hitting the transport *Solviken* (3,502grt). It sank one hour later. The crew were evacuated by German ships, except for two men killed in the torpedo explosion. As Soviet aircraft retreated from the target, Luftwaffe fighters were able to break through to the high-altitude torpedo bombers. They shot down the Il-4, piloted by Guards Senior Lieutenant A.D. Yevdokimov, and damaged three more, wounding four crew members. From the report of Il-4 air gunner Guards Senior Sergeant V.P. Zhuk: "All aircraft dropped torpedoes over the target at altitudes of 1,800–2,000m. I did not observe the results of the strike, as I engaged enemy fighters and shot down a Bf 109. When moving away from the target I saw a huge column of black smoke over the convoy, and another column of black smoke to the left of it. The wing led by Senior Lieutenant Yevdokimov went in low and was 300–400m lower than us. On leaving the anti-aircraft fire zone, we were attacked by up to 10 Bf 109 fighters. Yevdokimov's aircraft was ambushed by two Bf 109s and shot down at this time". It should be noted that the crash of the Bf 109 shot down by Guards Senior Sergeant V.P. Zhuk was observed by crews of several Soviet aircraft, but the German documents are silent about this. Meanwhile, the Airacobras of the 255th IAP were able to repel all further attacks by Luftwaffe fighters, with two victories added to their score.

Following the high-altitude torpedo bombers, eight Kittyhawk fighter-bombers of the 78th IAP (leader – Senior Lieutenant V.P. Strelnikov) attacked the convoy. Actually, these Kittyhawks were expected to attack together with the high-altitude torpedo bombers or before them, but because of delayed preparation the fighter-bombers attacked later… Captain I.P. Konev's report states: "There were no Kittyhawk aircraft arriving at the estimated time". The Kittyhawks dropped bombs on the German guard ships at the end of the convoy. Patrol ship V-6115 was hit by the close bursts of bombs and machine-gun fire. Twelve crew members were wounded and the ship sustained damage which the combat log of the 61st Patrol Boats Flotilla rates as 'light'.

It is difficult to say at what point the low-altitude torpedo bombers went on the attack. The group consisted of three Bostons (leader – Guards Lieutenant P. Ya. Gnetov) under the cover of 10 Airacobras of the 255th IAP (leader – Captain P.A. Rassadkin). Formally, they attacked at 22:30, on paper even earlier than the high-altitude torpedo bombers. However, the documents of the German ships suggest that they attacked somewhat later. The group passed along the coast and attacked the convoy from the land side. Unfortunately, all Airacobras of the group were engaged in air combat with Luftwaffe fighters and, although the fighters were able to shoot down one Bf 109, the circumstances of the loss of all three torpedo bombers of the group are not clear so far. Probably one was shot down by German ships at the end of the convoy, the second flew across the middle of the convoy and was shot down not far from the convoy, most probably by anti-aircraft fire, and the third one was probably shot down by Luftwaffe fighters when exiting the attack. The situation could have been clarified by two Kittyhawk reconnaissance aircraft of the 118th RAP which recorded the result of the attack, but they themselves were attacked by the Bf 109s and engaged in an air battle with them. As a result of the battle, Lieutenants A.M. Avtsyn and S.I. Pankrashin scored one Bf 109 each. However, on withdrawal they made an excellent photo run over the convoy.

Four Kittyhawk fighter-bombers of the 78th IAP (leader – Captain F.S. Plotko) and six Airacobras of the 20th IAP (leader – Senior Lieutenant A.K. Tarasov) were the last to appear over the convoy. Actually, four Kittyhawks were to attack the escort ships by skip-bombing method together with V.P. Strelnikov's Kittyhawks, but were severely delayed in their journey. From the report of Captain F.S. Plotko:

> Due to the fact that the group of eight Kittyhawks from the 3rd Squadron of the 78th IAP took a long time to concentrate, and approached the target in two groups of four each, my group fell behind them. At the approach to the target, I saw departing aircraft below at an altitude of 800–1,000m and two fires in the sea, aircraft were burning. A group of torpedo bombers struck before us and caused a big fire on the transport going in the tail of the convoy. I appeared alone in a small group over the target. The strike was made from a dive, exiting at an altitude of 400–200m with subsequent climbing and leaving the target individually. I attacked the patrol ship coming from behind on the left but observed no results. Pilots Proyavko, Nerubenko, Kovalenko attacked the patrol ship coming from behind on the left. The ship was on fire and sank.

Captain F.S. Plotko was premature to declare the destruction of the patrol ship, but the Germans still sustained damage. Though the Kittyhawks did not hit any ship with their bombs, they made holes in the patrol boat V-6107 with their machine guns, killing two crewmembers, wounding one, and damaging the gyrocompass.

Eight Airacobras of the 2nd GKAP were sent to help the aircraft leaving the battle over the convoy, but although patrolling in the Pummanki – Vaitolahti area, they did not encounter the enemy.

According to the work of Eric Mombeek, 19 Bf 109s of 7., 8. and 9. *Staffeln* of the JG 5 were engaged in air combat over the convoy. The Luftwaffe fighters claimed to have shot down 33 Soviet aircraft, including 20 Bostons, over the convoy without any losses of their own. Three more shot down Bostons were claimed by German ships.

Photo of the Rp.120.Ki convoy taken by a photo reconnaissance Kittyhawk of the 118th RAP after the attack by the Northern Fleet Air Force on 25 May 1944.

Pilot of the photo reconnaissance Kittyhawk of the 118th RAP, Lieutenant A.M. Avtsyn.

26 May

After the first strike against Convoy Rp.120.Ki, the command of the Northern Fleet Air Force decided to repeat the attack. According to the plan of the second strike, high-altitude torpedo bombers were to be the first to attack. As before, their task was to disrupt the convoy's order and, if possible, damage enemy ships and vessels. After the high-altitude torpedo bombers, the Il-2s of the 46th ShAP and the Kittyhawk fighter-bombers of the 78th IAP were to attack. Their main target was the escort ships. After the joint strike by the attack aircraft and fighter-bombers against the escort ships, the skip-bombers were to engage. The convoy's transports were to be their target. The groups of the attack aircraft and fighter-bombers were to approach from the land side, since, in the opinion of the Northern Fleet Air Force Headquarters, the convoy guard from this direction was weaker. The last to engage were the attack aircraft from the Pummanki airfield. Unlike the previous groups, no tricks were planned here – simply an attack on the ships and vessels from the seaward-side. The area of attack for all groups was the Pers Fjord. The high-altitude torpedo bombers were to strike at 6:00, the others to follow at one-minute intervals.

In fact, however, the plan was disrupted and the first attack on the convoy was carried out by eight Kittyhawk fighter-bombers of the 78th IAP (leader – Senior Lieutenant P.I. Sakharov). The time of the attack in various documents varies from 5:50 to 5:56. Most of the fighter-bombers attacked the ships that were guarding the rear of the convoy, and only two attacked the transports. The attack was recorded in the combat log of the floating base *Bali*. The Germans supposed that Kittyhawks attacked the group of ships consisting of the floating base *Bali*, patrol ship V-6115 and motor minesweeper R-154, which had followed the convoy after evacuating the crew from the sunken transport *Solviken* (3,502grt). The convoy was then attacked at 5:58 by high-altitude torpedo bombers. The group consisted of four Il-4s (leader – Guards Captain K.F. Shkaruba) under the cover of 16 Airacobras of the 255th IAP (leader – Captain P.A. Rassadkin). The torpedo bombers dropped torpedoes in the centre and at the rear of the convoy. However, the success of the previous day was not repeated – all the torpedoes missed their targets. Anti-aircraft fire was fatal for Captain I.P. Konev's Airacobra. His aircraft was damaged by an anti-aircraft shell. The pilot attempted to reach Sredniy Peninsula, but crashed into the sea. Due to the death of Captain I.P. Konev, control of the fighter force was disrupted, and the Luftwaffe fighters managed to shoot down two Airacobras and one Il-4 torpedo bomber. The torpedo-bomber crew headed by the Guards Junior Lieutenant L.S. Titov and two fighter pilots – Captain I.A. Gladkov and Junior Lieutenant S.S. Tropa, lost their lives. The Headquarters of the Northern Fleet Air Force credited three downed Bf 109s to the pilots of the 255th IAP. From the report of Guards Captain Shkaruba, pilot of 9th GMTAP: "After departing from the target at 50–75 km distance I saw a column of black smoke. I saw how Airacobras shot down a Bf 109. The crew of aircraft No.18 of Junior Lieutenant Titov was shot down by enemy fighters on withdrawing from the area of convoy". The column of black smoke observed by the torpedo-bomber leader was the success of Senior Lieutenant S.P. Sheikin's group of attack aircraft. The group consisted of eight Il-2s of the 46th ShAP under the cover of six Airacobras of the 20th IAP (leader – Captain E.V. Petrenko). The same group was supposed to have included eight Kittyhawk fighter-bombers of the 78th IAP (leader – Senior Lieutenant P.I. Sakharov), but, as mentioned above, they had attacked the convoy earlier. The most unfortunate thing was that, according to the plan, the Kittyhawks were to provide direct cover for the strike force. One attack aircraft failed to reach the target, and at 6:05 the others, divided into two groups, attacked the convoy.

Already on the approach to the target, the Airacobras of the 20th IAP were engaged in air combat against the Luftwaffe fighters. From the report of Captain E.V. Petrenko: "At 6:05–6:10, covering the attack of Il-2s on the target and their retreat, we conducted air combat against five to seven Bf 109s and FW 190s with no result." The attacking aircraft managed to drop bombs on the ships and vessels in the convoy. The first success was achieved by Junior Lieutenant P.V. Serdyuk who hit the bow of the steamer *Herta Engeline Fritzen* (3,672grt) with two bombs. From the report of Junior Lieutenant P.V. Serdyuk: "I attacked the rear transport of 6,000–8,000 tonnes displacement at 6:05 in the area of Pers Fjord. I did not observe results of the strike". However, when comparing his report with the German plan of the ships' positioning in the convoy it can be concluded that it was he who succeeded. The bomb explosions destroyed the mast and the cargo crane, and severely damaged the bridge. Seven of the crew were injured, including the captain and the sailing master. The damage was not critical to the vessel – neither seaworthiness nor steering was affected. But at the time the situation seemed critical from the outside, a fire broke out on the bow, which the crew managed to put out. From the report of Junior Sergeant Yu.G. Anikin of the crew commanded by the Junior Lieutenant P. Serdyuk: "When exiting our attack on 26 May 1944 I saw a direct hit of our bombs at the enemy's transport, after which it began to sink. I also observed a direct hit in the aft part of the destroyer and a big explosion which was caused by Lieutenant Tamarov's attack, as well as two fires on small guard ships". Most likely, Lieutenant M.M. Tamarov's target was the floating base *Bali*, and although he did not achieve direct hits by bombs, water columns from the bomb explosions flooded the ship and, according to the report of the floating base's mechanic, damaged the ship's electrical system, the repair of which later took almost two weeks.

The attacking aircraft were engaged by Luftwaffe fighters as they were leaving the convoy area. From the report of the air gunner, Junior Sergeant Yu.G. Anikin:

> We were attacked by six Bf 109s when exiting the convoy attack. One Bf 109 … approached from tail and fired at us with its machine guns and cannon. The enemy approached at the 0/4 target aspect ratio. I fired a long burst and he turned and attacked my wingman Obrevko in the side from above, after which Obrevko's aircraft fell into the water and was blown to pieces. After that, the Bf 109s became completely ballsy and started attacking and firing from a distance of only 20m away from us. I repulsed all attacks of the Bf 109s (and there were six of them). One aircraft came close to the tail and opened fire. It was flying at the 0/4 target aspect ratio, and I noticed that something was wrong with it due to some damage to the left landing gear. I fired a long burst, it emitted fire and crashed into the water. After that, I noticed that pilot Serdyuk climbed steeply, the aircraft almost hung in the air, and he fired rocket projectiles and machine guns at the Bf 109, which exploded in the air and the burning debris fell into the water. There was no fighter cover around, later one Kittyhawk appeared. The Bf 109s damaged our landing gear and we were forced to make a belly landing.

The Kittyhawk pilot, Junior Lieutenant N.R. Lisichkin helped to repulse the attacks of Luftwaffe fighters. From his report:

> Exiting the attack [he had dropped bombs on German ships – author's note] I found myself alone, our group of aircraft was not visible in the haze and I decided to wait for the Il-2s, which were exiting the attack; having made a couple of turns, I was still ahead of them and decided to stay behind the Il-2s. At that time the Il-2s were being attacked by two Bf 109s; having repulsed the first attack, I joined three Il-2s and began to repulse the attacks of two Bf 109s; I was engaged in air combat with them until the middle of the way from Vardö to Vaitolahti.

However, the group of attack aircraft commanded by Senior Lieutenant S.P. Sheikin suffered heavy losses. Four aircraft and their crews did not return from the mission. The reports on the aircraft losses stated the only reason for that: the aircraft were shot down by Luftwaffe fighters.

Two and a half hours after the attack on the convoy the motor minesweeper R-159 picked up two dead Soviet pilots near Kiberg. Apparently, they were the crew of the downed attack aircraft.

The group of S.P. Sheikin was followed by skip-bombing attack aircraft. The group consisted of four Il-2s of the 46th ShAP (leader – Captain D.V. Osyka), four Kittyhawk fighters of the 78th IAP (leader – Senior Lieutenant A.I. Batrakov) and four Yaks of the 20th IAP (leader – Lieutenant N.D. Tkachenko). At 6:10, in the Pers Fjord the skip bombers, coming in from the shore side and divided into pairs, attacked the German transports but missed. The fighters of the covering group succeeded in protecting the attack aircraft, but lost one Kittyhawk. From the accident report on the loss of the aircraft: "While moving away from the target, we repulsed an attack by four Bf 109s on the Il-2 group. The Bf 109s attack was repulsed by manoeuvring in pairs. Junior Lieutenant Kovalenko was shot down during the head-on attack by a pair of Bf 109s." The Kittyhawk pilot, Junior Lieutenant A.S. Kovalenko, was killed.

The last group to strike the convoy was the group of attacking aircraft from Pummanki airfield. The group consisted of four Il-2s (leader – Lieutenant L.M. Kalmykov), six Kittyhawks of the 78th IAP (leader – Lieutenant V.G. Mitrofanov), and six Yaks of the 20th IAP (leader – Lieutenant L.P. Lapin). The fighters of the 20th IAP were engaged in combat against a pair of Luftwaffe fighters. However, the Kittyhawks stayed alert and repulsed all Luftwaffe fighter attacks. Lieutenant A.S. Pavlov, pilot of the Kittyhawk of the 78th IAP reported: "On the approach, we sustained anti-aircraft fire and engaged with eight enemy Bf 109 fighters. We conducted an air combat. One of the Bf 109s was attacked from a distance of 50m at 0/4 target aspect ratio and downed. The aircraft fell into the water in the vicinity of the convoy three kilometres northward". The Northern Fleet Air Force Headquarters credited one downed Bf 109 to Lieutenant A.S. Pavlov.

At 6:14 the attacking aircraft, approaching from the stern of the convoy, dropped bombs from a dive. They hit around the tanker *Marsteinen* (806grt). Close explosions of the bombs damaged its steering, riddled the above-water part of the hull and the deck. The ship's crew suffered three dead and seven wounded.

According to data from the book by Eric Mombeek, the attacking Soviet aircraft were initially countered by fighters of the 9. *Staffel*. Then, the Bf 109s of the *Stab* III./JG 5, and the 7. and 8. *Staffeln* of the JG 5 flew in to help them. In total, the Germans scored 40 downed Soviet aircraft, including eight Il-2s. It is known that one Luftwaffe fighter was shot down, but no details are available.

After the aircraft involved in the attack on the convoy landed, the command of the Northern Fleet Air Force planned to carry out another attack on the convoy, this time in Kirkenes, but weather conditions didn't allow it.

Following the convoy attacks, the Northern Fleet Air Force command stopped using Kittyhawks for direct escort of the attacking aircraft, simultaneously acting as fighter-bombers. Usually, a strike group consisting of Yaks of the 20th IAP or Airacobras of the 255th IAP would begin the battle with the Luftwaffe fighters in order to engage them in air combat. As the Kittyhawks approached the target they would bomb the ships, while the attacking aircraft were left one-on-one with the Luftwaffe fighters. Credit has to be given to the Northern Fleet Air Force command – it drew the right conclusions from what had happened.

Captain P.I. Sakharov, Hero of the Soviet Union.

Pilot of a Kittyhawk receives orders for a mission.

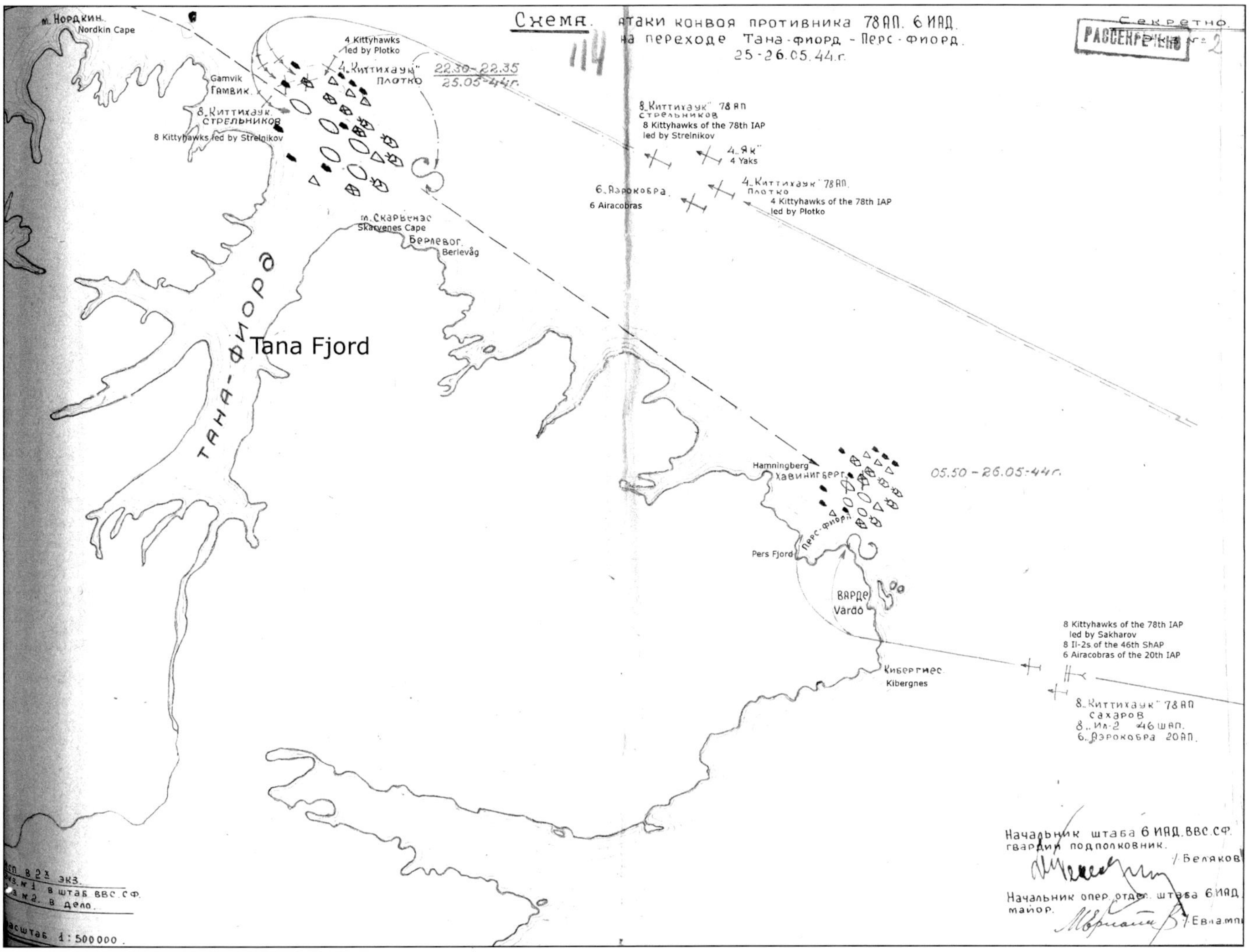

Plan of attack by the 78th IAP Kittyhawks of the Rp.120.Ki convoy on 25–26 May 1944.

APPENDIX I: PILOTS OF THE NORTHERN FLEET AIR FORCE, WHO FLEW KITTYHAWK AIRCRAFT AND WERE AWARDED THE TITLE OF HERO OF THE SOVIET UNION

Twice Heroes of the Soviet Union:

SAFONOV Boris Feoktistovich (1915–1942) – squadron commander of the 72nd SAP (awarded on 16 September 1941); commander of the 2nd Guards SAP (awarded on 14 June 1942). Killed in action on 30 May 1942.

Heroes of the Soviet Union:

BOKIY Nikolay Andreevich (1918–1995) – flight commander of the 2nd GKAP (24 July 1943);

DIDENKO Nikolay Matveevich (1921–1975) – deputy squadron commander of the 2nd GKAP (5 November 1944);

KLIMOV Pavel Dmitrievich (1920–1992) – flight commander of the 2nd GKAP (24 July 1943);

KOVALENKO Aleksandr Andreevich (1909–1984) – squadron commander of the 2nd GKAP (14 June 1942);

KOLOMIETS Petr Leontievich (1917–1974) – squadron commander of the 2nd GKAP (5 November 1944);

KURZENKOV Sergey Georgievich (1911–1981) – assistant commander of the 78th IAP (24 July 1943);

ORLOV Pavel Ivanovich (1911–1943) – deputy squadron commander of the 2nd GKAP (24 July 1943); Killed in action on 15 March 1943.

POKROVSKIY Vladimir Pavlovich (1918–1998) – flight commander of the 2nd GKAP (24 July 1943);

SAKHAROV Pavel Ivanovich (1919–1985) – squadron commander of the 78th IAP (5 November 1944);

SGIBNEV Petr Georgievich (1920–1943) – squadron commander of the 78th IAP (23 October 1942); Killed on a training flight on 3 May 1943.

STRELNIKOV Vasiliy Polikarpovich (1919–1993) – squadron commander of the 78th IAP (March 6, 1945).

BIBLIOGRAPHY

Printed books:

Groener, E., *Die deutschen Kriegsschiffe 1815-1945* Band 8 Teile 1 & 2 (Bonn: Bernard & Graefe Verlag, 1993).

Mombeek, E., *Eismeerjager. Zur Geschichte des Jagdgeschwaders 5*, Bde 3-4 (Linkebeek: A.S.B.L., La Porte d'Hoves, 2010-2011).

Archives:

Central Archive of the Ministry of Defence of the Russian Federation, Archive of the Navy branch (Gatchina):

Fund 767. Documents of the Northern Fleet Headquarters.

Fund 787. Documents of the Northern Fleet Air Force Headquarters.

Fund 1980. Documents of the 5th MTAD.

Fund 1982. Documents of the 2nd GIAP.

Fund 1983. Documents of the 78th IAP

Fund 1985. Documents of the 255th IAP.

Fund 1986. Documents of the 46th ShAP.

Fund 1987. Documents of the 118th RAP.

Fund 1988. Documents of the 9th GMTAP.

Fund 2325. Documents of the 27th IAP.

Fund 2452. Documents of the 6th IAD.

Fund 2924. Documents of the 20th IAP.

Fund 2982. Documents of the 95th IAP.

Fund 3283. Documents of the 14th SAD.

The following documents from the U.S. National Archives and Records Administration were provided by Igor Borisenko and Miroslav Morozov:

KTB des Kommandierenden Admirals Norwegen/ Oberbefehlshabers des Marineoberkommandos Norwegen 01.01-31.10.1944 NARA T-1022, roll 2750

KTB des Kommandierenden Admiral der norwegischen Polarküste 01.01-15.09.1944, NARA T-1022, roll 2774.

KTB des Küstensicherungsverbandes der norwegischen Polarküste 01-06.1944, NARA T-1022, roll 2777.

KTB des Kommandanten der Seeverteidigung Kirkenes 01.01-30.09.1944, NARA T-1022, rolls 2775-76.

KTB der 5. Landungsflottille 01.07-30.09.1944 NARA T-1022, roll 3137

KTB der 5. Minensuchflottille 01.01-31.10.1944, NARA T-1022, rolls 3079-80.

KTB der 9. Minensuchflottille 01.01-31.10.1944, NARA T-1022, roll 3083.

KTB der 22. Minensuchflottille 01.01-30.09.1944, NARA T-1022, roll 3175.

KTB der 5. Räumbootsflottille 01.05-31.10.1944, NARA T-1022, roll 3437

KTB der 7. Räumbootsflottille 01.01-31.10.1944, NARA T-1022, roll 3492

KTB der 59. Vorpostenflottille 19.01-31.10.1944 NARA T-1022, rolls 3740-41

KTB der 61. Vorpostenflottille 01.01-31.10.1944 NARA T-1022, roll 3791

KTB des Kanonenboote K 3 01.01-31.10.1944 NARA T-1022, roll 3164

KTB MRS Bali 01.01-31.10.1944 NARA T-1022, roll 3883

KTB XIX (Geb.) AK NARA T-314, roll 646

Photos:

Photos are courtesy of the above archives, Finnish Wartime Photograph Archive as well as from the personal archives of the author, Igor Borisenko, Aleksander Mardanov, Miroslav Morozov and Gennady Petrov.

ABOUT THE AUTHOR

Andrey Latkin was born in 1976. He completed his secondary education at St. Petersburg Shipbuilding Technical School, subsequently attending St. Petersburg State University of Telecommunications named after Prof. M.A. Bonch-Bruevich. His primary historical interest lies in the combat actions of the Soviet naval aviation during the Great Patriotic War. In his research, he utilises Soviet documents from the Russian archives and compares the data with available German sources. He has written three books on this subject personally and two more in co-authorship. He has also made approximately 40 articles on the history of the Soviet Navy, which have been published in magazines and on the Internet.